THE RUSSELLS

CHRISTOPHER TRENT

THE RUSSELLS

FREDERICK MULLER

First published in Great Britain 1966
by Frederick Muller Ltd., Fleet Street, London, E.C.4

Printed in Great Britain by
Ebenezer Baylis and Son Limited
The Trinity Press, Worcester, and London

Bound by Leighton-Straker

CONTENTS

INTRODUCTION | 11

1 The Early Russells | 17

2 The Earldom is Founded | 40

3 Elizabethan Tapestry | 71

4 The Draining of the Fens | 99

5 The Dukedom is Founded | 117

6 Edward the Kingmaker | 145

7 The Russells' London | 160

8 Constitutional Reformers | 189

9 Farming Reformers | 208

10 Victorian Statesman | 226

11 A Pen Mightier than the Sword | 258

12 Selling Woburn to the World | 291

BIBLIOGRAPHY | 311

INDEX | 313

ILLUSTRATIONS

Facing page

John, 1st Earl of Bedford   96

Francis, 2nd Earl of Bedford   97

Edward, 3rd Earl of Bedford   97

Francis, 4th Earl of Bedford   97

William, 5th Earl and 1st Duke of Bedford   112

Wriothesley, 2nd Duke of Bedford   112

Wriothesley, 3rd Duke of Bedford   112

John, 4th Duke of Bedford   113

Francis, 5th Duke of Bedford   113

John, 6th Duke of Bedford   113

Francis, 7th Duke of Bedford   192

Lord John Russell   192

William, 8th Duke of Bedford   192

Hastings, 9th Duke of Bedford   192

Sackville, 10th Duke of Bedford   193

Herbrand, 11th Duke of Bedford   193

Hastings, 12th Duke of Bedford   208

Bertrand Russell, 3rd Earl Russell   208

John, 13th Duke of Bedford   209

INTRODUCTION

The Russell Family

THE RUSSELL FAMILY has made a major contribution to the development of English life spread over five hundred years. Reformers always, they are the central figures in a story of high endeavour and achievement. In political and agricultural progress they have taken equally prominent parts. Their record of service is one of which any family would be proud.

John Russell, the 1st Earl of Bedford, was born in 1486. He was a most remarkable man. When still young he had the good fortune to be of assistance as interpreter to the Archduke Philip of Austria, who took refuge on the Dorset coast during a severe storm. The Archduke took him to his heart and, more important from the point of view of the Russell family, took him to see King Henry VII, who was impressed by his demeanor and made him a gentleman usher.

That is the point at which the Russell fortunes were founded, although John may well not have recognized the fact at the time. There is no doubt that he was a competent as well as popular member of the royal entourage. His virtues were recognized even more fully by King Henry VIII, of whom he became a personal friend and whom he represented on many diplomatic missions. He was at the Field of the Cloth of Gold in 1520.

After that he succeeded in steering a tortuous but safe course through the disputes between Wolsey and the King and in 1536 took part in the suppression of the Pilgrimage of Grace. Four years later he was appointed Lord High Admiral of England.

In this office he showed brilliance of judgment and initiative. He was rewarded by grants of monastic land in Devonshire, Bedfordshire and London. These grants were the foundation on which one of the three largest English family fortunes was built.

The most remarkable thing about John Russell is that he survived the reign of King Henry VIII with honour and was Lord High Steward at the coronation of King Edward VI. Later, more remarkably, he was Lord Privy Seal during the reign of Queen Mary. He died a natural death while holding this office in 1555, just five years after he had been created 1st Earl of Bedford.

Francis, the 2nd Earl (1527–85), consolidated the family fortunes. He was as remarkable a man as his father. He entered public life quietly enough in 1547 as M.P. for Bedfordshire. Even in this modest achievement he broke new ground, being the first heir to a peerage to sit in the Commons. Unlike his father he could not accept the reaction inherent in Queen Mary's succession and was thrown into prison at the beginning of her reign for supporting the claims of Lady Jane Grey to the throne. He was soon pardoned, however, a token of the high reputation of the Russell family, and spent the next few years of his life travelling in Europe.

He returned to England at the close of Mary's short reign but on the accession of Queen Elizabeth became a Privy Councillor. He was a commissioner for the new Liturgy and in 1563 was appointed Governor of Berwick on Tweed, where his ability for organization and his very real military skill made that outpost of the English realm secure against the Scots. He proved himself to be a man who could get things done. He was responsible for the new fortifications of Berwick, the only military defences of an English town erected in Elizabethan times. In 1569 he was in command of the Queen's army in Wales. By then he was clearly not only one of the Queen's favourites but one of the small coterie of men on whom she relied and on whose loyalty she depended absolutely.

The 4th and 5th Earls (the 5th Earl became the 1st Duke) were chiefly responsible for the reclamation of the Fenland. This was the greatest single contribution ever made to the reclamation of English land by a single family. The operation brought many thousands of acres of desolate and waterlogged countryside into active agricultural production. The Bedford Old River and the Bedford New River still serve as the main drainage channels of the Fens. Francis, the 4th Earl, was architect-in-chief of the scheme. He had been a stormy petrel in politics and had supported the Commons in the Petition of Right in 1628. He was arrested in 1629, brought before the Star Chamber but acquitted of treasonable action. He retired, however, from active politics and devoted himself thereafter to estate management. In 1630 he became the chief "undertaker" of the Fen reclamation scheme and, working closely with Cornelius Vermuyden, achieved his object of reclaiming hundreds of thousands of acres of the Fenland despite the attitude of the commoners, who regarded it as sacrilege to defy the will of God.

The Civil War brought work to a stop but the 5th Earl undertook the assignment afresh on behalf of the Commonwealth Government. The land that emerged is some of the richest arable and pasture land in the whole of Great Britain. A completely new agricultural industry was soon based on it, flourishing today as much as ever.

William, Lord Russell, son of the 5th Earl, was a member of the first Restoration Parliament and became a leader of the Country Party in opposition to the Cabal. He was a devoted Protestant dedicated to the cause of preventing a return to Roman Catholicism. He supported the Exclusion Bill, which would have made it impossible for James, Duke of York, to succeed. In 1683 he was charged with complicity in the Rye House Plot, was found guilty and beheaded in Lincoln's Inn Fields.

The 5th Earl was rewarded by King William III with a

dukedom, granted specifically in honour of William, Lord
Russell's services to the cause of Protestantism. By then he was
an old man with only faint memories of the equivocal part he
had played in the Civil War, when he supported the cause of
the King and of Parliament successively and without very much
success. He was a farmer rather than a politician or a soldier.
His honour came to him rather unexpectedly but he accepted
it with gratitude and possibly felt, as he was intended to feel,
that his son's life had not been sacrificed in vain.

The Russell family has put an indelible mark on the face of
modern London, as on the landscapes of East Anglia. Francis,
the 4th Earl, originator of the Fen drainage scheme, also saw
the possibility of turning the family's land in London to good
account. In 1631 he was responsible, with Inigo Jones, for the
laying out of the garden of the Abbey of Westminster, the
Convent Garden, or Covent Garden as we know it today. This
was the very first of London's urban planning schemes and
proved to be a model on which many later ones were based.
The squares, as they came to be known, were the centrepieces
of self-contained communities with shops in close proximity and
a church either in the square or adjacent to it.

There was a long pause after the Covent Garden development but during the lifetime of Francis, the 5th Duke, the
greater part of Bloomsbury was built and, among others,
Russell Square, Tavistock Square and Woburn Square were
created. Although leases of the land were granted both to individuals and to professional builders for speculative purposes,
the Russell advisers ensured a uniformity of building and a
relatively high standard of architecture, as many of the houses
still standing prove. With an abundance of ready cash available
from this speculation, the 5th Duke took the opportunity to
rebuild and enlarge Woburn Abbey.

In a sense every member of the Russell family has been a
reformer. Many of their objectives, such as religious toleration
and the ending of the slave trade, are admirable by modern

standards, but in their pursuit of these objectives they certainly earned the epithet of headstrong which has often been attributed to them. John, the 4th Duke (1710–71), took over where Lord William left off. He was associated with the motion for the reduction of the civil list in 1737 and was in constant opposition to the government, a powerful thorn in the flesh of the monarchy until he rather unwillingly agreed to be Lord-Lieutenant of Ireland from 1757–61. He was Lord High Constable at the coronation of King George III but the last years of his life were spent still in strong opposition to the King's wishes, which he regarded as reactionary.

The 5th Duke earned the reputation of being a fine debater in the House of Lords before he was 30. He was the implacable enemy of Burke, yet his sympathies were with the aims of the reformers of the time.

During the last century and a half the Dukes have taken little part in politics but their reforming zeal has been evident in agriculture. Britain owes the family a great debt for the experimental work that was carried out on the Woburn estate during the 19th century—work comparable with that of Coke of Norfolk and "Turnip" Townshend.

The political banner of the family was carried in the 19th century with distinction by Lord John Russell, created the 1st Earl Russell. He was the only member of the family who became Prime Minister, a member of the group which forced through the Reform Bill against terrific opposition. He was known in his own lifetime rather disparagingly as "Finality Jack" because he believed that the Reform Bill was the complete answer to the demand for a new basis of election. Small in stature, but great in perception, he began a process which has lead to the democratic representation of today and has, in effect, prevented a revolution comparable with the French revolution.

The Russells have always been centres of controversy. That is true of the present Duke, as of his father and grandfather, and of the brilliant men who founded the Russell dynasty. But no one has doubted the sincerity of any member of the family, which has always been forward looking in politics and in the management of great estates. The present Duke, John the 13th Duke, carries on the family tradition of national service by selling Woburn so successfully to the World.

CHAPTER ONE

The Early Russells

STEPHEN RUSSELL of Dorchester and Weymouth is the first of
the Russell clan who can be proved beyond doubt to be the
ancestor of the Earls and Dukes of Bedford. Stephen Russell
was born between 1360 and 1380, and died in 1438. He had a
son, Henry, a most distinguished member of the family who
was several times returned to Parliament and died in 1463.
Henry in turn had several children, including two sons, John
and William. John was born between 1430 and 1435 and died
in 1505. His heir, James Russell, died in the following year but
his son John, who ultimately became the 1st Earl of Bedford,
had reached his majority before his father's death. The evidence
for this line of descent from the 14th century to the 16th is quite
positive and involves the history of the manor of Berwick near
Swyre, which, as we shall see later, was linked for the first time
with the family during Stephen's lifetime and formed part of
the Russell property in the 16th century, when it is mentioned
in the will of the 1st Earl. There is also evidence that some
properties in Dorchester descended directly from Stephen to
the 1st Earl.

Before looking at some of the more elaborate and fanciful
genealogies that have been created for the House of Russell it
is necessary to know something of this first unassailable member
of the House, Stephen. A good deal is recorded of his life in
outline, even though inevitably the detail is blurred. The first
things that strike one on the evidence of the records is that
he was a man of substance respected by his fellows both in

Dorchester and Weymouth. He is sometimes described as Russell of Dorchester, sometimes as Russell of Weymouth, and in all probability he owned property in both towns. His prosperity was derived from trade in Bordeaux wine. He was described officially as "gentleman" and in at least one document as "squire".

It is often said that in the 14th and 15th centuries people engaged in trade were regarded as scarcely worthy of notice. This is not strictly true. There are numerous instances of the younger sons of the gentry turning to trade, especially the export and import trade, as a means of earning a living, which every younger son, if he were not extremely lucky, was compelled to do. In earlier times, certainly in the 12th century, the only careers open to younger sons were those linked with war and with the Church. Many chose the life of the cloister, many distinguished themselves on the field of battle, but by the time of Stephen Russell, with a rapidly increasing population and a reaction against the cloister as a way of life, the horizons of the squirearchy expanded apace. The search for a more distinguished lineage which preoccupied antiquaries seeking to gratify their patrons was quite unnecessary in the case of the Russells and the majority of the noble families for which unsupported genealogies were produced in a fruitless attempt to show descent from a Norman baron or a hero of romantic legend.

Stephen was probably bailiff of Weymouth in 1388. In 1394 he represented Weymouth in Parliament, an honour which reflected his standing in the borough and also proved him to be a man of substance, since members summoned to Parliament in those days were required to pay their own expenses of travelling to and staying in London or any other place at which the King elected to hold a Parliament. It was a costly business both in time and money for a man like Stephen Russell, who had to leave his business for a prolonged period without the benefit of easy communication.

The Parliament of which Stephen was a member was a critical one. The young King Richard II had dismissed the Regency Council only five years before but had proved himself to be capable of governing with restraint and with marked success as a constitutional monarch paying more attention to Parliament than any king before him. The result was that in the years until 1399, when the King declared himself an absolute monarch and paid the penalty for his presumption, the powers of Parliament increased. Its influence had increased so much by 1397 that Sir Thomas Haxey could propose a motion of censure on the Court, an unheard-of thing in any earlier period. It is true that Sir Thomas was brought to trial and condemned on a charge of sedition, but the mere fact that it was possible for a member, and especially one of comparatively humble birth, to put such a motion proves that Parliament was no longer merely an instrument to carry out the sovereign's whims, and in particular to vote him the revenues for which he asked.

In 1394, the year in which Stephen sat, discontent was increasing among the rural workers. The crushing of Wat Tyler's rebellion had done nothing to quell the spirit of independence and in this session of Parliament one of several bills was passed which attempted to limit the wages that could be paid to labourers and to re-enact the regulation so often and unsuccesfully enacted before, preventing workers on the land from leaving their master's estate in an effort to secure better terms elsewhere.

Although his election to Parliament was the highlight of Stephen's career, his influence continued to be considerable in Dorset until the end of his life. This can be inferred from the parliamentary writs which show that he was an "elector" not only for the parliamentary constituency of Weymouth but for the County of Dorset on numerous occasions between 1421 and 1437, and helped in the return of his son to Parliament on two of these occasions in 1425 and 1437, on the latter occasion only a year before his death.

He married about 1400 a lady known to us only as Alice. This Alice claimed to be the heiress of two families, the de Blynchesfelds and the de la Tours. With her husband she was engaged in litigation for many years in an effort to obtain property belonging to these two families, the male line of both having died out. In 1422 a case was heard by the sheriff and a jury at Dorchester, and in the following year judgment was given in favour of the Russells, whose title to the land was based on Alice's descent through her mother and her maternal grandmother from Hugh de Blynchesfeld. It is said that two trials were necessary to settle this claim owing to the fact coming to light that the Russells had bribed the jury empanelled for the first hearing. Certainly that particular jury was discharged without giving a verdict. It made no difference. In addition to possession of the disputed land Alice was awarded a fine of £20 at the second hearing against the then occupiers of the land.

Alice was also involved in litigation over land near Shaftesbury which she already occupied. She was called upon again and again to prove her title to the land but this Stephen and Alice never found it necessary to do, as they preferred to pay regular fines for non-appearance at the provost's court.

Their claim to land in Swyre and neighbouring manors, including the property of Berwick, has thrown light on the history of the Russell family. The traditional Russell arms show the de la Tour arms quartered with their own. This fact presented a problem which was never resolved until the present century. It was believed, reasonably enough, that some generation of Russell must have married into the de la Tour family but it was impossible to trace or even to guess at the occasion on which this happened. Nor is that surprising, since as far as it is humanly possible to determine, no Russell ever married a de la Tour. Alice's maiden name is unknown but it was certainly not de la Tour. Yet her claim was to de la Tour land and the subsequent passing into the hands of the Russells of Berwick, formerly a manor of the de la Tours, was reason enough for the quartering of their arms in the Russell arms.

However, Alice was not immediately successful in her claim. Her case was opened at the assizes of 1427, when the land in question was held by the widow of a member of the Gough family. Alice successfully established the case for her descent from the de la Tours of Berwick through a daughter of John de la Tour, who died in 1340, but there was some doubt whether the manor of Berwick had been made over by John to another branch of the family and the verdict was given against the Russells.

The main point which emerged was that no one questioned the descent of Alice from the de la Tours or her rightful claim to the land apart from the matter of its possible alienation a hundred years before. There were, as it happened, other claimants and in the end, after years of argument in Court and out of Court, an arrangement was made by which the widow Gough was allowed to retain the manor during her lifetime after payment of a substantial sum to the Russells and to the other claimants, the Deverells, on condition that the manor reverted to the Deverells and their descendants, or failing that to the Russells and their descendants. There were no descendants of the branch of the Deverell family concerned, so the Russell family was once more lucky and the Swyre estate became their principal land holding before the showering of untold riches on the 1st Earl of Bedford by a grateful sovereign.

So far a picture of Stephen has emerged as a well-to-do merchant, probably a shipowner, and a respected figure in the life of Weymouth and the county, and the husband of an heiress of the de la Tours, who had been Dorset squires at least from the beginning of the 13th century. The one thing we cannot do for Stephen is to give him a father. It is likely that it will never be possible because all the available records of Dorset must have been searched many times in an effort to do so. One interesting point, however, has come to light. In common with many other people of his own and other ages,

Stephen Russell had an alias. He appears in documents and even in the parliamentary register alternately as Stephen Russell and Stephen Gascoyn. This is not really surprising. Surnames in the 14th and 15th centuries were not nearly as immutable, or relatively immutable as they are in the 20th. Younger sons often took the names of their wives, especially if their wives brought land with them as a dowry. Some even changed their surname to avoid confusion with their father or their brother who held the same christian names. Others doubtless changed them, as they still do, to meet the exigencies of the moment.

In reconstructing the life of the early Russells it must be remembered that Dorset was further away in time from London than the furthest point of America is today. Not that there is the slightest reason to suppose that Stephen Russell used an alias to avoid the consequences of actions carried out in his own name. Far from it. All that is implied is that he was known by both names, more generally perhaps by that of Russell. But the fact does make the name of his father almost impossible to determine. It is not even clear whether Stephen or his father was the founder of the Weymouth business. Stephen Russell means a lot because of the latter-day fame of the Russells. Stephen the Gascon means practically nothing at all. It might indeed be true that one of his forebears took the name Russell after emigrating from Gascony. Equally it might be true that Stephen himself assumed the name because of the business he was building up in shipping wine from Gascony, in particular from the port of Bordeaux. In this case one might describe it as a trade name.

Russell, or some variant of it, was a common enough name in Gascony but no proof has been found that Stephen or his father or grandfather emigrated from Gascony. It is, of course, possible that a member of a Gascon family settled in Weymouth to manage the import side of an export/import business, married into a Dorset branch of the Russell family and took the name Russell. That is one of the more likely explanations but still guesswork and, as every other explanation, rests on inference from insufficient facts.

The 2nd Earl, if not his father, believed that he was descended from the Russells of Kingston Russell in Dorset. That has been proved to be untrue if, as the Earl intended, it is taken to mean by direct descent. Russells or Russels of Kingston Russell are recorded from the beginning of the 13th century. One of them, John Russell, was a leader of Dorset society in the reign of King John, and many of his successors won distinction. But towards the middle of the 15th century the male line died out and the estate was divided between the two daughters of Sir Maurice Russell, Margaret and Isabella. On the other hand, Sir Theobald Russell, who lived in the first half of the 14th century, is known to have had several sons apart from his heir; it is at least conceivable that Stephen was descended directly from one of these. But again there is not the slightest evidence; it is far safer to regard Stephen as the known ancestor of the Russell family than to try by hypotheses, likely or unlikely, to place the family in some earlier setting which in all probability was not his.

The claims of the early Russells themselves were modest enough. They did not seek to trace their ancestry further back than the Russells of Kingston Russell. The 3rd Earl was far less modest. Late in life he was involved with the College of Heralds in an attempt to trace his ancestry to the Norman occupation. The work of research was in the hands of the York Herald, le Neve, who duly obliged. There is no doubt that le Neve did carry out some research in Dorset, starting from the Russells of Kingston Russell and working backwards. He did not, and indeed could not, question the descent from the Kingston Russells, seeing that this was accepted as undisputed fact by the Russell family, who were only a few generations removed from Dorset life and might be expected to know the facts rather than to be accepting a tradition of such recent origin.

The College of Heralds produced an elaborate pedigree which traced the family back to Baron Hugo de Rosel, who "came over with the conqueror". A certain Robert Russell was said to be the direct descendant of Hugo; this Robert had two sons, one of whom was the first Russell of Kingston Russell, the other the first Russell of Berwick from whom the Earls of Bedford were directly descended. This in a sense bypassed the Russells of Kingston, though keeping them well within the family.

The detail of the pedigree has been disproved in the light of later research again and again. Little or nothing is known of Hugo de Rosel and it is quite likely, if he existed as one of Norman William's barons, that his line died out like that of so many others of the relatively few Norman noblemen who were concerned in the occupation of England.

The root fault of le Neve and of others who attempted to prove descent from a Norman baron was that when their researches brought to light a document containing the name Russell they assumed that this was their Russell if it suited their purpose to do so and disregarded it if it did not. Unfortunately (although perhaps fortunately for them), Russell is and was a very common name in Dorset and neighbouring districts, while some form of Russell, such as Rosel, was an equally common patronomic in northern France, especially in Normandy. It is possible that some of the Dorset Russells were descended from a Norman Russell who accompanied William from Normandy but there is no certainty that this is so. It is certain, however, that the ancestors of some of the Russell families were Anglo-Normans who settled in England a hundred years or more after the Conquest.

Even in the time of Stephen Russell there was a John Russell of Dorchester known as Gyle, distinguished as a successful merchant but apparently no relation of Stephen's. There were Russells, lords of the manor of Mappowder, in the 13th century and later, and a Russell family established in Bridport in the

14th century. Another Russell family lived near the Dorset-Wiltshire boundary. These are definitely known; there must have been many others who never achieved a position sufficiently important for their names to be recorded.

However, the efforts of le Neve and his contemporaries were nothing compared with that of an antiquary of the first half of the 19th century, J. H. Wiffen, who was a member of the Society of Antiquaries of Normandy and wrote a memoir of the House of Russell for John, the 6th Duke of Bedford. This sumptuous work was undertaken, the author said, "with the view of rescuing from oblivion the achievements and of commemorating the various services of the ancestors of his House". Wiffen accepts without question the descent of the Duke from the de Rosel who was born about 1020 and was settled by William of Normandy in Dorset. So all Wiffen's research was based on the false assumptions of the Herald who had worked on the problem two hundred years before.

The amazing thing is that Wiffen spent the better part of two years in France tracing the ancestry of Hugo de Rosel. And what a house he built from his pack of cards! At the head of his lineage stands proudly the name of Olaf the Sharp-eyed, King of Rerik. The sharp-eyed Olaf is not given a date but he is at least five generations earlier than his descendant Sigurd Hring, King of Sweden, who was said to be reigning towards the middle of the 8th century. A daughter of Sigurd married one Thrond, Lord of Trondheim, from whom were descended some of the most famous Norse families. One of these families, the direct ancestors of the Norman Hugo, was the barons of Briquebec, one of whom, William Bertrand, was Hugo's father.

In the light of modern criticism this may appear nonsensical but the lineage was the result of the sincere endeavour of a learned 19th-century antiquary. Fashions change, and it would no longer be regarded as a distinction to be descended from Olaf the Sharp-eyed. If one took the matter far enough, it has been said, every lineage would start with the name Adam. It does have interest, however, because it throws light on the mentality of noble families in the 19th century, just as the earlier pedigree of le Neve illuminates the attitude of the 17th century. Then it was a matter of providing a distinguished lineage for a recently created earldom. In the 19th century it was more a matter of gilding the lily.

So we revert to Stephen Russell of Weymouth. If we cannot assign him a father, nor could Wiffen name a father for Olaf the Sharp-eyed.

Stephen's son Henry made his mark in Weymouth and Dorchester long before his father died. He was still more successful in business than Stephen, certainly one of the wealthiest shipowners of the Dorset ports and a man who took more than his fair share in public life as a Member of Parliament and holder of many offices under the Crown. To round off the picture of a solid and honoured citizen, he was wealthy enough to found a charitable guild and to subscribe to many other philanthropic ventures.

Nothing is known of his education but he almost certainly had private tutors and was exceptionally literate for the 15th century, when formal education was virtually unknown. In early manhood he assisted his father in the business of shipping wine from Bordeaux and distributing it in Dorset and further afield. It is a reasonable assumption that he took over the day-to-day running of the business, since by 1420 he was prominent in the councils of Weymouth and his name was already being put forward as a likely candidate for Parliament. In the first half of the 15th century it was considered an honour to be called to Parliament, but it was an honour that could be accepted only by people of substance and leisure. It was relatively easy for a man like Henry Russell to leave the family business when his father was still alive.

Stephen Russell's name appears year after year in the parliamentary returns as "elector" of the Weymouth burgesses returned to Parliament. His influence must have been considerable, therefore, in securing the return of Henry in 1425. In this Parliament Henry Russell witnessed the ceremony of the Protector Humphrey, Duke of Gloucester, presenting the infant King. In the words of Speed: "A strange sight and the first time it was ever seen in England for an infant sitting in its mother's lap and before it could tell what English meant to exercise in open Parliament the place of sovereign direction." Apart from that, little business was transacted in the Parliament of 1425, for the Duke of Gloucester, although paying lip service to constitutional government, came very near to absolute rule with the support of a powerful faction in the privy council.

Two years later Henry was again called to Parliament to represent the burgesses of Weymouth. By the time this Parliament met, the Duke of Gloucester was much less sure of his ground. He had quarrelled openly with his uncle, Henry Beaufort, Bishop of Winchester, who was tutor to the infant King and who, though he held no official position, had authority in the protectorate second only to that of Gloucester. This second Parliament of which Henry was a member had the task of interceding in the quarrel between the two statesmen. After long and frequently postponed deliberation it defined the respective powers of each. It must have been a valuable and exciting experience for a comparatively young man. These two visits to London in his early life, when he met and probably impressed many of the Court officials, were undoubtedly the foundation on which his later influence at Court was built.

Henry probably represented Weymouth for a third time in 1433 but his election is not noted in the parliamentary returns for Dorset county and the Dorset boroughs, from which the year 1433 is omitted, although it is significant that in the returns for 1432 Stephen Russell still appears as elector for the county of Dorset and for the borough of Weymouth, with Henry as co-elector. It looks as though the Russell family was in a position to elect one of its own members at will. This was a vitally important meeting, coming at a time when the war in

France had taken a gloomy turn, when the exploits of Joan of Arc in raising the siege of Orleans had made a great impression, and her execution by burning at Rouen an even greater and more disastrous impression. The fact that Henry had been crowned in Paris in 1431 had done nothing to relieve the tension, and pessimists were already forecasting the loss of all the French territories.

Partly because of the need to raise additional finance to prosecute the war, partly because of the sovereign's long minority, the power of the Lords and Commons was increasing, however slowly. The main purpose of the 1433 Parliament was to discuss and ultimately to grant a subsidy and vote of credit for the continuance of the war. Parliament also passed a vote of thanks to John, Duke of Bedford (no relation, of course, of the Russells) for his competent administration of the Regency in France in circumstances of unparalleled difficulty.

Another preoccupation of the Commons was the investigation of "breaches of the peace" which had taken place in a number of counties. It may well be true that the decision finally taken to excommunicate offenders arose from a suggestion put forward by Henry Russell. The Speaker also proposed a motion, which was carried unanimously, that not only members of the Lords and Commons but all "worthy men" in every shire should be required to take an oath for the preservation of peace. The breaches of the peace concerned were defined ambiguously but reading between the lines it is easy to see that even then, while the war with France was still in the balance, the rumblings which turned into the thunder of the Wars of the Roses were discernible in many parts of England. Many landlords in the shires and burgesses in the towns believed that the government of the country was being mismanaged, that England's hard-won possessions in France were being thrown away, and that only a stronger and more experienced sovereign could provide a solution to the problems of the realm.

Additional interest attaches to the Speaker's resolution, since both Henry and his father were among the people of Dorset who were called upon to take the oath, which was administered to knights of the shire, squires, and a limited number of leading citizens. Stephen and Henry Russell were among only fifty-nine names put forward for the county of Dorset. They appeared at a special Court in Dorchester, consisting of the Bishop of Bath and Wells, the then Chancellor, and the two Knights of the Shire, to swear an oath that they would not support any wrongdoer in their households and would not criticize or attack any officer who was doing his duty according to law.

The oath was described as "the eschewing of riots, excesses, misgovernances and disobedience against the King's Estate and against his laws". The sting, one suspects, was in the tail. The importance of the oath was not so much that it constituted a binding obligation on the part of those who took it to refrain from "harbouring robbers, oppressors of the people, felons, outlaws, ravishers of women against the law, and unlawful hunters of forests and parks" as that it placed on these fifty-nine leading citizens of Dorset the duty of ensuring so far as lay in their power that no one else in the county acted in such a way. They became in effect officers of the law themselves, with the duty of discovering any who were disloyal to the King and the government, and of denouncing them to the authorities.

This system, in which both the Russells took an important part, worked admirably in a county like Dorset, which was traditionally loyal to the existing regime and because of its maritime and commercial interests demanded nothing better than a stable government, whether a good one or a poor one. It achieved nothing in some other counties without such traditional loyalty or, what was worse, where there was substantial feeling that King Henry VI was not only a weak and therefore unsatisfactory sovereign but that he had no just claim to the throne.

As Stephen grew older, Henry spent more of his time directing the family business. He negotiated the building of new ships,
so that the Russell fleet became one of the largest based on the
ports along the Dorset coast. It was a time when no voyage was
without its perils and Henry certainly sailed on many voyages
in his own ships. Whether there was a state of open warfare
between England and France or not, captains of both nations
regarded ships of the other country as lawful prey. In the
general confusion piracy became an ever-increasing problem
and among the most successful buccaneers were some English
adventurers based on western ports who preyed on English and
French ships alike.

In 1438 Henry obtained safe conduct for eight Breton prisoners who had been captured in an engagement of which no
details are known and had been taken under guard to France to
collect their ransoms. They were now returning to England in
one of Henry's ships which carried not only their persons but
their ransoms in goods. It is likely that these Bretons were
Henry's own prisoners and possible that he was a member of
the force under the leadership of Lord Talbot which won some
signal successes in Normandy, including the capture of Harfleur
and Tankarville. It was one of many expeditions despatched to
France in the rather hopeless attempt to re-establish English
rule after the Duke of Burgundy had renounced his alliance
with England in 1435.

Henry sat once more for parliament in 1442, again representing the borough of Weymouth, where since the death of his
father he had taken over the latter's mantle as elder statesman
of the borough while still only in early middle age. As on a
previous occasion, the business of Parliament vitally concerned
Russell himself. It was clear by then that an extraordinary
effort was necessary if the English Channel was to be kept free
for normal commerce. The combination of French privateers
and pirates was beginning to throttle trade. Losses of ships and
cargo were assuming crippling proportions. Against this back-

ground it was a foregone conclusion that the King should be granted a subsidy for the purpose of policing the sea, together with a loan of the very large sum of £3,000 from the Council of London, which as the centre of international trade was deeply involved. The purpose of the money was to give allowances, compensation as we should call it, to owners of ships which were taken into the King's service.

Two of Henry Russell's fleet were among the ships designated for the purpose, merchant ships pure and simple but carrying between sixty and a hundred crew and armed men. They proved themselves capable of acting as efficient auxiliaries to the few larger ships of the line which were assigned to the patrol of the Channel. It was a great tribute to this largely civilian navy that when once energetic measures had been initiated piracy became decreasingly a threat to commerce and France was never in a position to blockade English ports.

It becomes increasingly obvious that Henry had friends at Court, and probably the full confidence of the King, now adult and assuming the full responsibility of governing England. The astonishing record of public appointments given to him from 1440 onwards is proof of the esteem in which he was held. They were mostly in the nature of royal commissions to enforce the government levy on goods passing through the ports and especially on wool. One of these commissions, the instrument of which is preserved in the Patent Rolls, was a most intriguing one. It started with a greeting from the King to his beloved Henry Russell and went on to enlarge on the losses caused to the Exchequer by reason of the fact that much wool and other customable merchandise was passing through "divers ports and places of our realm of England" for conveyance to foreign parts before they had been charged "the customs subsidies and other monies due to us therefrom." The commission then imposed on Henry Russell the duty of "arresting" all such wool and merchandise about to be taken out of "our said realm not customed wheresoever they may have been found", also to arrest the people responsible for attempting to export the wool duty free and to give full details to the Exchequer of the persons so arrested and of their offences.

Russell was promised the help of sheriffs, mayors and bailiffs in carrying out the commission, these officials being required "to wait upon, advise and aid" him. The terms of reference of the commission are not clear. It can be read as implying that Russell was given an overall command in the war against smuggling but it is likely that the commission extended only to the ports of Dorset or possibly to the ports of Dorset and Devonshire. Russell carried out the commission with commendable zeal and arrested at least one ship off Portland Bill loaded with dutiable merchandise, which he seized for the Exchequer, to the value of more than £250. By then he had been appointed joint Collector of the Customs for the ports of Dartmouth and Exeter. That must have been an unpopular appointment in Devonshire, for then county loyalties meant far more than they do today and Russell would have been regarded as an interloper, winning his appointment by undue influence with the Court.

That may be the reason why an information was laid against him in 1442 before the sheriff in Exeter accusing him of failing to perform his duties as customs commissioner by absenting himself from the two ports. Poor Henry Russell. He could not reasonably have been expected to do a full-time inspection and collection job at Exeter and Dartmouth and at the same time carry out the King's roving commission. Moreover he had been appointed bailiff of Weymouth in 1441 and was compelled by the official duties of this appointment to spend a good deal of his time there. One must remember that it was a full day's journey in the 15th century from Weymouth to Exeter, while the journey to Dartmouth would normally have occupied two days. To have carried out even two of his three appointments satisfactorily Russell would have needed two or three trusty deputies.

However, there is no doubt that he had committed an offence by not keeping the customs accounts and in 1443 he went to Westminster by order of the sheriff, charged with an offence for which the set penalty was £100. But the good Henry knew what he was doing and the jealous people of Exeter would have done far better not to have informed against him. In reply to the charge at the Westminster Court Russell was able to produce two royal pardons, one releasing him from the consequences of any offence committed in or before 1441, the other a document issued by the King only five days before the time fixed for Russell's trial, commanding the authorities not to molest him in any way, and reiterating the terms of the pardon previously granted. The Court had no option but to take notice of the documents with which Russell had so thoughtfully provided himself and adjourned the case *sine die*, which was, of course, the equivalent of an absolute acquittal.

The King's commission to wage war on the smugglers had no definite term. It may well have continued for many years and possibly for the whole of his lifetime. It was equivalent to the King appointing a personal representative in the region. Had not the sovereign been unpredictable, forgetful, and recurrently of unsound mind, Henry Russell would surely have been knighted. As it was, these years of excitement marked the climax of Russell's life. He was not again, so far as is known, called to sit in Parliament. The opportunities of renewing friendships at Court were few. It has been suggested that he had a house in London but there is not the slightest evidence to support the suggestion. Very few provincial people apart from the bishops and a handful of the wealthiest families had by then acquired or built a town residence.

Henry, however, maintained his influence in Weymouth and in the County of Dorset. His name appears among the electors of the knights of the shire as late as 1460, only four years before his death. He was honoured in Dorset, too, for his endowment of the Guild of St. George. The Guild was founded in 1442

3

nominally as a token of appreciation for the confidence shown in him as their representative in Parliament by the people of Weymouth. Its personnel consisted of Russell himself, the Vicar of Wyke Regis, the mother-church of Weymouth, the Dean of Salisbury and all the parishioners of Wyke Regis, including, of course, Weymouth. The Guild had a master and two wardens who had the right of appointing the chantry priest, whose duty was to pray for the welfare of the King, the founders and the members of the Guild, i.e. the parishioners of Wyke Regis.

Twelve years later Russell endowed the chaplain and his successors in perpetuity with land in Weymouth, Portland and elsewhere, a very generous endowment by all accounts. The master of the Guild was always a member of the Russell family and it continued in active existence until the reign of Henry VIII, when all chantries were dissolved along with the monastic houses. The chapel was given to the parishioners.

The Russell's commercial activities suffered a severe decline in 1453, when the English forces in France were defeated at the Battle of Châtillon, which virtually brought the Hundred Years' War to an end, wholly unsatisfactory to England. Although the English King continued to be known as King of France, it was an empty title; the only French soil left to England was the port of Calais and the Channel Islands. Trade in French wine with Bordeaux continued, but on a reduced scale.

Merchants like Russell had expanded their commercial horizons and shipped wine from Spain, but Spanish wine never achieved the popularity of the rich red wine of France and there was at least a temporary lull in the prosperity of some of the families whose chief trade was with France.

Disruption at home also began to make trading less profitable. The Wars of the Roses had progressed from the long stage of unrest and occasional terrorism to that of pitched battles by 1455. It was always a rather nebulous war, the pitched battles of which historians have made so much being in fact no more than the clash of the armed followers of rival claimants to the throne. It was never a people's war in the sense of the wars of the 20th century. As Macaulay says, "In a week the peasant was driving his team and the esquire flying his hawk over the fields of Bosworth as if no extraordinary event had interrupted the regular course of human life." Even so, although the trading classes took no part in the war, the very fact that many of the leading families were deploying their resources in these domestic hostilities reduced the demand for expensive imported products.

Russell may have sold his business, or sold his ships, and allowed the commercial enterprise to lapse after 1453. There is no record of his taking any part in trade after that and no evidence that the business was carried on by later members of the family. In a sense it made little difference to him, for he was a rentier as well as a merchant and as revenue from trade declined, that from the land increased. His retirement, if that is the right word, made it possible for him to devote himself almost exclusively to public service during the last years of his life. He had been appointed Deputy Butler for the port of Melcombe as early as 1427. In 1455 he became in addition Deputy Butler for the port of Poole and in that year, or the year before, he was also appointed one of the commissioners in charge of the collection or special taxes for the Exchequer, his territory including Weymouth, Poole, and Salisbury.

Like his father he had made a successful and profitable marriage which had considerably enlarged the family estates. His wife was Elizabeth Herring, a co-heiress of John Herring of Chaldon Herring, a valuable manor some miles east of Weymouth. Although his father-in-law outlived his wife, who died some time before 1449, a considerable property passed to his son John, who had been born about 1430. Henry and Elizabeth had a younger son, William, and a daughter, Joan, born before John. Their youngest child was a daughter called Cristina, who married into the Cheverell family of East Stoke, forging a link with yet another important Dorset family.

The last year in which Henry Russell appears in any record
is 1463, when, carrying on the tradition of his father, he was
summoned to the manorial court of Stour Provost, and was
fined, as he and his father had been for so many years, for not
proving their title to the disputed land to which reference has
been made earlier. He must have died either in the last months
of 1463 or in the following year. It is uncertain where he was
buried, for there is no monument or parish record to give mute
evidence. The same, of course, is true of his father. It may well
be that they were both buried in a family mausoleum, most
probably in the Church of Holy Trinity, Dorchester, where an
investigator on behalf of the 4th Earl reported finding a Russell
tomb with an inscription commemorating Henry Russell and
his wife.

All trace of that tomb disappeared during reconstruction of
the church after a disastrous fire, but it is much more likely that
he was buried there than at Swyre, the parish of the manor of
Berwick. There is no reference to his ever having lived at Berwick and it is likely that the manor did not become part of the
Russell estate until some time after his death, in accordance
with the settlement to which his father and mother had been
parties. For his contemporaries and the people of the next few
generations his chantry chapel in St. Nicholas at Weymouth
was the finest of all monuments to a man of strong character
and great achievements.

John Russell, Henry's son and heir, and John's heir, James,
who was the father of the 1st Earl, were far less eminent in local
and national life than the two earlier generations. However, if
nothing very much is known of them, it is certain that their lives,
if uneventful, were useful and that neither fell foul of the law
or suffered any major catastrophe. The family continued in its
chosen path, changing gradually from the activities of urban
commerce to those of the rural squirearchy. As we have seen
already, Henry probably disposed of the family business. His
son took little or no part in it and certainly did not carry it on

after his death. John is the first Russell who can rightly be described as a Russell of Berwick. The manor came into his possession some time after Henry's death, probably in 1485. There is a tradition that he was the John Russell who was returned to Parliament for Weymouth in 1449 when his father was certainly one of the electors for the burgesses. The difficulty of accepting this tradition, which arises from the official parliamentary returns, is that he was scarcely of an age to be returned for Parliament in 1449. It is unlikely that he was born before 1430 or after 1433. It is just possible that he was elected through the undeniably great influence of his father but it is more likely that another John Russell was concerned. A John Russell was also elected for Dorset in 1470 but again his identity is uncertain.

In later life he was a gentleman farmer purely and simply, developing the Berwick estate and keeping a close watch on the other farm-lands which he had inherited. He married into the Froxmere family between 1445 and 1449. His bride, variously known as Elizabeth and Alice, was the daughter of John Froxmere of Wych in Worcestershire. Since the Froxmeres appear in Dorset history as purchasers of land for the first time after that date, it may be assumed that John's wife was so impressed by the Dorset scene that she persuaded her relatives to buy a stake in the county, where they later exercised considerable influence.

The only other known fact of any significance about John is that he was three times, in 1488, 1490 and 1491, called to the Court of Stour Provost to establish his title to the same parcel of land which had embarassed his father and grandfather before him. On each occasion he failed to enter an appearance and was fined in default. The fact can only be explained on the assumption that non-appearance was a matter of principle in the family. The few acres of land concerned can have had no real significance either for John or his father, or indeed for his grandfather. It would have been far cheaper to have abandoned it than to incur fines again and again for refusing to substantiate their claim to it. Although records are deficient after that, the principle was certainly maintained in future generations. The land in question formed part of the estate of the 1st Earl at his death, and one assumes that by then all concerned had forgotten the matter of disputed title raised 150 years before.

John died in 1505. He and his wife are buried in the Church of Holy Trinity at Swyre, the parish church of the manor of Berwick. A commemorative brass can still be seen on the wall just beside the north door: "Here lie John Russell Esquire and Elizabeth, his wife, daughter of John Frocksmer Esquire, which deceased in the 20th year of King Henry VII A.D. 1505." On the other side of the north door a similar brass commemorates John's heir, James: "Here lie James Russell Esquire and Alys, his wife, daughter of John Wise Esquire, who deceased the first year of King Henry VIII 1509." Incidentally, although the church was heavily restored in the 19th century, its general appearance today is much as it was in the time of John and James Russell, the fine Gothic windows being at that time a recent addition reflecting the increasing prosperity of a district which depended for its wealth on the fine flocks of sheep which grazed over the downs. Fleeces had never been more valuable than towards the end of the 15th century.

Of James, the 1st Earl's father, we know only that he was John's heir. There is no documentary evidence that he was his son and some critics have suggested that he was the son of John's brother William. There is no genuine reason for this supposition except the lack of documentary evidence of John's paternity. In this case there is no need to discredit tradition and the many near-contemporary chroniclers for whom James was indisputably the son of John. We know, too, that James had two younger brothers, Thomas and Henry. The latter followed the age-old vocation of a younger son and entered the priesthood, in which he won great distinction and was knighted for his services to the Church.

James married Alice Wise, a member of the Wise family of Sydenham near Tavistock in Devon. They had two children, Thomasine and John, the heir, who became the 1st Earl. That nothing else is known of James except that he farmed land adjacent to that of Berwick as well as the manor itself and lived in a house known as Little Berwick is not surprising, since he led the uneventful life of a countryman and only survived his presumed father by a year.

This chapter must end with a sad note on the unreliability of evidence which at first glance appears wholly reliable. The brass in Swyre church categorically states the date of the death of James as 1509, yet James's will was made late in 1505 and it was proved in February of 1506. His brother Thomas and his son John were the executors. He must, therefore, have died in the winter of 1505–6. Why, then, is the monumental brass guilty of such a gross error? The answer is that the brasses are not contemporary. They have been proved to be in a script characteristic of the Elizabethan rather than of the early Tudor age and were most likely made to the order of the 2nd Earl, who presumably had forgotten the date of his grandfather's death or was misinformed about it. Strange but true.

That is not the end of the story. The brasses were originally in the Berwick pew and were only removed to their present position during the 19th century restoration. Then, to make confusion worse confused, the shields of the two Russells were transposed, so that today James Russell's shield appears above the John Russell brass and John Russell's shield appears above that of James.

CHAPTER TWO

The Earldom is Founded

JOHN RUSSELL of Berwick, the future 1st Earl of Bedford, was not much more than twenty when his father died. He had completed his education, which his future career proved beyond all doubt to have been a good one, but, of course, nothing is known of its detail. He was brought up as the son of a prosperous Dorset farmer and as the grandson of the Lord of Berwick. There could be no reason for recording his early life, which would have been regarded as training for assuming the responsibilities of Berwick and of the other manors which constituted the Russell inheritance.

Descriptions of him as a young man show that he was good-looking, of medium height, of a cheerful manner, chivalrous to a degree, and able to make one with almost everybody he met. It is a description that would suit many future Earls and Dukes of Bedford, down to the present day. His social graces and wide general knowledge were noted. So was his philosophical outlook on life, and his willingness to come to the assistance of anyone who was in trouble. Most important of all, from the point of view of his future career, he was already an accomplished linguist by the time of his father's death.

Like many other eldest sons of well-to-do families, he had spent several years travelling in Europe and could speak and understand French, Spanish and Italian like a native. He had learned enough, too, in his travels to develop a passionate regard for the culture of Italy and for the ideals of the Renaissance which had blossomed in Italy long before they spread to other parts of Europe and which as yet had scarcely penetrated to rural Dorset.

In January 1506, either just before or just after James Russell's death, a fortunate sequence of events placed the youthful John on the road to a highly successful career. The Archduke Philip of Austria and his wife Joanna, the daughter of Ferdinand or Aragon and Isabella of Castile, whose sister Katherine was betrothed to Prince Henry, the future King Henry VIII, were sailing from Flanders to Spain accompanied by a number of attendant ships. They had the misfortune to run into a severe gale as they sailed down the English Channel. The Archduke, with two of his attendant ships, was separated from the rest of the fleet. A bad sailor, he was extremely ill with seasickness, and wanted nothing more than to put his feet on dry land. Against the advice of his counsellors he ordered the ships to put into Weymouth, the nearest port.

The appearance of even such a small convoy of foreign vessels caused consternation to the people of Dorset, who had lived for a century or more under the constant threat of raids by foreign ships. A warm welcome was in preparation for the unknown visitors. Sir Thomas Trenchard, in charge of the coastal defences of Dorset, and Sir John Carew, sheriff of the county, appeared on the scene just in time. They recognized the position and received the Archduke and his wife with suitable ceremony, all the more sincere because Ferdinand and Isabella were strong allies of England.

Sir Thomas invited the Archduke to visit him in his house at Wolfeton. In agreeing, the Archduke was no doubt influenced by his wife, who had had a frightening experience at sea about ten years before, when she was sailing to Flanders for her wedding. She was overtaken by a similar storm in which several of the escorting ships were sunk.

Sir Thomas did what he could to entertain his distinguished guests and sent a letter to the King, who asked him to continue to entertain the Archduke and his wife until he could come himself to welcome them. The only fly in this happy ointment was that the Archduke scarcely had a word of English, while Sir Thomas was equally ignorant of Spanish and French. An interpreter was necessary and who better than John Russell, then only a few miles away at Berwick, and whom Sir Thomas already knew as a kinsman by marriage. (A member of the Trenchard family had married into a branch of the Russell family.)

The arrival of John was welcomed by all, though it is perhaps significant that in his own account of the matter the Archduke made no mention of the young interpreter. However, there is no doubt that he was a success, for when the Archduke decided not to wait for the King's arrival but to go immediately to him at Windsor, John Russell as well as Sir Thomas was in the royal party. King Henry was very glad to have the Archduke as his guest and on one pretext or another kept him at the English Court for nearly two months, while the fate of Europe was discussed again and again and informal agreements reached on many matters of mutual interest to the King and the Archduke.

It is probably an apocryphal story that Russell continued to act as interpreter, but he was certainly introduced to the King either then or shortly afterwards, and created a most favourable impression. That is the only conclusion to be drawn from the fact that he was offered and accepted a minor appointment in the royal household, that of gentleman usher. The young Russell was fortunate to gain this first appointment, for only a few months before he had no thought of a career at Court and was preparing to be a farmer. It is most unfair to Russell, however, to attribute his appointment to a lucky chance. Chance, of course, entered into it because he happened to be at hand when his kinsman needed an interpreter, but that is the end of it. To ascribe this first stage in his career to luck was the taunt of jealous men who made far less use of their opportunities.

If he had not been a clever young man Sir Thomas would not

have sent for him. If he had not made a favourable impression on the Archduke he would not have accompanied him to Windsor. If he had not equally impressed Henry VII he most certainly would not have received a royal appointment, for the King was a most hard-headed sovereign, whose success had always been due to his ability to pick the right men to serve under him and to be guided by his reason rather than by emotion. He is said to have kept a voluminous notebook in which he jotted down details of all the promising people he met, with a view to using their services when occasion arose. He did not even find it necessary to relegate John Russell to the pages of his notebook. He was sufficiently impressed to secure his services without waiting for a suitable opportunity.

In the same way many have ascribed John Russell's success in the next thirty years to a combination of good fortune and charm, and have described his career as meteoric. Both statements are untrue. Russell succeeded by hard work, by unswerving loyalty to the Crown, and sheer ability. It was more than fifteen years after becoming a gentleman usher that he was given his first important assignment. He weathered the storms of King Henry VIII's reign and was just as influential in the reign of King Edward VI. Mere survival for so long as a confidante of the sovereign proved special qualities. Not only to survive but to complete a career as the sovereign's personal adviser and foreign representative with honour proved that he was a man in a million.

His first few years at Court were comparatively uneventful. The life of a gentleman usher, however, was not without its responsibility. He, with his three colleagues, was responsible for ensuring that the sovereign received only the people he was expecting. This latter point had perhaps been more important in the reigns of earlier kings but even in the time of Henry VII the fear of assassination was never far from the mind of a king, not necessarily by one of his own people but by agents introduced into his court by devious means on behalf of foreign powers. Whatever signs there might have been of growing amity among European nations, might was still equated with right and there was always an enemy country ready to pounce on another or to liquidate a sovereign like Henry VII, who happened to be a strong and formidable one.

So one of the most important duties of the gentleman ushers was to guard the door of the Great Chamber to ensure that only those who had been authorized personally by the King entered it. There was even a rule that no clergymen was to enter, except the King's own chaplain. The ushers were also the officials to whom the King delegated the duty of receiving lesser visitors to the Court. The latter were numerous, including many from Spain, France, Italy and Germany when England was not at war with any of these countries. The ushers were required to receive these visitors in person if they were of families judged to be equivalent to that of an English lord. There were also yeoman ushers whom the gentleman ushers could instruct to receive vistiors of lesser calibre.

It was a time when the once all-powerful position of the clergy was weakening. Until the Wars of the Roses all, or almost all, the trusted confidantes of the sovereign were ordained priests, his envoys and plenipotentiaries mostly bishops or other senior members of the Church. After Henry became King fewer and fewer clergy were employed and most of the high offices in the state and in the palace were held by laymen. It was a sign of the times in that although the Reformation was deferred until the following reign the government of England was already, in the person of King Henry, taking active steps to free itself from dependance on Rome.

So people like John Russell had an excellent chance of preferment. His work as usher not only made him known to the King personally but prepared him for the life of ceremony and protocol which was part and parcel of any high appointment under the Crown. King Henry died in 1509 before the occasion had arisen to give Russell any special commission but his appointment was confirmed by Henry VIII, then not quite 18 and very willing to carry on the traditions established by his father. He must have known Russell well before his accession. As he was the youngest of the Court officials near to the sovereign, only a few years older than Henry himself, it is perfectly understandable that the two, who were both intelligent and high-spirited young men, should get on very well together.

They did rather more than that. They formed a lasting friendship which sprang from mutual respect and persisted even when Henry in his later years became scarcely responsible for his actions. If the bonds of friendship inevitably grew weaker, mutual respect remained. Russell, unlike most of Henry's advisers, remained loyal to him to the end, Henry never entirely turned away from Russell.

In the early years of the reign there was scarcely a cloud on the horizon. As a 19th-century historian says, Russell "engaged the king's favourable notice while participating in all those magnificent frolics of his fancy, the dance, the masque, the pageant, and the tourney". That may be a slight exaggeration of fact. That Henry knew his own mind, however, is well shown by the execution of Empson and Dudley; he had been on the throne for less than four years before he took a personal part in the intermittent warfare between England and France.

That was the occasion of Russell's first opportunity to distinguish himself. Early in 1513 the King asked Sir Gilbert Talbot, the Governor of Calais, to engage Russell as a member of the garrison with special duties. Almost certainly what the King had in mind was that Russell should prepare the way for him. On 3rd June the King landed at Calais at the head of a sizeable, well-armed force, with the determination to carry the war into France itself. The expedition, which was remarkably successful, partly because it took the French by surprise, was more for the sake of propaganda than conquest. As such it was uncommonly effective. Russell accompanied the King and was with him at the Battle of the Spurs, at which Henry commanded in person and the strong force of French cavalry was put to flight. It was this flight of the French horsemen that suggested to the English the name of Spurs for the Battle, rather than Spours, the nearest village. The French, too, in later years appeared to appreciate the pun, for to them as well as to English historians it has become the Battle of the Spurs.

The principal and, indeed, the only result of this battle was that the English were able to enter Tournai without opposition, to garrison it, and to hold it as an English town for some years. Henry was well satisfied with his limited victory and returned to England before the end of September. He left Sir Edward Poynings as Governor of Tournai, with John Russell holding some ill-defined appointment as a personal representative of the King, an appointment which must have needed all Russell's tact and personality to hold without incurring the enmity of the Governor.

Sir Edward Poynings was succeeded by Lord Mountjoy at the beginning of 1515 and Mountjoy in turn by Sir Richard Jerningham two years later. Russell remained in Tournai until the town was returned to France in 1518 on payment by King Francis of a very large indemnity, 600,000 crowns for the city, 400,000 crowns for the recently completed castle, a similar sum to discharge the liability for grants which Henry had made to English people. This latter provision affected Russell, for he had received a grant in fee of land near Tournai as a reward for his services there and at Calais.

His years at Tournai meant much more to him, however, than a modest addition to his fortune. He had acted throughout as a messenger for the King and for Wolsey, whose overriding authority in England was now undisputed. He also carried out a number of diplomatic missions in France on their behalf, including negotiations for the seizure in France of Richard de la Pole, "The White Rose" and the chief pretender to the English throne, supported by the remnants of the militant Yorkists and for obvious reasons by the King of France. Russell executed the preliminaries of this commission with great skill and took the negotiations to the point where it only remained for a fee to be fixed between the English government and the people in Burgundy who were prepared to kidnap de la Pole, but the price asked was exorbitant and Wolsey refused to ratify it.

In his last year at Tournai Russell formed a close friendship with Sir Richard Jerningham and his wife, who was probably the first woman to arouse in him a feeling which transcended his ambition and his devotion to his career. No difficulty arose then because he endeared himself to both the Jerninghams but that friendship in later years changed the whole course of his life. The strength of Lady Jerningham's personality even in Tournai days was almost a legend.

Back home in 1519 John Russell resumed his round of duties at Court but by now the King and Cardinal Wolsey were thinking of him in terms of a special envoy rather than as a gentleman usher. He accompanied the King on most of his journeys. He supported him when he received ambassadors and acted for him in many private matters. He was already respected not only as a fluent linguist and courteous representative of the sovereign, both very important things, but also as a skilled negotiator, especially in financial matters.

In 1520 he accompanied King Henry on his visit to France for a conference with the French King. The meeting took place between Calais and Boulogne but it turned out to be less a conference than a display. The purpose of both sovereigns appeared to be to outvie the other in splendour and ceremony. Tent palaces were erected of gaily coloured materials embroidered in gold. The retinues of both sovereigns appeared in gorgeous uniforms, wearing jewels, and the main proceedings of the meeting consisted, we are told, of feasts, tournaments and balls. The meeting-place came to be known as the Field of the Cloth of Gold, not without good reason.

Whatever purpose the French King may have had, he failed

to achieve it. Henry was not in the least impressed by the French competition in royal grandeur. No effective agreement on the future relations of the two countries was reached, nor was any treaty signed. The two sovereigns parted after three weeks of festivity and returned to their respective courts. On his way home King Henry met his kinsman by marriage, the Emperor Charles V (the son of the Archduke Philip who had been instrumental in introducing Russell to Henry VII). Charles V had been elected Emperor of Germany and was by far the most powerful sovereign in 16th-century Europe. He had ambitions to add France to his dominions and possibly also England. At the time, however, he was regarded favourably by the English court, especially by Wolsey, who is said to have sought his good-will in the hope that he would use his influence to elevate him to the papacy when that office fell vacant. Whatever the reasons the fact remains that England now abandoned its traditional policy of maintaining the balance of power in Europe and made a secret alliance with Charles V directed against the French King. In the devious methods which the two sovereigns used to achieve the overthrow of France Russell had another opportunity to prove his value and also his courage.

The Emperor Charles visited England in 1522. He became betrothed to the Princess Mary and promised his support for a plan of the King and Wolsey to subdue France. This was in accordance with the secret treaty which had been made with the Emperor at Bruges in 1521 (the negotiations in this case having been carried out by Wolsey) by which it had been agreed that the Emperor and King Henry should unite not only to defend their own countries against French aggression but to make war on France with the purpose of recovering the lands that had once formed part of their respective dominions.

When Charles left England the government planned a coup against France which was no doubt intended as an earnest of English determination. Under the Earl of Surrey, then Lord Admiral, John Russell and some other well-known members of the Court escorted Charles down the Channel as far as the Bay of Biscay with a full muster of ships of the line under the pretext of ensuring that the sea was clear of pirates for the Emperor's voyage. The Emperor safely delivered, they descended on the coast of Brittany with a force numbering at least seven thousand and captured Morlaix. In the engagement before the town fell Russell was struck by an arrow and lost the sight of one eye, but he had his reward. When the force returned to their ships he was knighted on deck by the Earl of Surrey for his conspicuous bravery.

News reached the King of the successful foray and a royal welcome awaited the Earl and his party when they returned. The King congratulated Sir John on his bravery and coolness in danger and reminded him of the occasion when as a member of the garrison of Calais he had been taken prisoner by the enemy and had not only contrived to escape but to bring his captor back as a prisoner.

When in 1523 the time came to implement the plans made for the conquest of France, Sir John was chosen as the diplomatist to represent both King Henry VIII and the Emperor Charles V in the delicate negotiations which had to be carried out with Charles, Duke of Bourbon. The Duke, who was one of the most influential noblemen in France, had formed a bitter enmity for King Francis and was prepared to assist in overthrowing his government. He had reached an understanding with the Emperor Charles that he would join the confederacy with an army of ten thousand men in May of 1523. Sir John was sent in disguise through Flanders to discuss the details of the operations with the Duke at Chantilly. He reached Chantilly safely and put the proposition that the English King would advance him a substantial sum towards raising the army with which he was to attack Burgundy, on condition that he acknowledged Henry as the rightful inheritor of the French crown.

The Duke agreed and signed the form of treaty which Sir

4

John presented to him. Unfortunately the French King was suspicious of the Duke of Bourbon and although probably unaware of the conspiracy against France kept a permanent and obvious watch on his movements and virtually made it impossible for him to command or even to raise the army with which he was due to seize Burgundy. The Duke was alarmed and took refuge in the neutral town of Besançon. Meanwhile, as planned, a Spanish army attacked Provence and an English force under the Duke of Suffolk advanced across Normandy to the very gates of Paris. There is no doubt that had the Duke of Bourbon been in a position to join in the planned three-pronged attack the French government must have fallen, though whether Henry would have been permitted by Charles V to become King of France without a battle is less certain. As winter advanced the English force retired and a golden opportuntiy was lost.

During all this time Sir John was helping the Duke of Bourbon as best he could to augment the wholly inadequate mercenary force which he had raised before retiring to Besançon. By the autumn it was clear that nothing more could be achieved, especially as many of the mercenaries had deserted, and Sir John was instrumental in persuading the Duke and his advisers not to attempt to raise fresh troops. In this Russell was as tactful as possible, following his instructions to prevent English resources being spent fruitlessly. He told the Duke, reasonably enough, that if the mercenaries had been faithful to their engagements all would have been well. Sir John invited him on the King's behalf to seek voluntary exile in England but in this for once Sir John was unsuccessful. The Duke elected to take shelter with the Emperor, who gave him the choice of Spain or Italy for his exile. The Duke chose Italy.

Sir John deposited the large sums of money he was carrying (the unspent balance of the cash earmarked for the support of the Duke's army) with a merchant in Besançon but his stay there was becoming dangerous. His presence was known to the

French government and spies were sent to Besançon to discover his business and if possible to kidnap him. He repeatedly asked King Henry for further instructions but on the joint request of King Henry and Wolsey he remained there throughout the winter, moving from lodging to lodging, usually in disguise, to report on the relations between the French King and the Swiss Cantons.

The Duke of Bourbon appears on the scene again in the early spring, this time as commander-in-chief of the Emperor's forces based on Milan. He was brilliantly successful and drove the French occupying troops from the whole of Lombardy. Undeterred by the failure of his previous undertaking to the English King, he despatched a messenger to the English Court, offering to cross the Alps with the Emperor's forces from Italy, overrun the southern provinces of France, and recognize Henry as King of France in exchange for Henry's promise to pay him 100,000 crowns a month to provision the army. Sir John was instructed as a first step to join the Duke with the money which he had lodged at Besançon.

That was a commission which taxed all his ingenuity. It was no easy task to convey 100,000 crowns or more across hostile territory to the Duke, who had invaded Provence, captured Nice, Aix and most of the important centres in the South of France, and laid siege to Marseilles. Sir John left Besançon at the end of June and arrived at the camp before Marseilles on 26th August after the most incredible adventures but with his "cargo" safe and sound, and incidentally very welcome to the Duke of Bourbon, who was rapidly running out of funds.

Sir John described his adventures in letters to the King and Cardinal Wolsey. He travelled by way of Geneva and across the Alps to Turin. He had the gold packed in bales half full of old clothes and put a merchant's mark on the bales, then had them consigned as ordinary merchandise from Geneva to Italy. The simple subterfuge appears to have been completely successful. Even when he reached the camp before Marseilles his troubles

were far from over. He resumed his position as adviser to the
Duke and was present at the council on 19th September when
the Duke resolved to make a last effort to take Marseilles by
storm.

Sir John then set sail for Genoa to collect a further contribution to the cost of the war for transmission to the Duke. This
money was being carried by members of the Order of St. John
to the Grand Master of the Order in Trent. That at least was
the pretext given and accepted by the authorities for the transit
of the gold. He had difficulty in making contact with the St.
John's party but he ultimately met them at Viterbo and after
consulting the English ambassador in Rome and the Pope, took
the money into his own safe keeping. Its appropriation had been
left largely to his discretion, a remarkable tribute to his integrity. It was to be given to Bourbon if he and the Emperor
acted in accordance with their treaty with England but in the
event of this not being so Russell had authority to use it as
seemed to him to be of greatest advantage to the King's affairs.

Bourbon had suffered an unexpected defeat and his army had
been routed and had evacuated Provence after Sir John left
Marseilles. In these circumstances, in spite of a request by the
Emperor's ambassador in Rome and the assurances of the Pope
that he would stand surety for the loan, Sir John, with the help
of a Florentine merchant, arranged for the return of the money
to England.

His mission now completed, he took leave of the ambassador,
the Bishop of Bath, but had only completed three days' journey
when a courier from the Bishop overtook him, directing his
return on Wolsey's orders. He barely escaped with his life when
ambushed by a detachment of the Duke of Albany's forces (the
Duke was at the time seeking to restore the French occupation
of part of Italy). When he reached Rome he found that he was
required to return to Bourbon's camp, where he arrived in time
to be present at the Battle of Pavia, at which the imperial forces
won a resounding victory over the French and King Francis was

taken prisoner. It is possible, but not certain, that Sir John commanded some of the companies under Bourbon's direction (he was not, after all, inexperienced in war).

Sir John's letter to King Henry describing the battle and its consequences is of special interest. He started by saying that he would have been with Bourbon long before, as instructed, "but that the Duke of Albany lay in my way so that I could not pass". He said that when he reached the camp he found the Duke still determined to overthrow the French King, saying "that if your Highness will he will set the crown of France on your head and that shortly". He reported that in spite of his confidence the Duke would appreciate a further advance of 200,000 crowns "to furnish payment for 12,000 foot men and 500 men of arms for two months". With these forces at his disposal he would march into France with the selfsame men under him who had already beaten the French, "reckoning the same a great advantage for they were greatly dreaded in France".

Russell further reported that Bourbon would welcome an invasion of France by King Henry in person so that the two armies could meet. He estimated French casualties at Pavia to be twelve thousand, apart from many who were drowned in the River Tecino while attempting to escape from the battlefield. In addition there were ten thousand French prisoners. "The said Duke saith," Russell's letter ended, "that now is the time and that shortly your Highness may if you accomplish the said Duke's command before rehearsed obtain of your right and inheritance, and this offer, he saith, is only to do your Highness service and to help you recover your right."

The matter was complicated by the fact that Charles discountenanced all public signs of triumph and was inclined to encourage negotiations with the French Queen Regent for her son's liberation. Henry and Wolsey at first reacted favourably. An army was mustered to invade France for the recovery of Normandy and other parts of Northern France which had once formed part of the English realm and vigorous efforts were made to raise further taxes to carry on the war. The imposition of fresh taxes, many of them harsh, brought England near to rebellion and the King and Wolsey were compelled to abandon the plan. They did not, however, immediately inform Bourbon nor Sir John, who continued to send hopeful despatches asking for a quick agreement to the Duke's requests. He was finding continued inactivity most irksome and wrote to the King on 16th May, "If your Highness's pleasure be that I should be here resident about the Duke of Bourbon I would beseech your Highness to write unto the said Duke that I might have a company of four or five hundred horsemen and so I would trust to do your Highness some service." He was obviously expecting the denouement to take place very shortly and had no idea that his lord and master had already joined the Emperor Charles in negotiation with the Queen Regent and her advisers. The Bourbon court was currently at Milan and Sir John had been on foreign service without a break for almost two years.

About the same time Francis was taken a prisoner to Spain, thus making the Emperor virtually the arbiter of his future and of the future of France. The Duke naturally felt that it was now or never if his plan to invade France was to be successful but Sir John persuaded him to prolong his stay in Italy and relied with confidence on King Henry's active help in due course. Then on 3rd June Russell received letters both from Wolsey and the King which gave no decisive answer and were indeed meant to encourage the Duke to expect military assistance that was never intended to be furnished. Wolsey was frankly suspicious of Bourbon and asked Sir John to make fresh efforts to discover his feelings for the King. Sir John's answer was that the Duke was as devoted to the King's service as ever and far more anxious to be allied with Henry than with Charles. He forsook his usual temperate style and painted in vivid colours the disastrous effects of further delay on the part of the English court.

Relations between Henry and Charles were rapidly worsening. The Emperor sought to annul his betrothal to Princess Mary. Wolsey's far from flattering opinion of the Emperor was reported to him. Charles determined to do what he could to detach Bourbon from the diplomatic influence of England and invited him to Spain for consultations. Sir John, true to the end, saw him on to his ship and bade him a courteous farewell. That was the end of any possibility of King Henry of England becoming King Henry of France.

Sir John wrote to Wolsey asking for his recall now that Bourbon had left for Spain and received permission to return. Once again his journey was dangerous, for his association with the Duke of Bourbon had aroused the enmity of French interests in Italy and a plot was formed to seize him at Bologna and send him a prisoner to Paris. He was saved from capture by Thomas Cromwell (an officer in the Duke of Bourbons' army), who obtained information of the plot and helped Sir John to escape from his apartment in an inn surrounded by the conspirators.

This was incidentally the turning point in Cromwell's career. When he returned to England a few months later Sir John recommended him to Wolsey, whom he served first as a steward then as legal adviser.

Sir John reached England without further difficulty and was received by the King at Greenwich after more than two years' absence with cordiality and genuine pleasure. Henry complimented him on his diplomatic skill and admirable management of his trust. He was clearly marked out for further advancement in the King's service. This was not long in maturing. By 1526 he had won promotion in the royal household and was named one of the six newly created Gentlemen of the Privy Chamber.

His new appointment brought him much nearer to the sovereign. He had as colleagues men of wealth and influence such as Sir William Tyler and Sir Anthony Brown. His duties were still largely ceremonial but of a much more personal kind than in his former position. As all the officers were required, like Sir John, to carry out confidential missions on behalf of the sovereign, the work proved far too onerous for a group of only six and the number was soon increased until there was a rota of twenty or more on which to draw. With the increase in the number the office became less significant and more of a token of esteem by the sovereign than one of political importance. But Sir John was one of the first six appointed under the royal edict of 1526, published at Eltham Palace after a meeting of the Privy Council to reform the running of the royal establishment.

Two of the gentlemen were required to sleep in the "King's Chamber"—not, of course, in his actual bedroom but in an ante-room. They had the duty of dressing the King and one or more of them was required to be present throughout the day at whatever palace the King was staying at. Their functions combined those of private secretary and personal attendant and because they were all men of unusual distinction they were consulted regularly by the King on all matters of state and often had more influence than the members of the Privy Council. In particular the King used them all, but most often Sir John, as personal emissaries to foreign courts and as his deputies in entertaining visiting princes.

The wide use King Henry made of the senior members of his household was a most effective means of checking the previously almost unlimited authority of the Chancellor. Wolsey might appear to many as the *de facto* ruler of the country and most matters of national or international importance were done under his name, but if Wolsey wielded the power of a king, the King's personal representatives were the power behind the throne.

Neither Wolsey nor his successor as chief minister, Thomas Cromwell, desired to be on terms of enmity with the King. The fate of many who had been was an ever-present warning to them. That is why Sir John was permitted on so many occasions to act for the government irrespective of what the Chancellor might think and why both Wolsey and Cromwell went out of their way to be courteous to him and to assist him when he needed their help. In any case Cromwell and Sir John had, as we have seen, already met and worked together and held a high opinion of each other's honesty and determination. It was, after all, Russell's influence that had set Cromwell on the path to success. Undoubtedly it was partly due to him that Cromwell succeeded Wolsey after the latter's death.

In the same year as he obtained his new appointment at Court Sir John married Anne, the widow of Sir Richard Jerningham. This lady, who had previously been married to John Broughton, was not over-anxious to remarry but was persuaded by the combined approaches of Sir John himself and King Henry. Certainly it was a marriage that had the King's full approval and was a landmark in Sir John's private career. His bride was a wealthy lady who had inherited most of the land of her father, Sir Guy Sapcote, including an estate in Huntingdonshire and the Chenies estate in Buckinghamshire.

Sir John, of course, knew her well long before their marriage. He had held her in affectionate regard when her second husband was governor of Tournai and after that had met her frequently on royal occasions, including the Field of the Cloth of Gold, when she was a lady-in-waiting to the Queen. It was from every point of view an admirable match but one more important perhaps to the bridegroom than to the bride because Sir John, in spite of reasonably generous allowances from the sovereign, was often out of pocket executing some foreign commission and was required to live and also to dress, a very expensive item, in a style at least equal to that of an ambassador or princeling. He had found it difficult to balance his budget for some years. His marriage removed that difficulty and also provided him with a home at Chenies near enough to London and the royal palaces to be a convenient base and a fine setting in which to build up the image of a country gentleman.

With this in mind Russell and his wife soon put in hand the

rebuilding of the old manor-house at Chenies and transformed it into a sumptuous, if not magnificent, Tudor mansion. It was the family home both for him and for the 2nd Earl. King Henry showed his approval of the marriage by presenting Sir John with the manor of neighbouring Amersham.

That marked the end of Russell's direct association with Dorset except as an absentee landowner. He was, however, given the office of Sheriff of Dorset and Somerset in 1528. The King had rewarded him some time before his marriage with the customs revenue of the port of Poole but this right and certain others which he received at various times he leased to others. He was also the keeper of More or Moor Park and of Hold Park in Dorset, both royal domains. The former office carried a salary of fourpence a day, the latter one of £7 a year, but Russell made no profit out of these offices because, as an account which has been preserved shows, the whole of the money was disbursed in hiring deputy keepers and labourers on the estates.

Sir John and his wife did not see very much of each other even in the first months of their marriage, because of Sir John's attendance at Court. They had been married no more than a year when Sir John was called on to carry out a series of diplomatic missions which kept him abroad for the greater part of 1527.

Europe was still in a state of political uncertainty. King Henry was as much as anyone the cause of this uncertainty. Unless the dominant part he took in European affairs throughout the greater part of his reign is appreciated continental politics are meaningless. When Bourbon had gone to Spain and Russell had returned to England Henry and Wolsey had already in effect changed their policy towards the French King and the Emperor Charles completely. Henry had abandoned his hope of being acknowledged King of France and had decided to do what he could to reinstate Francis and use him as a lever to hold the Emperor Charles in check.

Russell learnt this only after his return but whatever his private feelings on the matter he took it in his stride. Soon afterwards a peace treaty was signed in Madrid, by which in return for being reinstated on the French throne Francis undertook to repay all England's expenses in prosecuting the war against him, to cede Burgundy to the Emperor Charles, to renounce the sovereignty of Flanders and Artois, and to pay a ransom of two million crowns, to ensure which, his two sons were taken as hostages.

It was extremely doubtful whether Francis could comply with the financial requirements of the treaty. Once released, he showed no inclination to carry out the other provisions. His parliament in Paris authorized him to raise the two million crowns for the ransom of his children but supported him in refusing to ratify the treaty on the ground that it was not binding, since it was extorted from him in captivity when his will was in abeyance.

It is unlikely that Francis, having suffered one severe defeat, would have taken this line without the support of the English King. By a strange irony he now found himself on terms of close alliance with England under the aegis of Pope Clement. The latter had been the moving power in forming the federation known as the Holy League, which was proclaimed with full religious ceremonies in the Autumn of 1526. Though the Holy Alliance depended on the Pope for its holiness, King Henry was given the title of Protector of the Alliance, as he had previously been given the title Defender of the Faith. Members of the federation were England, France, and the states of Milan and Venice.

Pope Clement was in dire financial straits and it has been suggested that his reason for giving support to the alliance was the hope of receiving adequate funds to carry on the work of the Holy See. In order to preserve the unity of the League Henry was quite prepared to subsidize the Pope and it was in connexion with this that Sir John was sent to Rome in January

1527, not only to pay over the substantial sum of 200,000 ducats but to act as counsellor and adviser to the Pope in the same way as he had to the Duke of Bourbon.

Not unnaturally his reception in Rome was tumultuous, in contrast with his last visit to the Holy City, when he escaped in disguise. On this occasion he rode into the city on the Pope's own Turkey horse accompanied by the Papal Nuncio, who had prepared accommodation for him in the papal palace, an honour which Sir John declined on the ground that no ambassador or other royal emissary had ever been lodged there.

He fulfilled this mission with the same success as most of his other assignments and was able to assure King Henry that "the Pope's Holiness is more bound to the King's Highness than to any other prince". This was a message repeated again and again. More to the point was Russell's despatch, "I have found the Pope's Holiness conformable to all such articles as specified in my instructions whereupon I have delivered him the money", and that on receipt of the money the Pope wished to assure him that "Your Grace for doing so hath won here great honour and fame". By then Russell had overcome his scruples and had changed his lodging "where I lie in the palace I am marvellous well entreated and all at the Pope's cost and gentles sent to keep me company daily".

Sir John, on his own initiative, persuaded the Pope to fortify Rome against attack and for a few weeks acted for the Pope in negotiation with the Viceroy of Naples and with the agent of the Duke of Bourbon. He returned fairly content with the position but the Pope soon announced his retirement from the Holy League, whereupon Sir John hastened back to Rome and prevailed upon him to sign a fresh agreement. He left Rome only a few days before the Spanish forces under Bourbon arrived at the gates and, although Bourbon himself was killed in action, seized the city, the Pope being very fortunate to escape with his life and take refuge in Orvieto.

Russell had made a wonderfully good impression in Italy.

The Bishop of Verona described him in a letter to Wolsey as "a man of so much probity and virtue as could scarcely be expressed". This helped him in the third of his missions to and on behalf of the Pope during the winter of 1527–8. The purpose of the English government was to induce the Pope, though exiled from the Holy City, to continue as leader of the federation against the Emperor Charles. This the Pope was willing to do provided the French General Lautrec would give him material support by advancing his army from Bologna to the South of Italy. Sir John's commission was "to visit Lautrec, stay near him, and be present at the settlement of various arrangements". He was, in fact, an intermediary between the Pope and General Lautrec with the task of persuading both to carry out the instructions of King Henry.

How successful he was is proved by events. Lautrec advanced southward past Rome and laid siege to Naples. Sir John returned to England with fresh glory. His friendship with Wolsey was also cemented by the success of this mission, for the Cardinal was by then most anxious to have the Pope so dependent on English support, direct or indirect, that he would agree to the dissolution of Henry's marriage with Queen Katherine. The Pope showed willing to the extent of sending Cardinal Campeggio to "try" the King's case but there were long delays lasting for more than a year and ending with the Cardinal remitting the case for final decision to the Pope. Henry blamed Wolsey for the delay and by the summer of 1528 the latter felt himself in such disgrace that he absented himself from Court for a time.

Russell showed remarkable concern for Wolsey throughout his time of grave trouble. The advice he gave was always sound. He wrote to him saying, "the King is merry, thanked be God, and I am sure that his Grace would that your Grace were so likewise", advising him that "it should be well done that your Grace would find a means to come more unto the King that your Grace might speak with him which should be greatly to

your both contentations". It was too late for mediation, however. Wolsey had difficulty in obtaining an audience of the King
and when he made a defence of his part in the divorce negotiations he achieved nothing. On 17th October he was ordered by
the King to surrender the great seal and to retire to his house
at Esher. Two days later his dismissal from all his secular offices
was announced. The French ambassador interceded for him
and the King unbent so far as to send Russell to him on November 1st to present a gold ring and a message that he "loveth you
as well as ever he did and is not a little disquieted for your
troubles".

Wolsey showed his appreciation of Sir John's support by
asking the King to settle on Russell part of the revenues of the
sees of Winchester and St. Albans when these were wrested
from him. The King agreed and the transfer was ratified by
Act of Parliament for the term of Russell's life.

Wolsey's fall and his subsequent death, perhaps from a
broken heart, was followed by the rise of Thomas Cromwell.
The latter's friendship with Russell and the fact that Cromwell
was so closely associated with the dissolution of the monasteries
and the consequent degradation of the orders of monks have
provoked the suggestion that Russell was closely concerned
with the dissolution. The two men did, of course, work closely
together as twin mouthpieces of the King but after Henry, by
the Act of Supremacy, had taken the title of Supreme Head of
the Church of England, Cromwell was appointed Vicar-Gen-
eral, with full responsibility for the work of winding up the
monastic establishments. The detail of the work was done by
commissioners appointed by Cromwell and every point of
procedure was referred to him.

Russell's part might be described as acquiescence, but he was
wholly loyal to his duties, which he conceived of as involving
absolute submission to if not concurrence with the King's
decisions. He was certainly enriched by the dissolution of the
monasteries but did not in any way deserve Edmund Burke's

accusation, "The merit of the original grantee of his Grace's pensions was in giving his hand to the work of being a prompt and greedy instrument of a levelling tyrant and by instigating that tyrant to injustice". That was only a case of an envious orator attempting to blacken the character of the ancestor of a Duke whom he regarded as an oppressor. It was a case of Cicero in Catalinam all over again.

On at least two occasions Sir John intervened on behalf of ecclesiastical establishments. Not unnaturally, in view of his relations with Cromwell, both interventions were successful. One was for the family Guild of St. George in Weymouth, where he secured the continued use of the guild chapel for the people of Weymouth. The other, a much more important intervention, was when his influence was invoked by his friend, the Abbot of Peterborough. He wrote to Cromwell assuring him that the Abbot "would be as ready and obedient as any man of his God in England whatever the King shall command him". As a result of this plea Peterborough was converted to a bishopric and its revenues appropriated to the endowment of the bishopric.

In 1536 we find Sir John directing on behalf of the King the funeral of Queen Katherine of Aragon, who was interred at Peterborough. In the same year he was one of the King's counsellors who investigated the accusations of unfaithfulness against Anne Boleyn for which she was executed.

After Anne Boleyn's execution he was put in charge of operations to quell an insurrection in Lincolnshire. Within a few weeks of his appointment he was able to write to the King telling him that the royal troops had occupied Stamford and a dangerous rising in Boston had been quelled. He was so energetic in following up his success that the leader of the rebellion, Lord Hussey, was captured (and later executed). Many of the rebel collaborators, including several dispossessed abbots and priors, had taken refuge in Yorkshire, where another more violent rebellion, the Pilgrimage of Grace, broke out but was ruthlessly suppressed. The ill-armed rabble which had composed most of the Lincolnshire rioters fled to their homes.

About now Russell was given the office of Comptroller of the King's Household and was thus second only in seniority to the Treasurer. With his unfailing precision he improved the financial organization and was credited by the King with restoring the failing discipline of the Court. After only a year in this office he was created Baron Russell of Chenies, a long deferred honour but understandably so in view of the great reluctance of the Tudor Kings to increase the number of Lords Temporal. Later in the same year he was invested with the Order of the Garter, the highest honour that the King could bestow on him.

These honours were the prelude to transferring John, Lord Russell, to an entirely different and far more critical sphere of activity than his work as Comptroller of the Royal Household. It was a time when unrest fomented by dispossessed clergy had spread to every part of the country from the North. Added to the genuine public alarm at the sweeping changes which Henry had introduced in religion was the consciousness that the much vaunted system of English justice was not working as well as it should. There were interminable delays in the courts. In all parts of England people were accusing the sovereign of deserting his first duty, that to his subjects. The King had already established the Council of the North and a similar council covering the Welsh Marches. With increasingly serious news reaching him from the west country Henry decided to establish a council there before open rebellion broke out. He appointed Lord Russell President of the Council.

In this position he acted to all intents and purposes as viceroy of Devonshire, Cornwall, and Somerset. Although the Council of the West did not survive for long he received other appointments in lieu of the presidency which gave him equal powers. He remained an unofficial ruler of the south-western counties to the end of King Henry's reign and throughout the next reign. He became Steward of the Duchy of Cornwall, and of the

Duchy of Exeter, which included most of Devonshire and part of Somerset, Warden of the Court of the Stannaries, and Rider of the Close of Dartmoor. These were all medieval appointments, much of the authority of which had lapsed but quite capable of being revived in an emergency. His duty as President of the Council was to deal with trouble firmly but with as much consideration as possible, to report on the loyalty of the great west-country families, and to ensure that justice was administered without bias or prejudice. He made his headquarters in Exeter but frequently toured the whole of Devonshire and Cornwall, often accompanied by his wife.

During Henry VIII's lifetime little more was heard of trouble in the West. The King recognized that Russell as a Baron needed considerably more cash at his disposal and that it had become necessary for him to keep up personal appearances to an extent which his existing income would not allow. To help him maintain his position the King granted him most of the manors of the Abbey of St. Mary in Tavistock, some of the manors of Dunkerswell Abbey and Torre Priory, and a house in Exeter which had once been a Dominican friary and which Lord Russell renamed Russell House and made his family home when in the West.

The result of these gifts was to double Lord Russell's income. A record of an inquiry made on behalf of the King when the grants were made showed the annual value of these properties and of the manors which he already held in Dorset, Buckinghamshire, Lincolnshire, Huntingdonshire, Northamptonshire and Leicestershire amounted to £1,205 12s. 6¼d. plus half a farthing, This was not exactly a round sum but a very adequate income in the 16th century on which to live well and employ a private "army" of servants and attendants, considered essential for the dignity of a man holding an appointment such as President of the Council.

He did not live permanently in Exeter, however. He was in London, for instance, to join with Cranmer in remonstrating

5

with the King in an effort to persuade him to change his decision to execute Cromwell, now Earl of Essex, who incidentally had recommended the transfer to Russell of the monastic manors. But the King, infuriated by the delay in freeing him from his bride, Anne of Cleves, whom he had married by proxy on Cromwell's advice, refused.

Lord Russell's loyalty to his old friend did not stand in his way. Fresh honours were heaped on him almost every year. In 1540 he was appointed Lord High Admiral and after two years Lord Privy Seal in succession to Cromwell himself, an office in which he continued to serve until his death.

He was in command of one of the army groups that King Henry led in person against France in 1544, which led to the capture of Boulogne, and complained bitterly in letters to members of the Privy Council that he could achieve nothing without further supplies. Henry, after the capture of Boulogne, was content to return home and was soon followed by Russell, who had some difficulty in persuading the sovereign that his lack of success had been due to bad organization. However, in the following year, when invasion by French troops was believed to be imminent, Russell was sent back to the West to place all the ports in his presidency in a state of security. Again he was in violent conflict with members of the Privy Council, but on this occasion his demands were met and with his mission accomplished Russell was recalled to Court. Later he was present at the ratification of the Peace of Guisnes, by which England retained Boulogne for the time being.

With Henry's death many believed Lord Russell's career was at an end. Far from it. He retained all his offices in the new reign and was appointed Great Steward of England for the coronation of King Edward VI. His son Francis was one of the forty Knights of the Bath created in honour of the occasion. He was on excellent terms with the Protector Somerset and after Somerset's execution apparently on equally good terms with John Dudley, Earl of Warwick, later Duke of Northumberland, who became the undisputed leader of the boy King's council. By his will King Henry had left still further land to Russell, although the abbey and manors of Woburn, which was one of the properties left by the King, had been let on lease for twenty-one years in 1539 and was not added to the Russell estates until the expiry of the lease.

Russell's greatest contribution during King Edward's reign was the handling of the dangerous rebellion in the West in 1549. He was given a commission by the Protector to act as he thought best for the pacification of the country. Before he reached Exeter the revolt had gathered strength and but for Russell's remarkably competent counter-measures it might well have resulted in the overthrow of the government. The insurgents invested Exeter under the leadership of prominent Roman Catholic noblemen. Russell organized the defence of the city, dealing firmly with a number of Exeter citizens who were loyal to the old religion and in sympathy with the revolt. But Lord Russell did not himself stay inside the walls. He left to organize supplies for the beleaguered garrison. The expected supplies did not arrive but he won two resounding victories over the insurgents, one at Honiton, the other at Woodbury Downs, and advanced with a small force almost to the gates of Exeter, where another pitched battle was fought in which many of the insurgents were killed and the rest took to flight. So Lord Russell raised the siege of Exeter, but only just in time because the people were on the point of starvation and would certainly have opened the gates to the rebels within a few days. Lord Russell, though generally regarded as a gentle man, was ruthless on this occasion. He had most of the ringleaders executed summarily, keeping only a few prisoners to await trial, but he gave a free pardon to many ordinary people who had taken part in the insurrection on their swearing loyalty to the King. Russell then marched into Cornwall and either executed or sent for trial in London a number of well-known people whose loyalty was doubtful.

The King and his council showed their gratitude by creating Russell Earl of Bedford on 19th January 1550. As a further mark of esteem he was granted the manors of Thorney Abbey in Cambridgeshire, a number of further manors in Devon and Cornwall, and several in other parts of the country.

Almost as soon as he had returned from the West Russell was faced with one of the most difficult decisions of his life. He had to choose between supporting his good friend, the Duke of Somerset, whose overbearing ways even his nephew the King deplored, or support Dudley, Earl of Warwick. He showed his usual statesmanship and ability to deal with people and steered a perilous but even course between the two conflicting nobles. He made a real but unavailing effort to reconcile the differences between them and with the help of Cranmer was the author of a compromise by which Somerset resigned the Protectorate but retained his seat in the council.

The Earl of Bedford was now deputed to negotiate a lasting treaty with France, where Francis had been succeeded by Henry II. He was successful in negotiating a treaty but its terms were far from popular, though they were approved by the Privy Council. They included the restitution of Boulogne, to which Henry had laid siege using the crisis of the rising in Devonshire as a suitable time at which to abrogate the treaty his father had made. In agreeing to the surrender of Boulogne, which had proved a heavy drain on English resources, Russell was acting on the instructions of Warwick, who by now had succeeded Somerset, executed on a trumped-up charge of high treason. So in a sense Russell and Warwick were united in justifying a peace which some regarded as dishonourable, others as expedient. It was ironic that after the execution of Somerset in 1552 Russell was granted on Warwick's (now Duke of Northumberland) advice Covent Garden and Long Acre, once part of the monastic lands of Westminster which had been held by the Duke of Somerset.

In June 1553 he accompanied the King in great state on his

last progress through the southern counties. The following month the King was dead and had settled the crown by will on Lady Jane Grey. Some members of the Privy Council protested, but the Earl of Bedford, who was strongly in favour of the reformed religion, acquiesced willingly in the invitation, which bears his signature along with those of other members of the council, in spite of the fact that the succession had not been sanctioned by Parliament. He was with Northumberland, too, at the proclamation of Lady Jane as Queen at the Tower.

Mary, the eldest surviving child of Henry VIII and the next in line of succession, was proclaimed Queen in Norfolk, where she was with the Howards, staunch Roman Catholics. Northumberland thereupon attempted to mobilize an army but received no support. Risings in favour of Mary were threatened in several parts of the country and the Earl of Bedford was deputed to quell one of them in Buckinghamshire. Only a few days later, when it was obvious that Northumberland would obtain no popular support, the council reversed its decision and sent emissaries to Mary with the royal seal.

Mary behaved with wise moderation, although Northumberland and later Lady Jane Grey and her husband, Lord Guildford Dudley, were executed. But the Earl of Bedford was re-sworn a member of the Privy Council and immediately afterwards re-appointed Lord Privy Seal. In 1554 he was despatched to Devonshire to deal with a local support for Sir Thomas Wyatt's rebellion. On his arrival the ringleaders fled to France and his task on this occasion was an easy one.

He lived to perform only one more public service, when he travelled in his capacity as Lord Privy Seal to ratify a treaty with Philip of Spain for the latter's marriage to Queen Mary. Perhaps he was happy to forge this link of diplomatic friendship with the grandson of the man who had introduced him to the Court of King Henry VII. After the signing of the treaty he escorted Philip with units of the fleet to Southampton and accompanied him to London. On 24th July 1554 he was one of five noblemen who performed the ceremony of giving away the Queen at the altar of Winchester Cathedral.

Immediately afterwards he fell ill and died on 14th March 1555 at his house in the Strand, leaving the bulk of his great fortune to his wife and his son Francis. He had fully earned the reputation of being the only nobleman at Court who by character, determination and loyalty had succeeded in maintaining friendly relations with all parties during the religious and political changes of four reigns.

CHAPTER THREE

Elizabethan Tapestry

FRANCIS, who succeeded his father as Earl of Bedford in 1555, was a most promising and already highly successful young man of twenty-seven. He lived to equal, if not surpass, his father's achievements as a statesman and proved as valuable to Queen Elizabeth as his father to King Henry VIII. He inherited many of his father's qualities. He was a skilled linguist, was often described by contemporary writers and by friends as affable, a word that was not so often used to describe his father but in retrospect is applicable equally to both.

It was not so much that Francis was all things to all men, as his father undoubtedly was. Rather by his understanding of human nature and sincere desire to please the people with whom he came in contact he disarmed criticism and often achieved as much by sympathy as others did by threats. He was a popular nobleman as well as a successful politician, though he lacked one thing which had certainly helped his father in his early career, that of exceptional good looks. Portraits of the 2nd Earl in later life, especially the one in Woburn Abbey by Zucchero, an artist whose reputation rests on his portraits of Queen Elizabeth more than any other work, shows a man of by no means unprepossessing appearance with shrewd eyes, a generous mouth, and the characteristic Russell nose, with a strong family resemblance, as one would expect, to John, the 1st Earl, as portrayed by Holbein. There seems little ground for the quip attributed to a Bishop of Aquila, who, when discussing a proposal for a marriage between Queen Elizabeth and Prince

Charles of Austria, commented that the Prince's head was
bigger, if that were possible, than the Earl of Bedford's.

Whatever he may have lacked in good looks, he certainly
compensated for by his persuasive manner. He was educated
privately and at King's Hall, later Trinity College, Cambridge.
There he came into contact with the foremost religious thinkers
of the English Reformation. Their influence was dominant with
him for the whole of his life. He became, in religion, a Puritan
before the term had assumed its full meaning. When he was
young his eagerness for reform outstripped that of King Edward
VI's ministers.

He was indeed the first of the reforming Russells. It was a
most fortunate chance that his natural skills and abilities could
be used so well by a Queen who was herself a reformer and
respected the zeal of her ministers even when she herself was
too cautious to give effect to what in her heart she considered
right. Again and again in the relations between the Earl and
Queen Elizabeth we shall find the Earl urging vigorously a
courageous approach to problems—political problems as well
as religious ones—with the Queen agreeing with the sense of his
thoughts but hesitating to commit herself to adopting them
openly and using the Earl, if not as a scapegoat, at least as a
straw to discover the direction and strength of the wind.

It is unlikely that Francis could have brought himself to
serve with equal enthusiasm four sovereigns of such divergent
views as his father had done. The reign of Queen Mary did, in
fact, threaten the Russell family fortune. Had the 1st Earl not
been alive the 2nd Earl might not have escaped so lightly the
consequences of his passionate antagonism to the Roman
Catholic faith. He was in his element during the reign of
Edward VI, a young man already with the mark of future
greatness upon him. He was enthusiastic about the use of
English in the Church services. He approved strongly of the new
prayer books, both the one issued in 1549 and the revised one
issued three years later. Like many of his friends in Cambridge,

he believed that there was still too much "useless ceremony" in Church services and believed sincerely that the Duke of Somerset had taken a step in the right direction in completing the process begun by Henry VIII, not only of disassociating the Church of England from the Church of Rome and of renouncing the authority of the Pope, but of modernizing the forms of religious services. Understandably he was a strong supporter of Lady Jane Grey as a claimant to the throne on Edward's death.

The first time that Francis received a public honour was at the coronation of King Edward VI when he was one of the forty Knights of the Bath created in honour of the occasion. In the next few years he came under the influence of Miles Coverdale, who had assisted Tyndale in his translation of the Bible and wrote a number of treatises against what he regarded as prevailing superstition, evidenced by incense still offered to images in many churches even when orders had been given by the Privy Council to remove them. Coverdale had been living in Germany for some time but on the accession of Edward he returned to England and became a special favourite of the 1st Earl, who made him his domestic chaplain and in 1551 used his influence to secure his promotion to the see of Exeter. Francis came into frequent contact with him through his father and also in his official position in Exeter.

At what in modern eyes appears the extraordinarily early age of nineteen he had been appointed Sheriff of Bedfordshire and Buckinghamshire, an office normally not requiring much active administration. In 1547 and 1548, however, these two counties were affected by the reaction against the rapid reform in religious observances since the death of Henry VIII. It was a reaction that stemmed partly, no doubt, from conscientious reasons but would scarcely have attained serious proportions unless it had been associated with a sense of injustice among many of the rural people, including some of the landowners.

The trouble arose from the enclosure of some commons without sufficient regard to the rights of the commoners. This had nothing whatever to do with religion but became linked with religion in a general opposition to the Protectorate of Somerset. Enclosure by mutual agreement between the lord of the manor and the commoners had been carried out to a small extent during the reign of Henry VIII with the knowledge and approval of the Privy Council, which had been impressed by the greater prosperity of counties such as Kent, where almost all the land had been enclosed before Tudor times. The measure was no doubt progressive but provoked great opposition (the process was not effectively completed until the beginning of the 19th century). Most of the commoners were quite unable to grasp the reasons underlying enclosure. A few of the lords of the manor acted without proper consultation and without the final agreement of their commoners.

This was by no means confined to the midland counties. Similar complaints led to rioting in East Anglia and in the south-western counties. But the first disturbances took place in Buckinghamshire and this came within the responsibility of Russell as sheriff. He was called into consultation by Somerset. As a result the Privy Council acted quickly by issuing a proclamation calling on all who had enclosed common land to restore it to the commoners, under severe penalties, and by appointing specific enclosure commissioners throughout England to investigate every complaint and regulate future enclosure.

Sir Francis Russell, as he then was, found his responsibility increased as one of the six commissioners appointed for the midlands. By agreement between the commissioners his sphere of responsibility was confined to the counties of which he was sheriff. He was respected by landowners and commoners alike, investigated scores of complaints, prevailed on many landowners to throw open common land which they had enclosed, and secured agreement in some cases between landowners and commoners where no agreement had been possible before. No further trouble arose in Buckinghamshire. That the task was not an easy one is shown by the fact that unrest continued in spite of the commissions in many parts of the country, especially in the South-west, where grievances at enclosure allied with dissatisfaction at religious reform led to the insurrection that began on 9th June 1549, the day appointed by Parliament for the reading in English of the New Liturgy.

It was no doubt due to his success as sheriff and as an enclosure commissioner that Russell was appointed Lord Lieutenant of Buckinghamshire in 1551, an appointment which he continued to hold in the following two years. Like his father, he was making an early start in life as a personal representative of the sovereign. He married about this time Margaret, the widow of Sir John Gostwick of Willington in Bedfordshire, a daughter of Sir John St. John, a member of an old and re-spected family. The marriage helped the future Earl to establish himself in the traditional society of English nobility in which the Russells had so far been barely accepted. After all, his father was only the 1st Earl and was born a commoner. It was a happy marriage, setting a strong domestic and family back-ground for Francis. Francis and Margaret had seven children: four sons – Edward, John, Francis and William, and three daughters – Anne, Elizabeth and Margaret – of whom more later.

It was as a married man that Russell was nominated for a seat in Parliament in 1553 and was returned as a Knight of the Shire for Northumberland. This was the first time that the eldest son of a peer had sat in Parliament, a precedent that was followed by many later Russells. That was the highlight of his early career.

When Mary became Queen his career ran into troubled waters. Within ten days of her accession she had signed an order in council committing him to the Fleet prison, along with Lord Rich and many others of the more extreme reformers who had supported the claims of Lady Jane Grey. However, he soon felt the power of his father's influence. Queen Mary was not nearly so severe as she is often supposed to have been with those who had initially opposed her accession. Within a very short time we find Francis released from the Fleet and committed to the safe custody of the Sheriff of London. It was a mild form of imprisonment, more a means of preventing the young man from active opposition to the new sovereign than of punishing him for his support of Lady Jane. His mother was allowed to visit him several times a week and he was treated as a member of the Sheriff's household.

A royal pardon soon followed. As though to underline the sincerity of the pardon Queen Mary asked him to act as her representative to receive foreign visitors. According to one account he assisted his father in quelling the rebellion fostered by Sir Thomas Wyatt. If that is true, it is the only case in his life when his loyalty as between sovereign and religion was tested. He was still in touch with extreme reformers at home and abroad and immediately he became earl he asked for the Queen's permission to travel abroad.

The passport, which is still in existence, was signed personally by Queen Mary and Prince Philip. It describes the Earl as "Our Right Trusty and Right Well-beloved Cousin, being in league and amity with us" and giving as his reason for foreign travel "the better attainment of experience and knowledge whereby he may be able to serve us hereafter". The Earl sailed from Dover, as an endorsement on the passport shows, "with his horse" on the 26th April 1555 and passed through Calais "with his horse quietly".

It seems strange that Philip and Mary should have wished to use him as an envoy in view of his still recent term of imprisonment for what amounted to treason, but that is the case. He was first charged with seeking an interview with the Emperor Charles, who was then holding court at Brussels, to pay him their respects and obtain his opinion on the future peace of Europe. The Earl did in fact have an interview with the Emperor, but only a brief one, at which he obtained the Emperor's permission to continue on his travels.

For the greater part of the next two years he was in Italy, at Venice, Rome and Naples. He also visited Zurich and Lausanne, both traditional centres of religious reform. In Zurich he made many friends, with whom he kept in touch for the rest of his life. His intolerance of Roman Catholicism and even of High Church practice was confirmed there. He regarded himself as an exile, a martyr to reform. His determination to return to England some day to carry on the good work was a dominant factor in his outlook.

He returned to England only a short time before Mary's death, and as Sheriff of Bedfordshire and Buckinghamshire was required by the Privy Council to raise money for the disastrous war which Mary had been persuaded by Philip to initiate against France and which had resulted in the loss of Calais. That was the only occasion on which he took a part, directly or indirectly, in the political events of the reign.

With the accession of Queen Elizabeth his fortunes and his confidence were restored. He was present at her coronation and was one of the Protestant noblemen whom the Queen immediately appointed to her Privy Council to balance the influence of the Catholic advisers she had inherited. His wife was appointed Lady of Honour, although unhappily she lived less than three years to support the Earl at Court, dying in 1561. That was a bitter personal blow for the Earl.

It has been said that the success which crowned the Queen's efforts to re-establish the reformed religion was mainly due to the moderation which characterized the Protestant members of the Privy Council. Moderate the Earl of Bedford may have been in the advice he gave on refraining from punitive measures against loyal citizens, especially noblemen whose only fault was their faith, but his moderation ceased at that point. A bill was passed at the instance of the Privy Council in the very first Parliament, suppressing the newly founded monasteries. Before the year was out all the statutes of King Edward VI had been confirmed and the nomination of bishops vested in the Crown.

The Earl of Bedford was one of those who represented the Queen on June 11th, 1559, when a sermon in English was preached at St.Paul's. He stepped easily and surely into his father's shoes as one of the most trusted and loyal of the sovereign's personal representatives. Between 1559 and 1570 he played an important role in maintaining the always perilous relationship between the Queen and her cousin Mary, generally known as Mary, Queen of Scots.

The first act in this personal drama opened in 1559, when the Earl travelled as the Queen's ambassador to the Court of France. His mission was twofold, first to ratify the existing peace treaty between England and France and, second, to protest informally to the Dauphin of France and Mary, his wife, against their assumption of the arms of England. In the first part of the mission he was successful, in the second he met so much hostility, not so much on the part of Mary herself as of the House of Guise in general, that his visit achieved little or nothing.

To understand the position of the Earl in the next few years it is necessary to appreciate the significance of the family links between Elizabeth and Mary. They were both descended from Henry VII, whose daughter Margaret, King Henry VIII's sister, had married first James IV of Scotland and after his death the Scottish Earl of Angus. The son born to James IV and Margaret Tudor, later James V of Scotland, married the French Princess, Mary of Guise, whose child was Mary, the bride of the Dauphin (later briefly King of France) and by right of inheritance Queen of Scots. She married as her second husband Lord Darnley, who was also a grandson of Margaret Tudor by the Earl of Angus. The child of Mary and Lord Darnley was James VI of Scotland and I of England.

Queen Elizabeth was Henry VIII's daughter by Anne Boleyn, born while Henry's first wife, Katherine of Aragon, was still alive. She was, therefore, in the eyes of the Roman Catholic world a bastard and on that account unlawfully designated

Queen of England, the rightful claimant to the throne being in their view Mary.

England, Scotland and France were all torn by dissensions arising from differences in faith. It was Elizabeth's policy to help Protestants everywhere, the Huguenots in France, as much as the Protestants of Scotland. It was equally the policy of Mary to advance Catholicism as best she could. Inevitably, therefore, Elizabeth became the focus of Protestant loyalty in Europe as well as in England and Scotland, Mary equally the focus of Catholic loyalty, at least in her native Scotland and in England.

The assumption of English arms by Mary when she was the wife of the Dauphin was an annoyance, but little more. The assumption by her husband and herself of English arms after he had become King Francis II in 1559 was a circumstance that might provoke war in which France and Scotland were allied against England. While Mary was in France, there was civil war in Scotland. The Congregation, as the Protestants were known, taking up arms against the Queen Regent, i.e. Mary's mother, with overt assistance from Elizabeth, won a victory over the Queen Regent's forces and concluded a peace to which Queen Elizabeth was a party. One of the provisions of this Treaty of Leith was that all parties to it acknowledged that the crowns of England and Ireland belonged of right to Elizabeth alone, with the undertaking that Mary should abstain from using the titles or bearing the arms of these kingdoms.

Francis and Mary refused to ratify the treaty and it was in these circumstances that the Earl of Bedford was despatched post haste to France on the unexpected death of Francis. The purpose again was twofold, first, to congratulate Charles IX on his accession and ratify once more the treaty between England and France and, second, to enforce on Mary recognition of the Treaty of Leith. On the face of it this was a reasonable assignment, since Mary's return to Scotland as Queen was imminent and the last thing she could have wanted was a state of open hostility with England. Mary, however, was a determined person in spite of her youth. She asked for more time, she evaded the issue, and the discussions ended when she refused immediate ratification but consented to discuss with Elizabeth the question of the arms of England.

Elizabeth was so furious at Mary's refusal to accept the Earl of Bedford's bidding that she refused Mary a safe conduct to her own country and immediately promised financial support to the Lords of the Congregation. However, Mary reached Scotland safely and was a popular Queen for at least two years, showing a degree of moderation towards the Protestants which at least matched Elizabeth's moderation towards the Catholics of England. The Earl of Bedford, too, survived the royal displeasure at the failure of his mission and because of his knowledge of Scottish affairs and of the Queen of Scots personally was appointed Governor of Berwick, a key appointment and the centre of English defence on the borders. He was outspoken in his criticisms of the town's defences. Writing to the Queen in March 1564 he said, "The defences are of such small strength that a man might in a very short space make as much in the plain field."

His first task, therefore, was to set about rebuilding the walls and adding forts and up-to-date battlements. These survive today as a tribute to the thoroughness with which he approached the task—the only surviving Elizabethan town defences in the country.

That autumn he was appointed the Queen's commissioner in the negotiations taking place on the subject of the Scottish Queen's re-marriage. The point at issue was that Queen Elizabeth had made it abundantly clear that she would regard marriage into the reigning family of any of England's enemies a hostile act. She had succeeded in dissuading Mary from proposed alliances with Austria and Spain and had said that she would suggest a husband for Mary so as to allow friendship to continue between the two countries. She promised as a further inducement that if Mary followed her advice she would be named as next in order of succession to the English throne. Elizabeth's choice was Lord Robert Dudley, whom she created Earl of Leicester. The Earl of Bedford was not much more successful in this mission than in his previous mission to France. The marriage did not take place as proposed by Queen Elizabeth, Mary cutting the Gordian knot by announcing her betrothal to Lord Darnley, a union which for the time being was extremely popular with Scottish people.

The Earl was present at the Privy Council held on 1st May, when it was decided not to recognize the marriage, and at another meeting shortly afterwards, when fears were expressed that the marriage of Mary with a Catholic descended from Margaret Tudor would increase the hopes of Catholics in England and Scotland and might lead to an insurrection. He said that the marriage could be prevented only by force but by implication advised using force. The Queen gave her consent and the Earl immediately returned to Berwick to prepare for invasion.

He was appointed Lord Lieutenant of the North Counties, hastened the completion of the defences of Berwick and Carlisle, and was poised ready for attack when news of Mary's marriage reached him. Now the Earl's commission was "to preserve peace and yet have all things in readiness for war". He obtained a levy of two thousand armed men from the Earl of Shrewsbury, Lord Lieutenant of Yorkshire, and his position was strengthened by the renewed activity in Scotland of the Lords of the Congregation. He applied to the Queen for authority to give them open assistance. The Queen, in a memorable letter, instructed him to give assistance in money to the extent of £3,000 and of troops to the number of seven hundred, provided he let the Earl of Moray and the other insurgents understand that the responsibility was entirely his, the Earl of Bedford's, acting without instructions from the Queen.

Mary, however, was too strong for the insurgents, who, faced

6

with a royal army eighteen thousand strong, disbanded their troops and took refuge in England, where they were received at Carlisle by the Earl of Bedford in person. The Earl of Moray later went to London for an interview with the Queen, who found his visit a great embarrassment and Bedford was blamed for permitting the intrusion. His defence was that he could not have prevented it unless he had imprisoned the Earl of Moray, who had given such good service to the English cause.

The Earl of Leicester was now one of Bedford's principal supporters at Court, a very useful one in view of the high opinion in which he was held by the Queen. The marriage of Lord Ambrose Dudley, the Earl of Leicester's brother, and Anne, the Earl of Bedford's eldest daughter, cemented the friendship. Queen Elizabeth was present at the ceremony and at the celebrations, which lasted for three days.

The Lady Anne had been a Maid of Honour for some time and remained in attendance after her marriage, a confidante and friend of the Queen and an always important link between the Earl and the throne.

There was need for this personal link at the beginning of 1566 when the Queen of Scots complained that Scottish villages near Berwick had been sacked by English troops with great loss of life. This was just after Queen Elizabeth had accredited Sir Walter Mildmay to the Scottish Court in an effort to improve relations. The Earl of Bedford took full responsibility, explaining that the raid was a reprisal for a Scottish ambush near the border when English prisoners had been taken. Queen Elizabeth accepted the explanation and relayed it to the Scottish Queen, but sent a despatch to Bedford warning him not to do anything that might compromise peace.

Poor Francis must have been getting confused by now, with official policy changing every month. However, he stood his ground and the incident was almost forgotten in the rapidly deteriorating situation in Scotland, with the murder of the Scottish Queen's secretary, Rizzio. All he could do was to maintain a state of preparedness and keep Queen Elizabeth informed of the position. This he did fairly, considering his antipathy to Mary's Catholicism, in a spirit of commendable objectivity. In many of his despatches he foresaw only too well that Mary's place on the throne of Scotland was becoming increasingly insecure. On one occasion he wrote, "The Queen and her husband agree after the old manner, or rather worse. She eateth but very seldom with him but lieth not nor keepeth company with him, nor loveth any such as love him."

Bedford's intelligence service at this time was one of the most remarkable things about a rather remarkable man. He was even able to report a week after this despatch, "I have heard that this King and Queen have slept together, whereby it is thought some better agreement will ensue between them." His informers were able to give literally day-by-day reports on what was happening in Edinburgh.

Russell's opposite number was the Earl of Bothwell, the Scottish Queen's Lord Lieutenant of the Borders, while Bedford continued as Lord Lieutenant of the Northern Counties. They had little reason to like each other, since Bedford was continuing to support any sign of rebellion in the southern counties of Scotland, while Bothwell inspired many ineffective but irritating raids across the border.

The birth of a son to Mary complicated the issue, since by any reckoning he must be heir presumptive to the English throne. Queen Elizabeth did her best to reach an understanding with Mary and appointed the Earl of Bedford her ambassador at the christening of the child, entrusting him with a present to give to Mary "in token of her great goodwill". She instructed Bedford to conduct himself in perfect harmony with this declaration.

He asked Mary for safe conduct. In her reply she said, "We assure you that whenever you please to come you will be as welcome as we may make you and thereunto all times shall be alike, but in consideration that the day of our son's baptism shall be, God willing, the 15th instant, we think it best that you enter on Scots ground upon the 8th of this month, against the which we have commanded our warden to meet you and convey you hither." The letter was signed at Craigmillar on 4th December 1566. The Earl was accompanied by most of the Berwick captains and a representative of the Lord Lieutenant of Yorkshire, and was conducted by Lord Hume on behalf of Queen Mary with an escort of a hundred horse. He was royally entertained and was given the special honour of one of the Queen's beds of state. He showed his independence, however, by attending St. Giles's Church to hear the sermon in English with the Earl of Argyll and other leading Scottish Protestants.

Before the baptism he told the Queen that in accordance with her desire that his mistress should stand godmother to the Prince she had sent him to assist the Countess of Argyll, whom she had appointed her proxy. He also told Mary that Queen Elizabeth wanted only peace and was now willing to withdraw her previous insistence that Mary should confirm the Treaty of Leith, or at least was willing to omit anything from it that might prejudice the child's presumptive title to the crown of England.

The present was a font of pure gold, weighing, according to the contemporary historian Stow, 333 oz. After the ceremony he pressed the Queen for a mutual treaty of perpetual amity. She refused an official reply but promised to forward him one in a few days. She then presented him with a chain of diamonds and he left Edinburgh with the satisfaction of knowing that he had done the best he could in a rather hopeless cause. Perhaps he had achieved more than he had imagined, for before a new treaty could be prepared Darnley was dead and Mary, imprisoned on an island fortress in Loch Leven, was forced to abdicate. The Earl of Moray was appointed regent during her son's minority.

The Earl of Bedford, who was far from well, obtained the Queen's permission to resign his office once he was assured that the danger of war had receded. The final act in the drama was enacted when he risked Queen Elizabeth's displeasure by refusing to take Mary into his custody. His refusal was dictated partly by sympathy for the ex-Queen. Their paths had crossed many times and she had impressed him even though they failed to agree. He disapproved also of the ruthless way in which Queen Elizabeth treated her kinswoman when she took refuge in England, not only denying her assistance but even refusing her a safe conduct to France.

The Earl now spent more of his time on his numerous estates, especially on the Woburn estate, where he initiated a policy of land development and improved conditions for the tenants and workers, including the founding and endowing of a free school. But Francis never retired. He remained a Privy Councillor and was always close to the Queen, though his services after 1568 were mainly rendered at the council table. It is likely that the Queen did not soon forget his lack of co-operation in providing a prison home for Mary. However, there was no open break and one can infer this only from the small number of commissions which she gave the Earl in his last years.

He remained her chief adviser on Scottish affairs and led the Privy Council on the grave issues arising in 1569 when a movement was afoot for the marriage of Mary with the Duke of Norfolk, an alliance which had the support of Spain and France in the event of civil war and the concurrence of the Pope, who could see the possibility of a return of England to the papal fold. The Earl advised the arrest of the Duke of Norfolk and this proved effective in defeating the plan fostered among others by the Earls of Northumberland and Westmorland, who raised the standard of rebellion prematurely, believing that the Queen's suspicions of them had been aroused. The rebellion was easily quelled and the two Earls took refuge in Scotland.

Meanwhile, after the most careful examination of the Duke of Norfolk, at which the Earl of Bedford was a commissioner, no evidence directly implicating him in a plot against the Crown could be found and the Earl urged his release. The Queen complied but the Duke was not at liberty for long. He was rearrested on a charge of plotting with foreign powers against the government and he paid the penalty for refusing to heed the warning of his earlier arrest. His position was aggravated by the fact that Pope Pius V in 1570 issued a Bull of deposition against Elizabeth, describing her among other things as an illegitimate usurper and a heretic. This gave spiritual support to the still numerous Roman Catholic families in England.

It was felt at Court that an example must be made of the Duke of Norfolk. The Earl did not again intervene in the Duke's favour. He was one of the judges appointed for the trial and had no hesitation in finding a verdict of guilty. Before his execution Norfolk, in letters to the Queen, acknowledged his participation in treasonable activities and paid a singular tribute to the Earl of Bedford and his fellow members of the tribunal, conceding their impartiality in reaching a verdict which sent him to the scaffold. Writing on 11th October 1571 from the Tower to the Earl of Bedford, the Duke said, "In most humble wise I beseech you to make declaration unto the Queen of my sorrowful and penitent heart, seeking nowise to excuse myself. I lay myself, my goods and my poor children, and all that I have, prostrate at Her Majesty's feet." It was a heartcry of a penitent man but it did not save him.

One of the last personal services which the Earl rendered the Queen was to act as a commissioner in the negotiations for the treaty of marriage projected between the Queen and the Duke of Anjou in 1581. The marriage, of course, did not take place but the negotiations were made difficult by the Duke's temperament and by his irritation at the Queen's constant misgivings.

Two years later the Earl was once more hard at work making preparations to repel invasion as he had done for so long on the Scottish border. He was Lord Lieutenant of Dorset, Devonshire and Cornwall and in 1583 this office assumed a special significance because of the imminent threat of a Spanish assault on

England. Throughout the greater part of 1583 and again in 1584 he was in residence at Bedford House in Exeter, the same house which his father had used in organizing the defence of the south-western counties. He visited every one of the ports from Land's End to Portland Bill, instituted major works of defence, and ensured that the ships which would be available in case of attack were in a state of full preparedness.

He did not live to take part in defence operations when the Spanish Armada finally dared to sail up the English Channel, nor did he live to witness the execution of Mary, Queen of Scots, when significantly his second Countess, Bridget, who outlived him by many years, was the chief mourner. On 28th July 1585 he died from the results of a gangrene in the foot and was buried like his father at Chenies, where he is commemorated in the chapel by a monument showing him and his first wife life-size in alabaster. It was a time of great mourning for the family, for the elder of his two surviving sons, Sir Francis Russell, was killed in a minor clash on the Scottish border only a few hours before his father died.

Francis, Earl of Bedford, had been a great patron of letters as well as a notable courtier and diplomat. Numerous works were dedicated to him by writers such as William Ward and Richard Androse. He was a less dedicated man than his father, more of a family man and with wider interests. He had pride of ancestry to a marked extent, as evidenced by his purchase for sentimental reasons of the manor of Kingston Russell from the Crown in 1559. He never lived there, nor at Moor Park, of which his father had been keeper and which he also purchased from the Crown. Most of his home life was spent in his father's house in Exeter, at Chenies, and at Bedford House in the Strand. The addition of Woburn to the family estates either just before or just after his father's death persuaded him to repair and enlarge although not entirely to rebuild Woburn Abbey and to make it one of his homes. He also enlarged the Russell home at Tavistock on the site of Tavistock Abbey.

It was at Woburn that his first wife died in 1561 and at Woburn, too, that he entertained Queen Elizabeth in 1572. This visitation was a source of combined pride and alarm, as he felt that Woburn was ill fitted for the reception of royalty. He wrote to Lord Burghley on 16th July: "I pray God the rooms and lodgings may be to Her Majesty's content. If I could make them better upon such a sudden then I would be assured they should be better than they be." Two years earlier he entertained the Queen with much more peace of mind at the better established family home at Chenies. On that occasion the Queen stayed for several days, taking the opportunity of extended conference with the Earl and other members of the Privy Council.

The 2nd Earl was succeeded by his grandson, Edward, the son of Sir Francis Russell. As one of his descendants, the 11th Duke of Bedford, said of him, he was neither statesman, soldier, nor diplomatist. He succeeded at the age of eleven and had as guardian his aunt, the Countess of Warwick. In 1594 he married Lucy, daughter and co-heir of Sir John Harrington of Exton, a lady who took over his care when his aunt perforce abandoned it. They had no children. She clearly had a much stronger character than her husband and such little limelight as is thrown on the 3rd Earl and his Countess in the following years illuminates her personality rather than his. He is mentioned occasionally as winning distinction in Court tourneys but soon after his marriage he was crippled by a fall when hunting. He was thrown against a tree and was so injured that he was believed to be dead. Although he recovered he took still less part in Court affairs.

The Earl of Essex apparently made an attempt to draw him into his ill-timed insurrection but as he was not charged with complicity we can only assume that whatever support he gave was from personal regard rather than from any desire to take part in the plot. According to one account he escaped being charged with treason only on payment of a substantial fine. The consciousness of the risk he had run, added to his natural liking for a quiet life, gave him a still greater distaste for public life. He rarely, if ever, appeared except at the Court ceremonials at which his rank obliged him to appear.

The Countess Lucy was of a much livelier disposition. She was prominent in the masques which were a feature of the Court of James I and was universally acknowledged to be a wit and a lady of exemplary taste. She was accused by later writers of extravagance but the charge had little meaning in the case of a wealthy childless couple, although there is no doubt that she made considerable inroads on the liquid family resources. She added to the Russell collection of paintings, especially several by Holbein; she was interested in unexpectedly scholarly subjects and had a well-known collection of ancient coins.

But the real pride of the Earl and Countess was their garden at Moor Park, which Sir William Temple described as "the perfectest figure of a garden that I ever saw either at home or abroad". It was a landscape garden far ahead of its times, adorned with fountains, statues and summer-houses. Even at a distance of thirty years Temple said, "Its remembrance was too pleasant for me ever to forget." The Countess, who was the principal architect of the garden was, of course, influenced by Italian ideas, the ideas that influenced the style of English gardens for centuries after her time. But she banished what she called the barbarity of topiary work, regarding this typical Tudor fancy as "a torture of shrubs and hedges into unnatural and monstrous forms".

The Earl and Countess died within a few weeks of each other, he on 3rd May 1627, she on 26th May. The Earl, like his two predecessors, was buried at Chenies.

If the 3rd Earl contributed comparatively little to public affairs and took little part in Court life, two of the 2nd Earls' other three sons lived useful and distinguished lives, adding in their several ways something to the pattern of the Elizabethan tapestry.

Edward, Lord Russell, the Earl's eldest son, had a tragically short life. He married Jane, daughter of Sir Richard Morrison, a prominent Buckinghamshire squire. A picture painted in his twenty-second year in 1573 shows a good-looking, intelligent young man already clearly showing the signs of poor health. He died soon afterwards, childless.

The 2nd Earl's fourth son, Sir William Russell, was a soldier by profession and is said to have excelled at the tourney, a skill that was required of any young man on the fringe of Court society. He was educated at Magdalen College, Oxford, like all his brothers, and on completing his education undertook the "Grand Tour" of France, Germany and Italy. He first saw military service in the Low Countries and having distinguished himself in a campaign received a knighthood. In 1583 he married Elizabeth, a daughter of Sir Henry Long of Cambridge-shire. He was the only surviving son of the 2nd Earl and the only Russell in the official funeral procession, at which the Earl of Cumberland represented the Queen as chief mourner.

In 1585 he was under the command of the Earl of Leicester in Holland and in the following year took part in the siege of Zutphen, at which Sir Philip Sidney, who had been one of William's closest friends, lost his life. Immediately afterwards Sir William was appointed Governor of Flushing, the office that Sir Philip Sidney had last held. In 1587 the Earl of Leicester raised the siege of Zutphen and was recalled but Sir William remained at Flushing, where he proved a competent and sympathetic governor. Queen Elizabeth wrote him several letters in her own hand acknowledging his services, but the highest tribute which in the eyes of the contemporaries could be paid to him was that he did not increase his wealth or otherwise better his position by virtue of his office. On the contrary, the entertainment he provided on behalf of the government for visiting noblemen far exceeded in cost the allowance which he received.

As so often happened in the wars of the 16th century, there

was a lack of liaison between the army in the field and the commissariat at home. In a letter to Walsingham he demanded either that the town should be provided with adequate supplies or that he should be "helped away from so beggarly a government wherein he should but undo himself without hope of service or reward". Ultimately the Queen recalled him, to the regret, it is said, of the people of Flushing.

On his return to England Sir William appropriately was appointed to command the forces of the West, following in his father's footsteps. However, the Armada came and went and Sir William's army of defence never went into action. In 1593 he was appointed Lord Deputy of Ireland in succession to Sir William Fitzwilliam. He received a personal commission from the Queen, with whom he dined before leaving for Ireland. He was sworn to his new office in Dublin Castle on 11th August.

His was an extremely difficult assignment. Ireland had not so far been conquered in the sense that its spirit had been broken. The English "adventurers" had only maintained their footing in the country by continuous active warfare. Even when they extended the English holding the Irish never surrendered but carried on guerrilla warfare against them from the mountains of the west.

The English settlers had been depleted in number by the Wars of the Roses, when almost every English nobleman had left his estates in Ireland to assist the party of his choice and many had never returned. Some other English settlers had been absorbed into the Irish people by marriage and had exchanged their Anglo-Norman surnames for Irish ones. When Sir William took over what was virtually the military as well as the administrative control of Ireland the English Pale consisted of little more than the four counties of Louth, Meath, Dublin and Kildare. Henry VIII had not improved matters by taking the title King of Ireland where previous sovereigns had been content with the more moderate title Lord of Ireland. Moreover there had been no consistency in government. Some governors had been almost barbarous in their treatment of the Irish, others had made a genuine attempt at conciliation.

Queen Elizabeth's policy was to resettle Munster by granting lands at a nominal valuation to the younger sons of English nobles and to establish a chain of garrisons on this redistributed land to hold insurgents in check. Ulster was in a turmoil and the English garrison in Enniskillen had recently surrendered when Sir William arrived. Dublin itself was threatened by strong Irish forces whose headquarters were at Glendalough in the Wicklow Mountains. To make matters worse, a number of Scots, mostly from the Western Isles, landed in Ireland and made some headway. One force which landed at Carrick-fergus overran Kildare. So Sir William was forced to the necessity of fighting against Scots and Irishmen separately.

He proved himself by far the most capable governor of the century. Though he did not bring lasting peace to Ireland (that would have been quite impossible in the circumstances) he left the country in a far more hopeful condition than he found it. First he recognized the absolute necessity of restoring the English position in Ulster and with all the troops at his disposal overran it. He led the army in person and with the help of a few lucky successes in minor skirmishes so terrified the Irish that they left Enniskillen undefended. Returning to Dublin, Sir William broke all the traditional rules of warfare by making a winter attack on the Irish forces at Glendalough, where he dispersed the rebels and received the submission of a number of chieftains, who swore their loyalty to the Queen and maintained that their only reason for joining the rebels had been the insensate severity of the previous governor Fitzwilliam. This may well have been true and there is no doubt that Sir William's combination of spectacular military coups and moderation towards defeated or captured chieftains did a great deal to relieve the intolerable resentment which might well have resulted in the final loss of Ireland.

However, he now faced the prospect of a serious and well-

organized rebellion under the Earl of Tyrone, who received
support from a number of Anglo-Irish nobles, including the
Earl of Kildare. He also received substantial assistance in the
form of money and supplies from Spain. Sir William wrote to
the Queen asking for reinforcements and for experienced
officers to take the field. The Queen despatched Sir John
Norris with the title of General of the Army of Ulster, with
powers properly belonging to the deputy only. The historian
Camden comments on this curious decision of Queen Elizabeth,
"Most certainly it was the subject of general wonder in regard
that the very essence of government seems to consist in its being
lodged in the hands of one." However, Russell welcomed his
new colleague in a generous spirit and having declared the Earl
of Tyrone and other leaders of the insurrection traitors, marched
with Norris on Armagh and Dungannon, which was the likeliest
port at which Spanish troops might land. Tyrone carried out a
scorched earth policy, withdrew his garrison from Newry, and
razed to the ground Dungannon and neighbouring villages.
Russell intercepted a letter from Tyrone to the King of Spain
calling on the latter in the name of the Roman Catholic Church
to send immediate reinforcements, but he was able to re-
garrison the principal forts before withdrawing his army to
winter quarters.

Disagreement now arose between Russell and Norris. The
latter was obsessed with the thought that the hostility of the
Irish was provoked by the oppression of the Queen's governors,
the former concerned only to bring the rebellion to an end. So
the extraordinary position arose in which Norris wrote
repeatedly to the Queen asking her to pardon the Earl of
Tyrone, while Russell prepared to overthrow by force his hold
in Northern Ireland. In vain Russell urged that concession
would only increase the danger of general insurrection and any
treaty would be violated on sight of the first sail from Cadiz.
His predictions, like those of Cassandra, were disregarded and
remembered only when they came true. Disregarding her

deputy, the Queen empowered Norris to enter into negotiations with Tyrone and a truce was arranged. A year later Sir William could say with reason that since the truce had been signed the Queen had lost more by treachery and guile than could have been inflicted in twice the time by open warfare.

At the beginning of 1596 he was writing to the Earl of Essex asking him to intercede with the Queen: "I think all the Irish are either in action or conspiracy. The whole kingdom will be lost if the government is not better supplied." Essex responded cordially and prevailed on the Privy Council to vote him the sum of more than £200,000 and an additional force of cavalry. Now operating from a position of strength, Sir William and Norris were able to impose on the Earl of Tyrone conditions of peace which Norris at least hoped would effectively prevent further insurrection. Tyrone agreed to accept a sheriff in his county and promised to rebuild the English fortresses which had been destroyed and to supply the English garrisons at his own expense there.

The value of the treaty was exaggerated if a long term view is taken, but the Queen's pleasure was obvious at the apparent ending of the war which was proving a serious drain on the exchequer. Oddly, Norris received more praise than Russell, whose continuing mistrust of Tyrone was put down at Court to jealousy of Norris. Russell was, however, permitted to keep Ireland in a state of readiness and to take vigorous action to quell several small rebellions which took place outside the field of Tyrone's influence. When he proposed regulations to prevent extortion by soldiers in the English Pale, Norris, now "promoted" President of Ulster, refused to give his agreement. So the divided rule continued uneasily and the equally uneasy peace with the main body of Irish insurgents remained in force.

One fine day late in 1596 three ships from Spain made landfall on the Galway coast and unloaded ammunition for the insurgents. Their commander delivered letters from the King of Spain to all the rebel chieftains urging them to continue their opposition. It was not so much the actual value of the supplies sent by Spain as the moral support provided by the King's promise to send further assistance that people throughout Ireland began to think once more in terms of ridding themselves of the hated English, to the greater glory of God.

Tyrone rose to the occasion. He delivered his letter from King Philip to Russell and almost simultaneously communicated with the former rebel leaders throughout Munster and Leinster, promising them support and urging them to unite with the men of Ulster for the sake of "Christ's Catholic religion". So once again in the summer of 1597 the whole of Ireland was enveloped in the flames of civil war. Spain, wounded by the sack of Cadiz carried out by the Earl of Essex, proved no more trustworthy in sending assistance than in the past. However, the die was cast and with or without further Spanish help the Irish leaders were committed to a fight to the death. Armagh was beseiged by forces under the Earl of Tyrone. The English were driven from the greater part of Wicklow and news was received every day of fresh outrages all over the country.

Russell wrote to Essex calling for supplies of victuals, powder and money, and in addition warships to defend the coast in case of Spanish attack. He complained bitterly of the inactivity of Norris in Ulster and asked to be relieved of his appointment. After a final and successful drive against the rebels in the Wicklow Mountains, he delivered the sword of state to his successor, Lord Borough, on 15th May.

On his return, Sir William had many consultations with the Queen, who came to realize by the end of the year that his advice had been right and that no hope of peace in Ireland could come from trusting further to Norris. So Norris was relieved of his command in Ulster.

The new deputy, Lord Borough, did little better and Sir William became in effect the ruler of the destinies of Ireland from his position as chief adviser to the Queen on Irish matters.

In 1599 he was pressed to accept formal command in Ireland for a second term but refused the dubious honour, although he was the chief architect of the ruthless but successful campaigns of Lord Mountjoy. In the last year of the reign he asked the Queen to re-appoint him to his old position of Governor of Flushing. The Queen agreed and he spent the next few years there as happily and effectively as in his earlier spell of office. He was one of the Knights raised to the peerage by King James I to commemorate his coronation and took the title Baron Russell of Thornhaugh. His son Francis, who later succeeded as the 4th Earl and had been with him in Ireland until his recall (when he was twelve years old), was knighted by King James in 1607.

Baron Russell was one of the nobles attendant on Prince Henry at the ceremony of installation as Prince of Wales, and was also in the funeral procession of Prince Henry in 1612. He died in 1613, according to his chaplain, a Mr. Walker, earnestly declaring his desire to be with Christ during the last days of his illness. He is remembered, perhaps, chiefly as a fearless and remarkably efficient soldier, whether as a junior officer at Zutphen or as an army commander in Ireland, but his political intervention in Irish affairs also achieved a great deal. Had it not been for Queen Elizabeth's incomprehensible degradation of his authority, he might well have achieved at far less expense and with far less bloodshed than Mountjoy the pacification of the country and perhaps have changed the course of Irish history.

Lord William, or as he is always remembered, Sir William Russell, was the most distinguished of the 2nd Earl's four sons. His eldest son has already been mentioned. Little is known of his second son John, Baron Russell, except that in 1574 he married Elizabeth, widow of Sir Thomas Hobby, formerly Ambassador to France, who had died in 1566. The Queen was godmother to their daughter Elizabeth, and the Earl of Leicester godfather. The Queen, incidentally, took a continued

ag del.   T.A.Dean sc

John, 1st Earl of Bedford, founder of the family fortunes. Appointed
to the household of Henry VIII, he became a friend and trusted
emissary of Henry VIII and was created 1st Earl of Bedford in the
reign of Edward VI

Left, Francis, 2nd Earl of Bedford, whose career matched that of his father. Elizabeth I entrusted him with many delicate negotiations, notably several missions to Mary, Queen of Scots; *below left*, Edward, 3rd Earl of Bedford, in contrast with his predecessors, avoided Court life and spent much time laying out the gardens of Moor Park; *below right*, Francis, 4th Earl of Bedford, who had many differences with Charles I and eventually retired from public life to undertake the vast task of draining the fens

interest in her godchild and later appointed her and her younger sister Anne maids of honour. John died about 1580. His only public service appears to have been as a Member of Parliament returned for Bridport in 1572 but he may well have held office at Court, of which there is no record. Certainly he was granted a barony at some time in his life and was buried in Westminster Abbey.

The third son, Sir Francis, was, like his younger brother, primarily a soldier. He spent some time as a youth with his father at Berwick-on-Tweed and seems to have been inspired then to follow a military career in the border country. He saw service under Sir John Forster, the Warden of the Middle Marches with headquarters at Alnwick and from 1570 onwards was the leader of innumerable forays across the Scottish border and was knighted on the field of battle. He was returned to Parliament as a Knight of the Shire for Northumberland in 1571. In the same year he married Julia, Sir John Forster's daughter.

He was serving under Sir William Drury at the siege of Edinburgh Castle in 1573 and again showed marked courage, volunteering for the dangerous mission of assaulting by escalade, or ladder, one of the bastions known as The Spur. It is a commentary on the social life of the times that even in the 19th century a writer can refer to this token of courage with disapproval, saying that men of meaner birth were normally appointed to the service of the escalade. However, the manoeuvre was a success and the bastion taken by storm. But Sir William Drury committed his charge to house arrest for fear that he would repeat such rashness, having received instructions from the Queen to pay special regard to his safety.

He continued to serve on the border under the general direction of Sir John Forster until the end of his life. His death, which has already been mentioned, occurred through misadventure. Sir John had arranged a day of truce with his opposite number, the Scottish Warden, on 27th July 1585, to

7

adjudicate on one of the numerous cases of alleged looting frequently made by one warden against the other. Apparently the Scottish troops failed to receive notice of the truce and the English deputation was met by a shower of bullets, one of which wounded Sir Francis just after he and his companions had crossed the border. The wound proved fatal.

Queen Elizabeth sent commissioners to the Scottish Court to demand that the murderers should be delivered to her but although Sir Thomas Carr of Farnihurst, the Scottish Warden, was imprisoned as the man responsible, at least by a sin of omission, for the breaking of the truce, the Queen received no satisfaction.

CHAPTER FOUR

The Draining of the Fens

The draining of the Fens is the greatest contribution ever made to the reclamation of English land for farming. The transformation of what came to be known as the Bedford Level from waste and bog into some of the richest agricultural land in the country is equally the greatest contribution made by a single family to this achievement. Although the Earls of Bedford were not alone in this vast project, they not only made themselves responsible for a great deal of the work involved but inspired others to join them and made it possible for those who came after them to complete their work. The net result of the reclamation was the addition of an area variously estimated at between 300,000 and 400,000 acres to the sum total of English farm-land which was made available at the time when it was most needed.

The 4th and 5th Earls were the two individuals mainly concerned. In speaking of the work of Francis, the 4th Earl, Wiffen says, "He gave his thoughts to an undertaking highly patriotic in its principle and vast in its design." It was certainly both, although paradoxically the patriotic principle was conceived immediately the Earl's further intervention in politics had been made impossible or dangerous by reason of conduct which might equally well be called unpatriotic in its principle.

At the beginning of the 17th century the Fen land, then known as the Great Level, was an ill-defined tract embracing large parts of the counties of Huntingdon and Cambridge and reaching into the neighbouring counties of Norfolk, Lincoln and Northampton. The Earls of Bedford were concerned chiefly with the southern part of this Great Level, roughly south of a line drawn from Crowland to Denver. Wells, in his *History of the Bedford Level*, calls the 4th Earl of Bedford's agreement to carry out this undertaking "a most striking instance of selfless devotion to the wishes of the people and the real benefit of the State which appears upon the records of history. Hope dawned over a dreary waste. A new world arose to crown his efforts and enabled himself to deserve from posterity a monument of its unceasing gratitude and admiration."

These words were printed in 1830, when one might have expected the memory of the 4th and 5th Earls to have been dimmed by time. It shows something of the importance with which the draining of the Fens has been regarded for more than three hundred years and it is appropriate that the Old and New Bedford Rivers still serve as the main drainage channels of the southern Fens.

On a map the level of the Fen land appears as an extension of the Wash bounded by a coastline consisting of higher ground in Norfolk, Suffolk, Cambridgeshire and Huntingdonshire. In fact it consisted of two parts, known to Fenmen as the Silt and the Fen or Peat. The surface of the latter consisted mainly of alluvial deposits carried down by the midland rivers. The former, which extended some way back from the coast, was originally a salt marsh, frequently inundated by the sea and with an admixture of sand. In the 17th century the rivers Ouse and Nene ran into the sea only on the maps. Their rate of fall was not sufficient for them to scour out their channels. They meandered sluggishly towards the Wash by a hundred different courses which were constantly changed as the old ones silted up. The combination of spring tides and a north-easterly gale frequently resulted in the sea breaking through the rudimentary banks which protected the silty marshes near the Wash, while the incoming sea meeting the flood water in the many streams of the Nene and Ouse after heavy rain inundated the whole of the Fen land to a depth of several feet.

The only life associated with the Fens was on the "islands", especially the Isle of Ely. This had not always been the case. There is evidence that drainage on quite an extensive scale had been carried out in the first centuries A.D. with the help of Roman drainage engineers and that considerable areas had been cultivated at that time. The task of the Romans, however, was far easier than that facing anyone who tried to emulate their example in the 17th century. The gradual fall of the land in eastern England relative to the level of the sea is now an established fact and has been estimated to be approximately 6 in. in a hundred years. Even allowing for the possibility that this is an exaggerated figure and that the decline has not been steady or continuous, it is a reasonably safe assumption that the land has sunk by 6ft. or more since the time of Roman Britain. And 6 ft. can and does make a difference. What in the first centuries A.D. had been a courageous and successful drainage operation had become by the 17th century an unavailing rearguard action against the encroaching water.

All the Fen land suffered periodic "drowning" and some of it was drowned in summer as well as in winter. In the Later Middle Ages work on the Fens in close proximity to the islands had been well maintained by the numerous monastic houses in the district, especially Thorney, Ramsey, Ely and Crowland. It was by virtue of being in possession of the Thorney estate since the Earldom was created that the Russell family was interested.

It is certainly true that the greater part of the Fen acreage capable of cultivation was under monastic control until the 16th century. It can well be imagined that with the dispersal of monastic labour and the parcelling out of the land among frequently absentee landowners the work of draining and embanking was neglected. A survey for the Earl of Bedford carried out during the reign of Queen Elizabeth described the Thorney estate as containing 16,000 acres of Fen grounds "dispersely grown with sedge, reed, willow and alder of five years' growth, which in memory having been dry and firm lye now surrounded for the most part in water". (Surrounded was a current term meaning inundated during the winter or liable to frequent flooding.)

One of the medieval monastic works inspired by the famous Bishop Morton was and still is in use and is known to this day as Morton's Leam. It was one of the first straight cuts or artificial rivers constructed to speed the flow of water from the hills through the Fen land. It was completed before the end of the 15th century and after 150 years had, like its parent river, silted up and was virtually useless.

It is only fair to the new owners of the land, including the Earls of Bedford, to say that although many complaints of neglect were made against them at the Courts of Sewers, similar complaints had been made when they were monastic property. By the beginning of the 17th century the Commission of Sewers was the only public authority concerned. All the Commissioners could do was to hear complaints and give instruction for work to be done. Of course, the work was seldom carried out; in any case it was quite inadequate to keep existing farm land in good order, let alone to reclaim what had been made waste in the previous century.

Queen Elizabeth was interested and there are frequent references to Fen problems in the proceedings of her Privy Council. Part of the Isle of Ely was restored and the river "scoured" below Wisbech. In her reign, however, the problem was never tackled as a whole. It was not fully realized that what was needed if the Fens were ever to be reclaimed was fresh capital and indeed an almost unlimited supply of capital.

In the last years of the Queen's reign several disastrous floods occurred in previously "dry" country with attendant loss of life and cattle. An Act was passed in 1600 for a general scheme of drainage but was never even begun. At that time according to Camden, the local people were forced to keep watch continually throughout the winter and made banks and dams against the waters. The condition of the Fens a few years later had become such a public scandal that King James I, who held a number of manors in the district, was moved to say that he would no longer "suffer these countries to be abandoned to the will of the waters nor let them lie waste and unprofitable". He declared himself personally undertaker for a scheme of reclamation in return for 120,000 acres of the reclaimed land.

This was in accordance with the spirit if not the letter of the Act of 1600, which envisaged the possibility of landowners and commoners making a bargain by which the contractor, or "one who would undertake the draining and keeping dry perpetually" should be rewarded with an agreed part of the reclaimed land. The King's declaration was made in 1621. He called into conference the Dutch engineer Cornelius Vermuyden, fresh from the reclamation of hundreds of thousands of acres on the other side of the North Sea. However, as he so often said himself, something prevented him! He died in 1625 without a start being made on the great work.

King Charles I proposed to take up the matter where his father had left it. The Commissioners of Sewers proposed a prospective drainage tax of six shillings an acre but no landowner ever paid the tax. At the King's request the Commissioners reapproached Vermuyden, but they had to report that a contract with Vermuyden was impossible owing to the prejudice against an alien and the opposition of the commoners, who feared that their livelihood from fowling, fishing and reed gathering would be jeopardized if a major scheme of drainage took place (in this, of course, they were right and many of the Fenmen were innocent victims of circumstances).

A number of the major property owners decided at last that concerted action was necessary. They approached the Earl of Bedford with the suggestion that he should seek the King's approval for acting as undertaker and promising their support. The King was apparently pleased to be relieved of the responsibility, and he readily gave his consent. So the Earl of Bedford became undertaker, contracting to drain the southern Fens—the Bedford Level—within six years.

The conditions of the contract were agreed by the Commissioners sitting at King's Lynn, the instrument being known as the Lynn Law. By this the Russell reward was to be 95,000 acres but only 43,000 of these were awarded absolutely to him, the remainder being allotted in part to the Crown and in part to the Commissioners for a fund to maintain the drainage works when they had been completed. The Duke was joined by thirteen "adventurers" (in effect speculators who risked their money for the prospect of receiving a reward in land). The fourteen were granted a royal charter of incorporation.

Undeterred by local opposition, the Earl re-engaged Vermuyden, probably the only man in Europe capable of carrying out the work. There was much preliminary argument, in which Vermuyden and the Earl put forward the expedient of constructing a completely new river to hasten the course of the Ouse, the majority of the other members of the corporation preferring a plan to deepen existing waterways. In the end Vermuyden and the Earl prevailed and work was begun on a project at the magnitude of which the imagination boggles.

The main work was the construction of the Bedford River from Earith to Denver, 21 miles long and 70 ft. wide. Morton's Leam was reconstructed. Another cut to drain the Whittlesey marsh was 10 miles long and 40 ft. wide, and another over the Peterborough levels 10 miles long and 17ft. wide. There were several other major cuts and in addition innumerable drains and dykes and sluices. A traveller at the time reported that the original River Ouse bypassed by the Bedford River was left a mere trickle. Towns like Cambridge and Wisbech complained that the river was no longer navigable and that their trade would suffer. The Fenmen banded together to destroy the work as it was being done. Labour was extraordinarily difficult to obtain, although one visitor in 1634 reported seeing more than six hundred men at work in the neighbourhood of Wisbech.

Against all probability the work was completed in three years. After a survey had been made the Commissioners of Sewers met at St. Ives in 1637 and gave their decision that the Great Level had been drained according to the terms of the contract entered into by the adventurers, or as they put it, "according to the true intent of the Lynn Law". But at what a cost. There is agreement that the actual expenditure of the Earl of Bedford was not less than £100,000, that is not less than £2,000,000 at the present time. Although his co-adventurers risked far less capital than the Earl, they were all in a state of bankruptcy when the Commissioners made their decision. The Earl himself had been compelled to sell many of the Russell estates in various parts of the country although, of course, he was hampered in this respect by his inability to sell land that was entailed. The manor of Kingston Russell seems to have been one of the casualties at this time.

The Russells were, of course, by now extremely wealthy by any standard of comparison but their wealth was principally in family estates, and borrowing against security in the 17th century was far from easy. The Earl had undertaken a greater task than perhaps he himself had foreseen, but thanks to the prompt action of the Commissioners complete financial disaster was avoided. Vermuyden and the hundreds of labourers were paid off.

Now the adventurers sat back to enjoy the rewards of their speculation. They were disappointed. It is not clear what precisely went wrong. Vermuyden's scheme cannot have been adequate to reclaim the whole of the Bedford Level for winter pasture, though it was probably adequate to ensure that the Fen fields were not inundated during the summer. But the people whose lands had been reclaimed were far from satisfied. They had expected far more and the Privy Council was showered with complaints. There is some evidence, too, that the Earl of Bedford had become unpopular with King Charles.

Whether that is so or not, the Commissioners of Sewers had little alternative when they met in 1638 to revising their judgement of the previous year. In view of the piles of complaints before them they came to the decision that the undertaking was defective. Treating the matter as one of urgency, they imposed a tax on all the reclaimed land to provide capital for improving and continuing the works. The King himself agreed to act as undertaker. The Earl of Bedford and his associates were given 40,000 acres, only 3,000 acres less than the net amount which they would have received under the original Lynn Law. They were indeed fortunate to have received any return at all on the capital invested but in view of the new tax imposed on their land none of them was the richer for their "adventure", though their heirs may well have been when the manifold difficulties of Fen agriculture had been overcome.

King Charles lost no time in pressing on with the new work. He re-engaged Vermuyden, who is now seen as a kind of resident engineer, employed by whoever happened to be the undertaker at the time, still vastly unpopular yet still indispensable, the only man who in the whole saga of the Fens appeared to have the slightest conception of a scientific approach to a problem that could be solved only with the help of science. He was undismayed by the need of further works. He justified himself by pointing out that he had always maintained that far more capital was required for a satisfactory job than the Earl of Bedford and his thirteen co-adventurers had provided. The Earl himself must have smiled ruefully when it proved impossible to collect a debt from a tenant on his own Thorney estate because it was inaccessible in winter.

In the event the King and Vermuyden had scarcely started on their second plan of campaign when the King exchanged the battle for the Fens for a battle for his throne and life. Little or nothing was done during the years of civil war. Vermuyden was still in England and carried out some few drainage operations for private landowners. That was all. Then in 1645 Parliament, no doubt at the instance of Oliver Cromwell, who had been appointed governor of the Isle of Ely in 1645 and had every opportunity to see the state of the Fens at first hand, formed a committee to consider ways and means of completing the work on the Bedford Level.

This committee was in existence for four years. It produced one or two reports but again and again was met by the difficulty of finance. It came rightly to the conclusion, however, that the greater part of the Fens could be made dry in winter as well as summer and that the draining, if carried out, would be of great advantage to the Commonwealth. It endorsed the very sensible provision that a part of the further area reclaimed should be held in trust after the initial draining was completed to provide funds. Always the committee's deliberations brought them back to the Russell family, the only family with a sizeable stake in the Fens and sufficient capital and influence to prevail against the still vigorous opposition.

The 4th Earl had died and been succeeded by William, the 5th Earl, who was approached by the committee and agreed to carry on where Francis had left off. With him were associated the 4th Earl's thirteen adventurers or their heirs and some others who were associated with the second scheme only. The Act which passed through Parliament on 29th May 1649 required the Earl to "cause the Great Level to be drained and embanked without prejudice to the navigation in the rivers and all the said level shall be made winter ground on or before 10 October 1656".

This second great scheme was not designed to do again what the 4th Earl had already achieved but to carry his work a stage further. The first scheme had produced hundreds of thousands of acres of new "summer" land. The second scheme was to transform this into winter land, i.e. free from flooding in all normal circumstances. The ever-present Vermuyden inevitably was re-engaged and the work of planning and engaging labour began again, just as it had in 1634. A happy circumstance was that Vermuyden had retained in his employment through all those troubled years a number of key assistants.

The 5th Earl took a more personal and active interest in the actual reclamation than his predecessor and once more upheld Vermuyden's plan against all criticism. The main feature of the scheme as finally adopted was a duplication of the Bedford River (thereafter known as the Old Bedford River) by a parallel cut (then known as the Hundred Foot River but now as the New Bedford River) about half a mile from the Old Bedford River. The area between the Old river and the New, known as the Wash Land, was designed to be used for temporary and deliberate flooding when the two main channels proved, as they occasionally might, inadequate to hold all the water flowing down the Ouse. The Ouse itself between Earith and Denver flowing round by Ely was downgraded into a channel which drained only the southern part of the Fen, but in accordance with the agreement Vermuyden made allowance for maintaining a sufficient height of water to make navigation possible on the Cam and the Ouse. This involved scouring and deepening the channels of both rivers.

The 4th Earl had partially solved his labour problems by employing a number of Walloon refugees from Picardy and North Flanders. The 5th Earl had obtained government support for using prisoners, so Cromwell's victory at Dunbar in 1650 was incidentally a victory for the drainers of the Fens. Many prisoners were taken who proved willing workers after expecting a far worse fate.

Many of the French workers settled in the Fens permanently, especially the Walloon refugees. They were given their own church and their own French minister at Thorney, and even in the 18th century a French baptismal register was kept. Their influence on Fenland agriculture was significant, as many of them were experts in the cultivation of colza, from which oil was extracted and which proved one of the most successful crops in the 17th century and early part of the 18th. Although these settlements have long been merged with the English there are still a more than ordinary number of French names among the people of the Fenland villages, Thorney in particular. Many are directly descended from the Walloon settlers.

The second scheme aroused almost as much opposition as the first. There was the same story of disorders arising largely from fear and of attempts at sabotage, guarded against during the construction operations by keeping a day-and-night guard on the works, but impossible to prevent once the constructors had passed on to the next stage. One persistent school of thought was that the work was contrary to the will of God and that because it involved tampering with nature it was bound to fail except with the help of the Devil. The undertaker and his associates were compared with witches, so that it became a matter of honour as well as anger to impede the progress of the work in every possible way.

Vermuyden triumphed as he had done before. In March 1652, well in advance of the contractual date, the Earl was in a position to ask for an adjudication by the Commissioners on the work done. The north and the middle level had already been adjudged properly drained and the Earl was able to report to the meeting that 40,000 acres were currently sown with wheat and other winter crops, and that vast numbers of sheep and cattle were grazing on land which had never been grazed within living memory. The south level, which was now adjudged to be drained, contained about 130,000 acres of land, all of which would be suitable for use as pasture or for winter sowing in the coming months. The Commissioners duly made their decision that the work had been well and truly done and a thanksgiving service for the completion of the work was held in Ely Cathedral.

The building of the New Bedford River was, of course, only one part, though a major part of this second scheme. Almost equally important was the linking of the "Old" Nene with the outfall of the Ouse by a cut known as Vermuyden's Drain from

Ramsey to the Old Bedford River. The principle adopted for providing an area for emergency flooding between the Old and the New Bedford rivers was incidentally adopted during the 18th century in the north of the Fen area between Morton's Leam, which was deepened and strengthened, and a completely new cut to accommodate the main flow of the Nene.

For the time being there was far less complaint than there had been after the completion of the 4th Earl's undertaking. In 1663 an Act was passed through Parliament to the effect that William, Earl of Bedford, and the "adventurers and participants of the said Earl William and Earl Francis, their heirs and assigns shall be a body politic and corporate and have succession for ever by the name of the governor, bailiffs and commonalty of the Company of Conservators of the Great Level of the Fens". No longer do we hear of Courts of Sewers or Commissioners of Sewers. The Company of Conservators was the sole arbiter of disputes arising out of Fen drainage and had full responsibility for maintaining it and improving it.

The 95,000 acres which had been set aside to provide an income for the conservation of the Fens was vested in the Company, as was all the land allotted to the Earl, the "adventurers and participants" and also the royal allotment, amounting to 12,000 acres. The board's revenue was derived from taxes on the land. Even the King's land was subject to this taxation.

This was a vitally important Act from the point of view of the Earl and his associates, for it gave them absolute security of tenure, as it did of responsibility. Surprisingly, in view of the vast political changes that took place during the next two hundred years, the corporation remained in existence and with little change of constitution until it was merged in the Low Ouse Drainage Board, which was established under an Act of 1914. The 5th Earl made the company a very special interest of his, largely rebuilt Thorney Abbey, and spent a good deal of time there from 1663 to 1685 supervising the operations carried out by his agent, who was accommodated at the Abbey.

It is not known precisely how much was added to the Russell estates by the two operations. The 5th Earl, of course, was the principal landowner in the 1663 company, but how much the 4th Earl actually received of the 40,000 acres allotted to him and his co-adventurers is uncertain. What is beyond doubt is that these two great schemes sponsored respectively by the 4th and 5th Earls made upwards of 300,000 acres available for intensive agriculture. The prosperity of the Fenland today is a still-present monument to their courage and determination to succeed against odds, political and social.

The final result is perhaps best illustrated by the fact that when the Thorney Abbey estate was made over to the Russells after the dissolution there were 300 acres of land under cultivation, including both arable and pasture, the remainder being either permanently "drowned" or unused except for occasional summer pasture and for fishing and fowling. In the 19th century this same estate amounted to 23,000 acres, some no doubt acquired by subsequent purchase, but by far the greater part of it certainly representing land of the original monastic estate which had been reclaimed by the drainage operations.

That, of course, was not the end of the story. Although Vermuyden was scientific in approach and both the 4th and the 5th Earls spared no expense to obtain the best available supporting opinions and criticisms of the plans made, the fact was that scientific knowledge had not then advanced far enough for the implications of land drainage on such a vast scale to be understood. The long-term problems involved were already apparent in the 5th Earl's lifetime. One of the points which had been overlooked was that the water content of a land surface bulks large. When it is reduced either by draining the water away or subsequent to the drainage operation by evaporation, the land shrinks and, therefore, ultimately the land surface falls. In the case of the Fens this meant that the surface of the whole area subsided well below sea level. The erosion of dry soil by wind was another factor making for the lowering of the level of the land. It was a specially important factor in the Fens because they had no natural wind-breaks and were exposed to the north-easterly gales common in spring after the soil had been broken up by frost. A good deal of the top-soil ultimately found its way by wind dispersal on to the high ground of Northamptonshire and Cambridgeshire.

Even that was not the sum total of nature's revenge on the drainers. All the inner area of the Fens, that is, the area referred to as the Peat, was lowered by cultivation. The habit of burning off the peat provoked very few protests at the time, but although it was excellent from the point of view of yield, once the peat had been removed there was nothing to replace it with and the process continued until in the 19th century the cultivators reached the clay subsoil. When deep ploughing was introduced the topmost layer of peat no longer presented a problem and this particular form of wastage ceased. But by that time the damage had been done. Consequently not only was the whole area below sea level but the "inland" areas, that is to say, the areas round the Isle of Ely and Crowland, became lower in level than the areas adjacent to the sea, the Silt, and the normal slope of the land towards the sea was reversed.

The Bedford estate at Thorney was ultimately on average 10 to 12 ft. below the high-water level of the North Sea and the risks attendant on flooding became absolutely lethal. On the few occasions when the Bedford rivers burst their banks the loss of stock was disastrous to the farmers, the loss of life tragically high. It became essential, therefore, for the safety alike of the farmers and their stock that the retaining banks of the rivers and cuts should be kept in perfect condition, because one weak point was enough to precipitate disaster.

William of Malmesbury's 12th-century picture of the Fens as "a very paradise for that in pleasure and delight it resembleth heaven itself, the plain with the flourishing of grass alluring the eye" may have been re-created visually but its very re-creation *right*, William, the 5th Earl and 1st Duke of Bedford, became an implacable enemy of the Stuart dynasty after the execution of his son and heir, Lord William Russell; *below left*, Wriothesley, 2nd Duke of Bedford, who suffered an early death, leant towards the arts rather than politics; *below right*, Wriothesley, 3rd Duke of Bedford, who succeeded to the dukedom as a child, had poor health but expensive tastes, including a powerful love of gambling

Left, John, 4th Duke of Bedford, the "merry little duke", worked hard to restore the Russell finances and had a brilliant political career; *below left*, Francis, 5th Duke of Bedford, is remembered especially for the outstanding contribution he made to developing a scientific agriculture; *below right*, John, 6th Duke of Bedford, brother of Francis and father of Lord John Russell, had a distinguished record in the expansion of the Russell estates

held an imminent threat of total destruction. A complication was that the level of the water flowing through the new cuts and drains was higher than that of the fields they drained. That is still so, as anyone can see who travels through the Fenland country. That might have been tolerable, but when the level of the water in the minor dykes was lower than that of the drains into which they discharged they ceased to be of any use and the land which was intended to be drained by the dykes soon became waterlogged.

1673 was a particularly bad year. The estuary of the Ouse began to silt up, with the result that the water coming down the Bedford rivers from the uplands could not find its way to the sea, and the combination of a north-east wind and a spring tide was followed by widespread flooding, so that in the Crowland area grain stacks were 3ft. deep in water, the farmers' homes were inundated and the farmers themselves forced to take to boats. Thorney Fen was another district severely affected in that year. The company did all it could do to meet the numerous complaints and petitions addressed to it but after the death of the 5th Earl (who had then become the 1st Duke) the complaints became more and more numerous and more drastic action had to be taken.

The difficulties were overcome for the time being in two ways. Early in the 17th century a new cut was made for the Nene, supplanting the functions of Morton's Leam, and a 20-ft. dyke was cut from Whittlesey to Denver. Further drains and major cuts continued to be made at intervals in the 18th and 19th centuries, including what proved to be the most effective of all, a channel from the Middle Level of the Fens west of the Bedford rivers to the Ouse near King's Lynn and a new and deeper channel to accommodate the outfall of the Ouse itself. The other innovation, equally effective, was to pump the water from the dykes into the drains and from the drains into the cuts or rivers. During the 18th century windmills proliferated, until the whole landscape at a distance seemed to be filled with them. In

8

the single parish of Whittlesey there were fifty, in the Middle
Level more than 250 in the year 1748.

Work carried out by the Bedford Level Corporation was aug-
mented by other groups of landowners when the funds of the
Corporation derived from taxes on the land were insufficient to
finance the work. The windmills proved adequate to their task
through the great part of the 18th century but unfortunately the
difficulties which they overcame became more and more
aggravated, if only by the natural progressive fall of the land
level irrespective of the special problems set by Fen cultivation.
Windmills are at the best capricious machines, often wayward
in their activities when they are most needed and, above all,
liable to immobilization by frost.

Once again, towards the end of the 18th century, despair
replaced confidence. A writer in 1777 said, "Look everywhere
you will, you will see nothing but misery and desolation."
Arthur Young, in his *Annals of Agriculture 1805*, wrote, "In the
last 30 years many inundations have taken place. The remedies
that have been applied by numberless Acts of Parliament have
been in vain but the burden by taxes immense", and in another
passage, "the total ruin of the whole flat district must ensue".
In Young's lifetime one important remedy was known but
unhappily not applied. It was the steam-engine. Young says,
"The application of steam-engines is a *desideratum* that has
often been mentioned but none yet executed. It must be evident
that the power of steam could nowhere be employed with
greater profit." Yet it was not until 1819 that the first steam-
engine in the Fens was recorded. The prospective capital outlay
in replacing the windmills was immense but it is difficult to
understand why the Corporation did not act more promptly.
The result when action was finally taken was electrifying. The
dykes began again to do their work, which was further simpli-
fied by deepening the channels of the drains and rivers. With
unlimited power in harness there was no longer real fear of catastrophe and the lives of the Fen farmers on the Thorney estate

and elsewhere became secure, as they had never been before.

The Russells were, however, associated with more major and permanent work of improvement carried out during the 19th century. It was undertaken in a much-needed effort to improve the flow of water which normally drained into the Nene or the artificial channels which had taken the original river's place. A completely new cut was made from Vermuyden's Drain to the estuary of the Ouse near King's Lynn, so giving the Middle Level a drainage system independent of the Bedford river system. The outfall of the Nene into the Wash was also improved by a deeper channel known as the Nene Outfall Cut. This proved of permanent benefit to the agriculture of the North Level. Work was completed on all these projects by the winter of 1851–2 and there is a singularly beautiful silver centre-piece at Woburn made to celebrate its successful outcome.

The more efficient diesel engine replaced the steam-engine during the first half of the 20th century, yet the problem is not permanently solved. The land level continues to fall; while the high-level system of the rivers flowing through the Fens remains constant the low-level system of the dykes and drains is falling, and, therefore, the differential increasing. A crisis can and still does occasionally arise through the combination of high tides and rivers in spate after heavy rain. Inevitably the differential will continue to increase. The floods of 1947, when almost 60,000 acres were inundated in the Crowland and Earith districts, was a warning. On that occasion there was a real risk that the sea-water of the Wash would breach the protecting banks and was only prevented from doing so by continuous lines of sandbags laid as a military operation by detachments of the Royal Engineers, and it took the whole of the following summer to repair the worst of the damage that had been done. Since then, with the responsibility no longer that of the Bedford Level Corporation but invested in government-sponsored boards, the unending work of improving on the achievements of Vermuyden and his successors has continued. It must always do so, because the Fen problem is only one phase of the greater problem of containing the sea in its inexorable work of erosion and inundation.

The Russell estate of Thorney, won from the watery wastes with so much effort and at so great an expense, was generally prosperous during the 18th century and always one in which several Dukes took personal interest. The actual reward calculated as interest on capital invested was, however, never great and with the agricultural depression of the 19th century profit was turned temporarily into loss. The 11th Duke, reviewing the results of the years 1816 to 1890 published the following illuminating figures:

Expenditure £1,598,353, including £265,155 spent on new works and permanent improvement.

Receipts £2,282,562, giving a net income of £684,209, an annual average of £8,552.

In some of the worst years of depression there was a deficit, amounting to more than £2,000 in 1879.

Although the excellence of the land reclaimed was undeniable and its rental value in normal times higher than that of other parts of the Russell estates, the cost of maintaining it always prevented what many people would regard as a fair return on an investment. That was the chief reason which led Duke Herbrand to reverse the traditional Russell policy and transfer capital invested in land into more profitable sources of revenue. The Thorney estate was sold, and the money obtained from its sale was invested in securities. One of Duke Herbrand's investments was in Russian bonds. Today those bonds are worthless.

In the 20th century, however, conditions have again improved all over the Fens and prosperity has returned. It has become one of the best arable areas in Britain. Wheat has always been one of its staple crops, market gardening and fruit growing increasingly important activities and sugar-beet a comparatively recent but wonderfully successful newcomer.

CHAPTER FIVE

The Dukedom is Founded

THE 17TH CENTURY was a critical time for the Russell family, in the struggle between Charles I and Parliament, in the troubled times of the Restoration, in the conflict between Protestantism and Roman Catholicism, and finally in the events that led up to the invitation to William of Orange to become sovereign of England. Either the 4th or the 5th Earl might so easily have lost the Russell estates, if not his head. One member of the family, Lord William Russell, was executed, several others were in dire peril. Yet in the end the House of Russell emerged strengthened by the grant of a Dukedom, its progress assured in any field it chose in the social or political world.

Apart from the great contribution which the 4th Earl made to the Russell fortunes and to national welfare by initiating the scheme for draining the Fens surrounding the Thorney estate, his career was neither particularly significant nor outstandingly successful. Francis, 4th Earl of Bedford, the son of William, Baron Thornhaugh, succeeded to the earldom in 1627. He had by then acquired considerable experience appropriate to a man of his standing. He was with his father in Ireland. A year later, in 1607, he was knighted. He married Katharine, a daughter and co-heiress of Lord Chandos. He was educated to be a lawyer and was admitted to Gray's Inn. After his father's death he took his seat as a Baron in the House of Lords and retained for the greater part of his life a keen and sometimes passionate interest in parliamentary matters. His legally trained intelligence was a great asset to the Members both of the Lords and

Commons who sought means of establishing the power of Parliament on a sound basis and of limiting constitutionally the powers of the monarchy. He studied parliamentary precedent and specialized in parliamentary law, using his knowledge in later years as a means of establishing precedents for the discomfiture of the Crown.

His legal training may also have been the root cause of his apparent inability to make up his mind on any matter of vital importance and of his habit of vacillating between unswerving loyalty to the sovereignty as such and wild attacks on the individual sovereign because of the latter's refusal to subscribe to the Earl's views on the functions of a constitutional monarchy. No doubt in politics he acted for the best as he saw it. He was certainly not a careerist in any unflattering sense of the word. Service to his country and to his fellow men was the aim he set himself. If that service brought honour and glory to the House of Russell, so much the better, but it was a secondary consideration.

We have already seen how he visualized the draining of the Fens as a service to the nation. He risked a lot in undertaking it but that was characteristic of the man. So in politics one can discern the motive of service in many of his actions and words, however unfortunate the results proved to be. His support of Parliament against King Charles appeared to be offset by his efforts to placate the King, but in fact it is probable that he sought to placate him only in order to make him amenable. If he failed in the end to promote either the cause of Parliament or of the King it was due to an inherent fault in his character rather than to insincerity or selfish motives.

In 1621 he showed clearly enough the symptoms of a man who was determined to preserve established rights at whatever cost and to defy the King if need be to secure his objects. This attitude, allied with a pedantic and academic approach to current problems, must have made him supremely irritating both to James I and Charles I. If to irritate them was his object he must be judged in this respect to have achieved success. Although still only a young man, he was an acknowledged leader of the party in the Lords unfavourable to King James. With 32 other peers he signed a petition criticizing the King's action in giving precedence to Englishmen with Irish and Scottish titles which the King had recently created. On the face of it the petition was a vindication of the privileges of heredity. It was justified on the ground that the King had made a mockery of the peerage by creating far more new peers in a year than the Tudor kings and queens had created in a century. The petitioners announced their intention of not paying the same respect to the new peers as they considered due to members of the "real Scottish and Irish peerage".

In retrospect the matter seems a trivial one and the King treated it with the contempt it deserved. But it showed clearly which way the future Earl's thoughts were tending. When he succeeded to the earldom he became deeply involved in the struggle between King and Commons. He had come to the conclusion by 1628 that the country could be freed from the monstrous claim of "many made for one", the principle of the Divine Right of Kings, only by limiting the constitutional power of the King, if necessary by force. Charles had been on the throne for only three years when many of the landed proprietors in the Midlands preferred imprisonment to complying with the King's demands for taxes levied without the sanction of Parliament. The Petition of Right was drawn up by Sir Edward Coke but in its final form it represented the combined resolution of both estates. The Earl took a prominent part in the discussions which ended in its presentation unanimously and without any major alteration having been made to the draft prepared in the Commons.

The Earl was so prominent in his support of the petition in the House of Lords that the King came to the conclusion that he was a dangerous enemy. It is a measure of his influence in Parliament at the time that he was given a royal command to leave London and assume the duties of Lord-Lieutenant in Devonshire. There he was forced to remain until Parliament was prorogued, though the King made no pretence of his having any urgent business to transact in the West.

As it happened, the discussion on the Petition of Right was the last opportunity which the Earl had of speaking in Parliament during the reign, since the King ruled for the next ten years as an absolute monarch without calling on Parliament to assemble. The King also committed a number of the parliamentary leaders to prison. Among several others he had the Earl of Bedford arrested on a charge of circulating seditious literature, in fact a satiric piece by Sir Robert Dudley which purported to teach an imaginary sovereign how to "bridle the impertinence of Parliament". A Bill was filed against the prisoners in the Star Chamber but never came to trial, for the King, having shown his strength, assumed a show of leniency and sent a message to the Court that as the Queen had given birth to a Prince it was his wish to proceed no further with the prosecution. The Earl was therefore released after about six months in prison.

If the King had hoped to intimidate him he must have been sadly disappointed, for the Earl attached himself more and more closely to those of his fellow peers whose demand for constitutional reform was becoming insistent. However, he did not intervene in public for the time being, and in the year after his prosecution offered himself as undertaker for the drainage of the Fens. The King doubtless heaved a sigh of relief at the thought of his old adversary being engaged on such a harmless and patriotic endeavour, a fact which explains in part why when the Earl's undertaking was declared defective he was, in spite of that, rewarded with a substantial grant of land. He did not return to the fray until 1638.

Since the Petition of Right the King, with the administrative help of Wentworth as President of the Northern Council, and the spiritual assistance of Laud, had achieved a position of almost complete autocracy, using the judges of the Star Chamber to punish citizens, peers and commoners alike, who refused to pay the taxes he levied, or who opposed the government by word or deed. He was crowned in Scotland at a ceremony in the abbey church of Holyrood and was so well received there that he thought it might be possible to restore episcopacy and abolish the Presbyterianism which had become the national form of Scottish religion. This was too much for the Scots to tolerate; a majority of prominent Scottish people signed a national covenant, by which they swore to "defend the true religion". The General Assembly of the Church of Scotland excommunicated the bishops, while by order of the Scottish Parliament all English possessions in Scotland were seized. The King was already on the slippery slope to ruin and death.

The part which the Earl of Bedford played in the events of 1639–40 is still not clear. That he played an important and sometimes dominant part is certain, as it is equally certain that his influence was for moderation. He tried to exert his influence in turn on the leaders of the Scottish Covenant, the King, and his own party of reformers. He acted in such a way that some historians have pictured him as a man who was impressed by the harshness of King Charles' regime and who in the early years of his reign genuinely desired reformation but later without giving any clue to his change of mind to his associates determined to support the King at all costs.

There may be some truth in this reading of the situation. He did not wish to see the King overthrown. That was equally true of many of his friends. But that was not inconsistent with a true desire for reform and for limiting the King's authority by constitutional means. He may well have been foreseeing enough to visualize the bloody end of the dispute between King and Parliament. If that were so he would scarcely have told anyone except his most intimate friends. The thought of executing the King would have seemed intolerable even to the most rabid of the reformers in 1640. It took years of civil war and incomprehensible stubbornness on both sides before that thought found positive and open expression.

One thing which stands out clearly is that the dispute between the King and the Scottish Covenanters was wholly a religious one. The blame for it must be laid squarely at the feet of Archbishop Laud, who had so often persuaded the King against his better judgment to enforce episcopacy on a people no less religious than the English but deeply convinced of the rightness of their Church organization and of their liturgy.

The Earl was on terms of apparent friendship with Laud. That itself is strange but there is no doubt that they dined and wined together at intervals throughout the years of crisis and that there had never been an open breach between them. Bedford, as one of the half-dozen most powerful peers in the realm not deeply committed, would have made an admirable arbitrator between Laud and the Scots. The fact is that he never attempted to arbitrate, either by word or deed. Rather, he exacerbated it. The events are well documented, however, even if the motives that inspired them are obscure.

When the General Assembly of the Covenanters had declared episcopacy void and Charles was unable to reach any compromise, he prepared for war. The Scots, believing rightly that there was a great deal of sympathy for their cause among English Puritans, as the Low Church party was already known, sent a commission to England to explore the possibilities of obtaining active assistance as well as moral support. The Earl of Bedford was one of those approached, so were Pym and Hampden, the Earl of Essex, Lord Say and Lord Brooke, all more or less close friends of Russell. The commissioners, rightly or wrongly, reported that there was at least no fear of these gentlemen helping the King's cause in the event of hostilities.

Then in April 1639 the King called on all the nobles to assemble at York with whatever forces they could muster, falling back in the absence of Parliament on the feudal system. The nobles, or most of them, duly assembled but when required to

sign a declaration of loyalty, two at least, Lord Say and Lord
Brooke, refused to sign on the ground that if the King suspected
their loyalty it was an insult to ask them to sign a declaration.
The King thereupon apparently dismissed this strange feudal
army and (after years of personal rule) summoned a parliament,
asking for a substantial vote of larger taxes to prosecute a war
against Scotland. It is not surprising that the temper of this
parliament, the Short Parliament, was unfriendly. It included a
large number of nonconformists, some who had been imprisoned for refusing to pay taxes which they regarded as illegal
and others who had been prosecuted for various acts of defiance
of the government. Parliament refused to grant the supplies
unless the King would agree to sweeping reforms of the constitution. It was dismissed without achieving anything.

The Scots now communicated with Lord Saville, a traitor to
the country's cause if ever there were one, asking him to discover which English noblemen could be depended upon to help
them if they decided to invade England. This was a very
different matter from the previous approach and envisaged the
Scots and disaffected Englishmen joining in open warfare
against the King and a Royalist army. Lord Saville is said to
have failed in his mission but forged the names of many
prominent Englishmen to a declaration promising support in
the case of invasion. The names included, apart from the Earl
of Bedford, the Earls of Essex and Warwick, Lord Brooke and
Lord Say.

It was an extraordinary thing to do, if indeed it was done.
The Scots certainly had a document with these names appended
but whether they were really signatures or forgeries is one of the
key problems in assessing the part played by the Earl. The
document undoubtedly precipitated war. Orders were given for
the Scottish army to cross the border. It met with early success
and soon captured Newcastle, while a Royal army under Lord
Strafford, President of the Council of the North, retreated to
York.

Once more the Earl of Bedford took a hand. With eleven other noblemen he addressed a petition to the King enumerating the wrongs of which they complained, including innovations in religion, the employment of Catholics in positions of trust, and warning him that civil war was inevitable if he brought in Irish troops, as was rumoured to be his intention, to oppose the Scots. The petition ended by demanding the calling of another parliament to redress these grievances and ensure full English support. The Earl of Bedford, with the Earl of Hertford, also asked for and obtained an interview with the Privy Council at Hampton Court. At the interview, according to Windebank, Secretary of the Council, the two Earls amplified the petition, putting the case for immediate reform in exchange for support at that time of crisis in such a way that it could only be constructed as blackmail.

The King called another meeting of the peers at York and reached agreement with them to open negotiations with the Scots for a treaty. Inevitably the Earl of Bedford was one of the commissioners appointed to negotiate the treaty terms. One can imagine the astonishment of the Scottish leaders when the very noblemen whose promise of support was the real cause of the war now appeared as ambassadors of the King. In the circumstances compromise was impossible and all that was achieved was agreement for a cessation of hostilities, the question of the treaty being left specifically by both sides to Parliament at Westminster.

Many of the King's friends, including the Earl of Strafford, complained bitterly that it would have been better to have carried on the war against the Scots, but the King accepted the implied terms and summoned another parliament, which came to be known as the Long Parliament. The Parliament was disastrous for the King. Its members, like those of the Short Parliament, were concerned only to obtain changes in the constitution limiting the sovereign's authority. To show their power the most militant impeached Strafford, using Pym as their mouthpiece. Charles made a real effort to save his minister by yielding to many of Parliament's demands and by appointing to the Privy Council some new members acceptable to the bulk of the people. The Earls of Bedford, Hertford, and Essex, and Lord Say were naturally among the number, as also was Lord Saville.

The new Privy Council was sworn in to the great satisfaction of Parliament but the compromise did not save Strafford. The King offered the Earl of Bedford the position of Treasurer of England, with Pym as Chancellor of the Exchequer. The Earl saw in his own and his friends' appointment real hope for peace, and accepted subject to the passing of a Bill legalizing the levy of tonnage and poundage. The others were not so convinced and the short time that remained of Bedford's life was spent in pressing moderation on his friends, and urging acceptance of the King's compromise.

As Clarendon said, he had more authority "with the violent of his party" than anybody else, and "laboured heartily that the Earl's life should be secured". He knew of the plan to rescue the prisoner by force but kept his own counsel about it. Later, that prudent action was called treachery to his own party. He approached leading members of the Commons as well as of the Lords, telling them that the King was ready to do all that they could desire if the Earl of Strafford's life were spared. Could he have succeeded in reconciling two such opposing points of view as those of the King and the Earl of Essex? Or of Laud and Pym? That is something we cannot know. Dejected at the failure of his efforts, distressed by the death of his son Francis, he had no energy to combat the attack of smallpox which struck him and he died early in 1641. With his death all pretence of moderation was thrown aside by the reform party.

William, the 5th Earl, was as much a reformer as his father had been in his younger days. He was, however, more of a man of action than the 4th Earl had been, less patient, less conciliatory, rather more effective. Yet there are basic similarities between their careers. The 5th Earl, like his father, was unwilling that the sovereignty should be submerged in the flood of reform. He was basically a constitutionalist but sympathetic to the demands that Parliament had made of the King. He differed from many of the most violent opponents of the Caroline regime in that he only desired the granting of substantial reform by the King and would certainly, if that had been done, given his loyalty unreservedly to the throne. By contrast, the more extreme members of the Commons and the Lords overtly or secretly maintained that their ends could never be achieved while Charles was King.

The 5th Earl resembled his father, too, in his inability to commit himself wholeheartedly. He found himself unwillingly embroiled in civil war, but appeared to teeter in an agony of doubt which side to support. Finally, like his father, when politics proved too much for him he retired to drain the Fens, and a very good job he made of it (Chapter 4).

The Earl had been returned to the Long Parliament as member for Tavistock before succeeding to the title. His fellow representative for Tavistock was none other than Mr. Pym, whom he supported initially in his impeachment of Lord Strafford but grew luke warm owing to his father's influence. In this short but important period of his life he was frequently commissioned by the Commons to confer on their behalf with the Lords, a criterion, if any were needed, of the respect in which the House of Russell was held by both estates. He was also appointed by the Commons a member of the committee to study ways and means of disbanding the army, the cost of which the King was unable to bear and the Commons was unwilling to subscribe.

Almost immediately after his father's death he was appointed to negotiate with the King on the dismissal of those members of the Privy Council who were not acceptable to Parliament. In this mission he failed, though no one could have expected any mission to succeed in what amounted to persuading the King to abrogate his genuinely constitutional authority in the choice of his personal counsellors.

Events now moved swiftly. The Commons accused Lord Digby of raising an army in Surrey for the purpose of intimidating Parliament. Although he was related by marriage, the Earl was a member of the committee which examined the evidence against Lord Digby and reported that his actions amounted to high treason. Before anything further could be done, the King raised his standard at Nottingham and the Civil War had begun.

That year 1642 was a momentous one for the Russells. The Earl was all too clearly identified with the reformers and however unwilling to take up arms against the sovereign he subscribed to the parliamentary convention and was commissioned as general of the forces under the Earl of Essex. He was in command of the regiment which besieged the Royalist troops under the Marquess of Hertford in Sherborne Castle. According to one account the Earl of Bedford's sister Anne, wife of Lord George Digby, to whose family Sherborne Castle had been granted by King James I, was in the beleaguered castle and sent him a note by messenger, who slipped out of the castle gate unseen, telling him, "If you persist in the attack you shall find your sister's bones in the ruins." Unhappily, there were all too many cases in the Civil War of members of a family fighting on opposite sides. In fact he was compelled to raise the siege because many of his troops deserted and he had insufficient artillery with which to make a frontal attack. As he withdrew he was pursued by a Royalist force. Lord Hertford now withdrew his own forces from the castle and the Earl of Bedford was in a position to pursue him as far as Minehead. He then rejoined the Earl of Essex.

At the battle of Edgehill, he was commander of the cavalry reserve. Joining late in the battle, he was uncommonly successful in turning the tide when the Parliamentary forces were on the brink of defeat. But he was not able to transform a near defeat into an outright victory.

Little success had so far attended Parliament in the field. Essex and Bedford were both anxious to conclude a treaty with the King before more damage was done. Their suggestion to negotiate a peace was rejected, however, by most of their colleagues, though Bedford helped in the preparation of a draft treaty by which both armies would have been disbanded and the King would have been reinstated as sovereign by Parliament on promise of reform. Some members of the Commons were sympathetic to the proposal but Essex was persuaded by the extremists to withdraw his support and the scheme came to nothing. It was so unpopular among the leading burghers of London that threats were made by members of the City Corporation against the Earl's life and against the lives of others who were regarded as pacifists.

The Earl of Bedford, with the Earls of Clare and Holland, thereupon resigned their commissions and, at imminent risk of their lives, rode to the Royalist garrison at Wallingford. The King was at Gloucester at the time but travelled to Oxford to discuss with the Privy Council the reception that should be given to the three Earls. It was certainly not the kind of reception the Earl of Bedford had expected. After much deliberation it was resolved by the King and Council that the three might come to Oxford but whether they should be given their due precedence was a matter for individual members of the Court to decide for themselves.

The Earl disarmed criticism by accepting the invitation to Oxford and offering his military service to the King. He was given a commission in the King's own regiment of horse and distinguished himself in the magnificent charge at the Battle of Newbury. The King, now satisfied of his loyalty and grateful for the accession of a man who had proved himself an outstanding cavalry officer on whichever side he was fighting, appointed him a commissioner for the settlement of the covenant and liturgy.

Thus Charles promoted him to a position of personal adviser, against the wishes of many of the Privy Council, who treated the Earl with a sad lack of respect, and in the end goaded him to change sides once more. He rejoined the Earl of Essex at his camp at St. Albans on Christmas Day, 1643.

The welcome he received from the Earl of Essex was little more cordial than the one he had received from the Court. He was arrested but held in prison for only a short time. His estates were sequestrated but after a year the sequestration was annulled and in April 1645 the Earl, with five other peers who had deserted from the King's service, swore the oath of Parliament before the commissioners of the Great Seal. But he was given no more appointments and did not resume his seat in the House of Lords until after the Restoration.

His personal activities from that time onwards were concerned solely with Thorney and Woburn, where he was host to the King for a night in 1644 and again in 1645, and for a period of about a fortnight in 1647 after the King had been delivered by the Scots to the Parliamentarian army, quartered then at Bedford. At that time the army was acting independently of Parliament, its officers treating their captive with the utmost respect, even to the extent of restoring to him his High Church chaplains. With Dr. Hammond, the chaplain-in-chief, the Earl of Cleveland and other loyal supporters, he stayed at Woburn while negotiating with the army leaders terms which might be acceptable to the army if not to Parliament. The proposals made by the army were reasonable enough and did not include the abolition of the Episcopacy, a point on which the King would not yield. They did, however, include an amnesty for the King's supporters. The Earl of Bedford urged Charles to accept the terms, but Charles was so sure of ultimate recall on his own terms that he rejected them, thereby sealing his own death warrant.

The King had arrived at Woburn on 24th July and left some time after 2nd August. That was the last time the Earl saw him,

9

and the last act in the part he played in the drama of King versus people.

The Earl came briefly out of his retirement to take part in the negotiations that preceded the Restoration. He and the Earl of Manchester were among the peers who petitioned the still exiled King to enter into political and religious guarantees before he was recalled. The guarantees were duly given by Charles but soon forgotten, only to be remembered when his popularity began to wane. By 1670 the Earl of Bedford was once more definitely in opposition and once more numbered among the peers who called for reform.

A special point of contention was the King's known leaning towards Roman Catholicism and the support he gave to his brother as successor to the throne, although he was a practising Roman Catholic. By 1673 the Earl was in the forefront of opposition to the Crown in the unending disputes about the Test Act, and a few years later spoke several times in the Lords in favour of the Exclusion Acts designed to prevent the succession of the Duke of York. His position now was that of an elder statesman and his views were listened to with respect by Whigs and Tories alike.

His speeches in the House of Lords were few, however. As the years passed he resented more and more the necessity to leave his country estates for the hurly-burly of life in London. He roused himself in 1680 to support the Duke of Monmouth in a petition to the King against the latter's decision to summon a Parliament at Oxford. It was a time when the Commons was becoming increasingly outspoken in its criticism and an early clash from the lack of religious toleration on either side could be foreseen. Oxford was known as a city in which the bias of opinion was High Church and where there was little sympathy for Nonconformists.

In their petition the Duke and the Earl of Bedford urged that Parliament could not deliberate in safety when threatened by the swords of the Catholics and their adherents. It was ironic

hat a statesman who had done so much to bring Charles to the
hrone should now be in the position of opposing him with
every means at his disposal. He had actually done more to help
Charles in exile than many people realized at the time. He was
n regular communication with him and received a letter of
congratulation from Dr. Hammond, the exiled King's chaplain,
n 1660, when after General Monk's dissolution of the Long
Parliament the Earl had been freed from the recognizances into
which he had been compelled to enter when his estates were
restored. It is probable that he supplied Charles and his retinue
with substantial monetary aid during the latter years of the
Commonwealth. As we have already seen, he was one of
the most prominent members of the Upper House to support
the Restoration.

But now nothing that the King did satisfied him. He feared
for the Constitution, which meant a great deal to him as to
many of his contemporaries, and he feared equally sincerely
that there was a real threat of a return to Catholicism, regarding this as a fate if not worse than death at least as one to divert
which it was the duty of all right-thinking men to lay down
their lives, if the need arose.

An event occurred shortly afterwards which not only finally
hardened his heart against the sovereign, and indeed the
monarchy, but compelled his complete withdrawal from the
political scene.

Although the Earl's contribution to the government of the
country was restricted after the civil war, other members of his
family maintained the Russell reputation for fearless action and
a passionate regard for the rights of the individual. One of his
nephews, William, the son of Edward Russell, served as stan-
dard-bearer to Charles II in the King's Own Company of Foot
Guards until his death in 1674. The Earl's brother John had
taken a much more definite line than the Earl on the outbreak
of civil war. He, too, was liberal in his ideas but had no
sympathy with the Parliamentarian cause when war became

imminent. He threw in his lot with the King and remained true
to him throughout the long period of hostilities. He commanded
a regiment under Prince Rupert, was wounded at the Battle of
Naseby, and served with honour and distinction in all the
major engagements of the war. After the execution of Charles
he travelled abroad for some time and is not heard of again
until the Restoration, when he was appointed Colonel of the
First Regiment of Guards, which later became the Grenadier
Guards. He was a man entirely devoted to the army and never
married, dying at the age of 69 in 1681, when, although he had
maintained friendly relations with his elder brother throughout
the civil war and the Restoration, he was devoted to the King's
cause and unsympathetic to the Earl's niggling opposition.

It was the Earl's son, however, Lord William Russell, who
achieved the greatest fame of all the family in the 17th century.
His deeds became virtually a legend in his own lifetime. After
his death he was regarded as a national hero and martyr. Lord
William, or Mr. Russell as he then was (his elder brother
Francis died in 1678, unmarried, when Lord William became
heir to the Earldom), was educated with his brother, who was
only a year senior to him. They went together as students to
Cambridge University in 1653. After Cambridge they were
still together on the usual grand tour, visiting France, Switzerland and Germany.

Francis left his brother at Augsburg in the summer of 1657
and spent the next few years in Germany and Italy but William,
after a few months in Paris, returned home at his father's request in time for the Restoration. He was returned unopposed
as member for Tavistock in Charles II's first Parliament and for
a time, in common with all the Russell family, was a favourite at
Court, only to glad to take part in the gay life of the King and
his companions by whom he was considered an uncommonly
bright and entertaining man. This, after all, was the time when
most liberal-minded people were still rejoicing in the Restoration. Even the most forward-looking had had enough of the

Puritan regime and there was virtually no opposition to Charles. Every man was his friend.

But there is something of the Puritan in every Russell and it was not long before William tired of the round of Court festivities. After his marriage to Rachel, Lady Vaughan, he was seen less and less at Court functions, dropping many of his closest associates and for a few years retiring into private life. Gradually however, he became, like his father, perturbed at the course which the administration was following and in particular at the growing tendency to High Church or rather Roman Catholic sympathy on the part of the King, who incidentally never denied Catholic loyalty but maintained that it was quite feasible for a hereditary sovereign to be ruler of a Protestant country, whatever his personal religious conviction. With this point of view none of the Russells agreed and gradually, as told in chapter 7, the house became the meeting-place of many noblemen and a few commoners who shared Lord Russell's fears and felt, like him, impotent to achieve anything when the temper of the country was still favourable to Charles.

But Charles had not changed—nor is there any real evidence that he was disloyal to the throne which he had inherited. Certainly he was not as black as he was painted by the surviving Puritan clique, or by the many people who had been brought up to believe that Catholicism and evil were synonymous. He was certainly often short of funds when once the generous exuberance of Parliament had evaporated and it is probable that he accepted bribes from the King of France for doing what he could to mould England's foreign policy. It is equally likely that he would have followed the same policy if no bribe had been concerned. It is true also that he supported his brother, the Duke of York, as heir to the sovereignty in spite of, or even because of, the latter's faith.

It is difficult in retrospect to appreciate the reason in condemning as the Presbyterians did—and indeed as many clergymen of the Church of England did—a man because he held a different form of the same faith. Yet this was the attitude o the Russell family. It is undeniable, however, that when Parlia ment could no longer be depended upon to serve his wishes he preferred to dispense with Parliament and this was certainly unconstitutional. He appears still to have believed in the doc trine of the divine right of kings in which he had been brough up. His chief crime in fact was that his thought did not move with the times.

To people like William Russell he came to represent the incarnation of evil, a view of the ruling family shared by the majority of Puritans, who regarded pleasure as evil and looked with horror at the private life of the Court, which certainly won an international reputation for high spirits or depravity, accord ing to the moral outlook of the observer. The attitude is well expressed by J. H. Wiffen, writing in 1833, "The honourable counsels of Southampton and Clarendon were abandoned for those of giddy and frivolous companions who, taking him when he was with his mistresses and in a humour of delight insinuated the most dissolute and dangerous principles of government", and again, "The faith of common decorum was cast away and pleasure, the gross enchantress, paced throughout his palace in zoneless undisguised effrontery." That all sounds rather ridiculous from a competent historian whose chief fault to find with the King was that "he scarcely had any sense of religion. The little he possessed was Roman Catholic, a portentous secret".

The real trouble started when Clarendon was dismissed and the Cabal ministry, including Buckingham, Ashley and Lauder dale, took office. For the first time a Parliamentary opposition began to be discernible. William Russell was its unnamed leader. The Triple Alliance linking England with Holland and Spain was generally approved but in 1670 rumours began to circulate that Charles had made a secret treaty with Louis XIV of France which committed Charles to helping the French King to conquer Holland and to promote a return to Roman Catho-

licism in England. Holland was regarded as one of the chief
strongholds of Protestantism. It was rumoured also that Charles
would receive a subsidy of £200,000 from France and was
promised that a force of six thousand men would be maintained
by France so that he could make war on Holland without the
consent of the English Parliament.

It seemed to people like William Russell that the constitution
had foundered. They blamed Parliament almost as much as
they did the King. It was said that Lords Arlington and Clifford
were aware of the secret treaty with France and had received
gifts from the French King. Certainly they were of the Roman
Catholic faith and among the King's closest advisers. So arose a
Country Party as opposed to a Court Party.

The new "party" won more support in Parliament than at
first seemed likely. The public reception of the Duke of York
into the Roman Catholic Church was an eye-opener to many
members and credence was given to the thought that England
was destined to be Catholic when the Privy Council announced
a Declaration of Indulgence repealing all acts against Nonconformists and Catholics alike.

The King was forced by growing unrest to summon Parliament in 1673. For the first time in his reign the Commons
rebelled. A Bill was introduced to incapacitate all Catholics
from holding public office. This negatived the Declaration of
Indulgence. After a long debate the Test Act, as it came to be
known, was passed in the Lords also. Lord Clifford was compelled to resign from the government and the Duke of York
gave up his office of Lord High Admiral.

William Russell was no orator and seldom spoke in the
Commons, but the plan of campaign for embarrassing the
government and the King was well and truly laid at Southampton House. One of his major speeches was made early in 1674,
when a Bill for pressing "men of quality" into military service
was being discussed. This, said Russell, was contrary to Magna
Charta and made it the opportunity to air the grievances of his

party—the proroguing of Parliament, the breaking of treaties, the acceptance of money from France—calling for an investigation into the authors of these misfortunes and the removal of the ministers who were responsible for committing them.

It was a thinly veiled attack on the Court. The Commons rose to the bait, impeaching Buckingham and Arlington. The King had no option but to dismiss both these noblemen, and as he could not raise the funds for carrying on a war with Holland, was compelled to break the terms of his secret treaty with France. More, the Commons attacked the very existence of a statute which the Country Party regarded as a disguised form of intimidation against the Commons, and the sovereign's generally unchallenged right to detain suspected persons was removed by the passing of the Habeas Corpus Act.

The intrigue between Charles and Louis apparently continued. The latter appreciated that Charles was forced by Parliament to make a peace treaty with Holland. Fearing that when Parliament next met it would vote for a declaration of war on France, he is said to have offered Charles a further gift of £100,000 if he would prorogue Parliament until the following year. Whether that story is true or not, Charles certainly did prorogue Parliament for a total of fourteen months.

When he once more summoned it in April 1675 William Russell impeached Lord Dancy for his "lavish and arbitrary actings in the Treasury" and moved that he should be dismissed from the counsels of the King. This time Russell was not successful but later in the session, on introduction of the Non-Resisting Test, a Bill making it necessary for a member of Parliament to swear that he would not resist the King's authority in any circumstances, he was far more successful. It was not the intention of the Bill to prevent criticism by Members of Parliament but rather to inhibit suggestions for the dismissal of the King. This, as Russell stated, was an attempt to ensure that there should never be any alteration in Church or State, a Bill that might tend to restrain freedom of opinion or expression. William was supported in the Lords by his father but before a vote could be taken the King adjourned Parliament, which was tantamount to accepting defeat of the Bill.

Parliament was now sixteen years old. Not unnaturally the Commons were clamouring for its dissolution, i.e., for the election of a new Parliament. An address was presented to the King by the Lords to the same effect, but all the King would do was prorogue it yet again. William Russell made what was perhaps his greatest speech in moving an address for dissolution but still there was a majority of this first Parliament for the King when the King's interests were linked with its own selfish ones.

When the King asked for higher taxes at the beginning of the next session the Commons were more solidly behind Russell in taking up the position that if the King would declare war on France he should have as large a vote as he wished. This, of course, Charles would not and could not do. It was not only his understanding with the French King that prevented him but his horror of the Dutch, who were at war with France and with whose advanced form of Protestantism he was no more in sympathy than were English Puritans with his Catholicism. One can share in Russell's sense of helplessness even if one is not in sympathy with his intolerance.

Parliament talked and talked and talked, but did little. The King found his own ways of remaining solvent and it was only by withholding a money grant that Parliament could attack him. However, Russell succeeded by a small majority when he demanded a committee of the whole House to consider the state of the kingdom with special reference to the dangers of Popery and of a standing army "in order that some means might be found to save it from ruin". The King would have been a saint if by now he had not grown weary of Russell and the small but vocal political set of which he was the leader. Most English subjects were impressed by the marriage of Princess Mary with the Protestant Prince of Orange, but not so Russell. He regarded that happy event as only a further reason for declaring war on France. King Louis, however, greatly resented the marriage of the English Princess, and abandoning the thought of gaining the active support of Charles, offered him a large sum if he would disband the English standing army, in fear, of course, that this army might be used against France.

Thus arose the Gilbertian situation in which the opposition party led by Russell was demanding the very same thing of Charles as was the King of France. The King not unnaturally, but with some misgivings, agreed. By a strange coincidence the Marquis de Rouvigny, Russell's maternal uncle, was sent to England to ensure that Charles carried out his part of the secret treaty and that the standing army was in fact disbanded.

Here was another Gilbertian situation. Russell and Rouvigny were on friendly terms and it was natural that Russell should entertain the French commissioner on his arrival in March 1678. After that they had numerous meetings, although what transpired between them can never be known for certain, as the meetings are not documented. It appears that Rouvigny convinced Russell that the French King had no wish to help Charles to become an absolute monarch; on the contrary, that he desired to help the English Country Party to bring about the dissolution of Parliament, the first step towards the election of a new Parliament which Russell and his friends hoped would be prepared to take more vigorous action against the King's unconstitutional actions. Russell, for his part, apparently promised to take no further action calculated to drive Charles into war with France.

Rouvigny sought still greater help from Russell, pointing out that he was prepared to distribute substantial sums to Members if a majority could be obtained for refusing any grant in aid for a war with France. This proposal was not well received. In any case it was doomed from the start, for when the debate in Parliament was resumed, it was apparent that it would be futile to resist the proposal to grant money for hostilities against

France. The Country Party did, however, succeed in attaching conditions to the grant which they hoped would be enough to prevent the King from accepting it. That was not to be the case, however. The King gladly accepted the grant, neglected the conditions, and took prompt action to increase the size and strength of the standing army.

It seems strange indeed that a party which until the discussions between Russell and Rouvigny was insistent on war should now be the advocate of peace. The inconsistency can only be explained by the assumption that Russell and his friends were prepared to go to any lengths to secure first a newly elected parliament and through it the maintenance of the Protestant religion. If France was willing to make peace with Holland, as appeared to be the case, and Louis would use his influence to embarrass Charles, then France became an ally.

The historian Dalrymple describes these moves as the "dangerous products of the heads of the popular party acting in concert with France" and as "the intrigues of Lord Russell with Versailles". The Country Party had still not achieved their objects but their hand was strengthened by the publicity arising from the so-called Popish Plot of 1678, when on the evidence of an informer, Titus Oates, many leading Catholics were convicted of high treason. When Parliament met again the Bill for incapacitating Catholics passed both Houses.

Russell seized his opportunity. He proposed a motion to exclude the Duke of York from the King's council, a prelude to raising the question of the succession. He also discussed the contents of papers which had been given him by a former French ambassador, showing the existence of a secret money treaty between the French and English kings. These were fateful days for Charles. He dissolved Parliament, now in its eighteenth year, and not inaptly called the Pensionary Parliament, but the subsequent elections were disastrous to the Court. The Country Party secured more seats in the Commons, Russell himself was returned with acclamation for Bedfordshire. The opposition had reason to feel that it might at last be able to make progress.

The King did his best to meet the changed situation. Russell and some of his friends were sworn members of the Privy Council. The Earl of Shaftesbury was made President of the Council. The King had no joy from these appointments. Within a week of its first meeting Lord Russell spoke in Parliament in favour of a Bill modifying the precedents of royal succession. "We see by what is done under Protestant Princes what will be accomplished in a Popish state. Betwixt both religions this is the deciding day." At this stage all he demanded was the appointment of a committee to draw up a Bill of Limitations in the event of the Duke of York succeeding. He also proposed a Bill to exclude Catholics from the navy and the army, the courts of justice, and indeed any sphere in which they could possibly assist a Catholic sovereign.

This did not satisfy all Russell's friends and a Bill of Exclusion was finally introduced. Charles prorogued Parliament before a vote could be taken. On the advice of the Privy Council the prorogation was converted to dissolution.

The next elected Parliament differed little from the previous one. The recently created Privy Councillors from the Country Party, including Russell, were conscious of the mockery implied by the King soliciting their advice, which he was determined not to follow, and decided to resign from the Privy Council. Russell asked permission on 28th January 1680 on behalf of himself and Lord Cavendish. The King replied emphatically, "Aye, gentlemen, with all my heart."

It is possible to argue that these were noble patriots who breathed more freely when they had left the palace into which they had been beguiled by the King's magic. It is equally easy to argue that the King had made an effort to widen the basis of his council and had found his new councillors just as intractable as Parliament. The fact remained that the opposition was now back where it started and Russell and his friends, who had rejected the Non-Resisting Test, began to think in terms of restraining the King by force if that proved necessary. They became known as the Southamptons, after Russell's London house.

Their joint leaders were Russell and Lord Ashley, Earl of Shaftesbury, who was now as vehement an opponent of the Court as he had once been a supporter of it. He was a relation by marriage of Russell and the two had often acted together in the past. It was apparently Lord Shaftesbury's scheme to organize an insurrection in London designed to capture the Tower, from which strongpoint the Earl hoped to be able to dictate terms of compromise to the King. Neither Russell nor the Duke of Monmouth was in favour of this dramatic but unpromising plan, though perfectly willing to be parties to any scheme which would allow them to dictate to the King, provided that it had a reasonable chance of success.

Many other plans were discussed at Southampton House, some of them involving armed resistance, but no final project seems to have been agreed upon by 1683. By then the Exclusion Bill had passed the Commons but had been thrown out by the Lords. The Duke of Monmouth had made a tour of the north country in royal state, defying the King's will, and the fifth Parliament, which met at Oxford, had refused to accept Charles's offer that the Prince of Orange should act as regent for James in the event of his succession.

Compromise was impossible and the country seemed to be on the brink of civil war, with more and more moderate men leaning towards the extreme views of the Russell Party. An action group was organized as the council of six, including Lord Russell himself, the Duke of Monmouth and the Earl of Essex. The argument these men used was that if a breach of faith was committed on one side the other was free of obligation—in other words, if the King acted unconstitutionally his subjects were no longer bound by ties of loyalty.

This committee, bound to the utmost secrecy, had already

succeeded in arming its members and many of their followers and had decided to wait until Parliament was called with the intention of initiating resistance if Charles persisted in his attitude. They had obtained at least £8,000 worth of ammunition and arms from Holland through the Duke of Argyll.

Their preparations were rudely interrupted by the disclosure of the Rye House Plot. Some of the more violent members of the opposition, though not necessarily Russell or members of his committee of six, had undoubtedly conspired to assassinate the King and his brother. The plot was divulged by an informer, and two of the conspirators, by name Rumsey and West, gave themselves up and implicated, among others, Russell, Algernon Sidney and the Duke of Monmouth.

Russell may, or may not, have known of the plot. He was certainly not an active conspirator nor, it seems, was Sidney, nor the Duke of Monmouth. But Russell was certainly implicated in Shaftesbury's plan to seize the Tower and in other abortive plots involving force against the Crown. In a sense, therefore, his conviction and execution on a charge of high treason was just, though he was probably innocent of the specific charge brought against him.

One must remember, too, that the 17th century is not the 20th. Another Russell, Edward, won respect and renown for his part in the "Glorious Revolution", which involved armed resistance to the Crown. So, too, William Russell was granted every possible honour posthumously when William and Mary ascended the throne.

For the time being, however, the revelation of the Rye House Plot was a mortal blow to the opposition. There was strong reaction against the Whigs. Even the venerable Earl of Bedford was threatened with violence, and the last years of Charles's reign were easier for him than any since the first years after his accession. He felt strong enough to replace the Duke of York as Lord High Admiral and the succession of the Duke as King James II was achieved without a blow being struck and with no murmur from Parliament—since Charles never called another one.

The Earl of Bedford was devastated by his son's conviction and made every possible effort to secure a pardon. Charles had no cause to like him but his position as Earl of Bedford was an impregnable one and he had an enormous passive following among country gentlemen. He offered sums variously estimated at £50,000 and £100,000 if a pardon were granted, using the Duchess of Portsmouth as intermediary. It was to no avail. Finally he wrote a personal letter to the King, assuring him that he would think himself happy to be left only with bread and water if the life of his son were spared. It is said that the King himself was inclined to yield the point and substitute banishment (the Duke of Monmouth was banished) but was prevailed on by his brother to let the sentence stand.

There was clearly no room for the Earl or for any other Russell in politics after Lord William's execution, but the Earl gave his moral support to the efforts which proved successful to dethrone King James. He received the Dutch Commissioner at Woburn Abbey in 1687 and commended him to many of his friends. He was approached by King James after William had actually landed on English soil. The King apologized for not having called a Parliament, asked for his loyal support and help, and is reported to have said, "You are a good man and could render me today essential service", to which the Earl is said to have replied, "For myself, sir, I am old and weak, but I once had a son who could indeed have served your majesty."

When William amd Mary were crowned the Earl came to London for the coronation. King William redeemed all the promises he had made to the Russell family and one of the first acts of his government was to reverse the attainder of Lord William Russell. A vote of the House of Commons stigmatized his execution as a murder and Lord Hampden in the House of Lords made the assertion that those who introduced the Prince of Orange into England were in effect continuing the work of the Council of Six.

In April 1694 the highest title which the King could confer upon a subject was bestowed on the 5th Earl, who was created 1st Duke of Bedford. The citation for the creation of the Dukedom underlined the fact that it was granted in recognition of Lord William's martyrdom in the service of freedom and in honour of his being "the father to the Lord Russell, the ornament of his age, whose merit it was not enough to transmit by history to posterity".

The Duke of Bedford lived only six years to enjoy the honour bestowed on him, and by implication on his family, but all who knew him in those last years agree that his sense of bitter frustration had vanished and that when he died in 1700 in his eighty-seventh year he was tranquil and convinced that his son's sacrifice had not been in vain.

CHAPTER SIX

Edward the Kingmaker

EDWARD RUSSELL, Lord High Admiral of England, first Earl of Orford, is the most enigmatic as well as one of the most distinguished figures in the Russell panorama. He was a determined Whig, a competent and occasionally brilliant naval commander, a man of charm with the ability to influence almost everyone he met. With his family background he was predestined for a distinguished career, although the execution of his cousin temporarily enforced his virtual retirement from Court. A reformer in politics and religion, a leader of liberal philosophy, passionately devoted to the forms of the Anglican Church, he was the natural enemy of King James II, equally the natural friend of William of Orange, whose religious beliefs approximated to his own.

His life leaves many questions unanswered. His was the hand that more than any other toppled King James from the throne. There is little exaggeration in saying that his single-mindedness and determination made William King. It is equally certain that he was disappointed in William and opened negotiations with the exiled King James, and that he had some part in encouraging the exile to believe that he would be welcome if he returned to England, and in stimulating the French King to assist him. Yet it was Edward Russell's handling of the naval war with the French that destroyed James's aspirations as surely as it destroyed the power of the French fleet. The enigma, the puzzle which historians looking at the known facts have never been able to elucidate, is how closely Edward Russell was implicated in the exiled King's plans for regaining the English throne. Was he, by a remarkable volte-face, so anxious to be rid of the King whom he had promoted that he was prepared to play traitor to him, or was he an *agent provocateur*, concerned only that James should swallow the draught of bitterness to its dregs and incidentally give himself the opportunity to prove his excellence in naval warfare? His contemporaries had no such doubts. They heaped honours on him but, of course, they knew nothing of his intrigues with the exiled King.

Edward Russell, according to a 19th-century historian "one of the great ornaments of his age and country", was a grandson of Francis, the 4th Earl. He was born in 1652 and made the navy his career. He quickly won promotion and was in command of the *Swallow* in 1673. The Duke of York, currently Lord High Admiral, later King James II, showed full appreciation of him both as a man and as a naval commander and appointed him a Gentleman of his Bedchamber. He gave him increasingly important commands and the two became on terms of personal friendship in spite of the religious gulf that separated them. Through his royal patron, Edward met Charles II frequently and made an equally good impression on him as he had on his brother.

So far Edward's life had been that of a typical Russell, a courtier on terms of virtual equality with the sovereign and the sovereign's family. It had happened so often before that one would have predicted with confidence that he would serve a succession of kings or queens with the same persistent loyalty that had been shown by the 1st Earl.

The Rye House Plot changed all that. Edward was of a fiery temperament and although secretly he, like his cousin William, may have sympathized with the aim of changing the succession, he did not believe that his cousin was implicated in the plot any more than he was himself. He regarded Lord William's execution as a gross miscarriage of justice, all the more difficult to bear because both of them, though strongly Whig in sympathy and still more strongly Protestant in outlook, had striven so hard to bring about political reform by constitutional means. He believed passionately that his cousin should have been saved and the consequent disgrace to the Russell family averted. He blamed the King and the Duke of York impartially. That was a factor as important as his religion which determined his attitude to the Crown when the Duke of York succeeded as King James II two years later.

Many were convinced by the new King's promise that although he was a Roman Catholic (and made no secret of it) he would maintain and defend the Church of England according to the law of the land and respect the laws made by Parliament. Not so Russell. The hopes of moderate men were dashed when the King attended Mass in royal state. Some prominent Whigs, including the Earl of Shrewsbury and Russell himself, made up their minds that the King must be deposed.

The attempt by the Duke of Monmouth to seize the throne by invasion was abortive, the Battle of Sedgemoor the final blow to those who supported the Duke. The severity with which the King pursued the rebels through Chief Justice Jeffreys further strengthened sentiment against him. The Judge boasted that he had hanged more traitors than all his predecessors since the conquest. Many of the Whig and Anglican party, who before then had been moderate in their attitude to the Sovereign, were transformed into the protagonists of active intrigue against him. His every act was described as one of tyranny. The birth of a son, later to be known as the Old Pretender, to the King and his second wife, Mary of Modena, both sincerely Roman Catholic, precipitated events which in any case could not have been delayed long.

Edward Russell had a married sister resident in Holland. This fact, quite apart from his eagerness to be in the forefront of the movement, made him an ideal emissary for the group of influential noblemen who looked to William of Orange as a sovereign in place of James. He was able to travel to and from

Holland without arousing suspicion. He was also an old friend of Princess Mary, who had been just growing to womanhood when he was a member of her father's household. At the least there was always mutual goodwill and respect between him and William.

There is every reason to think that William, a bigoted Protestant, was genuinely and sincerely alarmed at the course of events in England. After all, he was the son of Charles I's daughter Mary and after marriage with his cousin, who was described as the most English of Englishwomen, must have felt as affronted by the conduct of King James II as if he had been an English subject. He believed, too, the rumour that James II's alleged son was not really the son of Mary of Modena but was a changeling foisted on the people of England so as to deprive Mary of her rightful inheritance of the English throne. There were, therefore, many excellent reasons why he should have been willing to intervene in English affairs.

How soon Edward Russell and he discussed the possibility of his seizing the English throne by force of arms is not known but it cannot have been more than a year after James's accession. Naturally he wanted to explore the ground for himself. He therefore despatched M. Dyckvelt, one of his most intimate confidantes, as special emissary to England in February 1687 with instructions to test the opinion not only of the obviously dissident Whigs but of influential Tories. His brief was to unite all parties in a determination to invite William to accept the throne. On 24th March he visited the Earl of Bedford, with a personal message from William and Mary expressing the sorrow they had felt for the Russells' misfortunes and the reverence in which they held the memory of William, Lord Russell.

Mr. Dyckvelt returned to Holland in May, carrying with him the assurances of many prominent Englishmen that they would support William in the event of his entering into open hostilities with James. Soon afterwards the "Association" was formed with

Edward Russell, now unreservedly accepted as leader of the younger Whigs, and the Earl of Shrewsbury representing the older reformers as its guiding lights.

It only remained to complete negotiations with the Prince, and this hazardous commission Edward Russell undertook. He sailed to the Hague in May 1688 to ask William on behalf of the Association how he proposed to give effect to the general understanding that had been reached. William detailed his plans, which Russell conveyed to his fellow conspirators, and in September returned to Holland with the Earl of Shrewsbury, carrying a formal letter of invitation to the Prince to assume the English throne. The signatories of the letter, in addition to Shrewsbury and Russell, included the Earls of Danby and Devonshire, Lord Lumley, the Bishop of London and Henry Sidney.

The following weeks were not easy ones for the Association. First, unfavourable winds battered the Dutch fleet when it set sail and forced it to return, but on 4th October Prince William set sail once more with a fleet of six hundred ships, including fifty men-of-war. Russell sailed on board the Prince's ship, which was put under his command. This time fortune was with them. An east wind assisted the progress of the fleet down the Channel, while it prevented the English fleet from sailing from its moorings in the Thames and Medway.

The pilots made some error in calculation, for the course which was intended to bring the Dutch fleet into Torbay carried it further down-Channel beyond Plymouth. The Dutch Prince refused to land there, probably rightly in view of the state of preparedness in which the port of Plymouth was constantly held. Russell and his friends despaired. Russell instructed Dr. Burnet, later Bishop Burnet, to whom he always turned, as William, Lord Russell, had before him, to say prayers for the souls of all the expedition, because he believed that all was lost. Then the wind changed and carried the Dutch fleet back into Torbay. A landing party was well received and met not the slightest opposition. The "Glorious Revolution" was well under way.

Edward Russell must have felt justified in his revolutionary activity when James fled the country and Parliament invited William and Mary to accept the throne jointly. When they jointly assented to the Declaration of Right, which reaffirmed all the ancient privileges and liberties of the people and made it unlawful for the King to raise money without the consent of Parliament it looked as if the days of absolute monarchy and of the "Divine Right" were over.

Edward Russell was promoted Admiral and was despatched to reinforce the fleet under Herbert, Earl of Torrington. This was a time when one of the periodic scares of French invasion which had bedevilled southern England from the beginning of the Hundred Years War was at its height. While the King was in Ireland during 1690 the Queen not unnaturally referred on naval matters to Russell as an old friend rather than as a admiral. Russell deplored the inactivity of his nominal chief, the Earl of Torrington, and persuaded the Queen that as the English fleet had now received reinforcement from Holland, defence should be abandoned for an offensive campaign to destroy the French fleet.

Unhappily Russell's advice on this occasion proved unsound. The English and Dutch fleets suffered a major reverse. Thousands of Englishmen on the heights of Beachy Head had the mortification of seeing Torrington's fleet driven back, sailing for its very life and forced to seek refuge in the estuary of the Thames. Torrington received the blame and Russell was invited to be one of the commissioners appointed to investigate the causes of the reverse, but he declined. The two commissioners, the Earls of Devonshire and Pembroke, found Torrington guilty of hazarding the fleet and he was deprived of his command.

The whole episode was not to Russell's credit. It did not improve matters when the fleet was placed under the control of three commissioners with Russell at their head. According to a letter from Queen Mary to King William, Russell received this appointment with extreme reluctance but that did not prevent most knowledgeable people believing that he had persuaded the King to treat Torrington with conspicuous harshness in order that he might succeed him in command of the Navy. Russell was, in fact, appointed Lord High Admiral and Treasurer of the Navy in 1691 and was afloat for the greater part of that year, seeking to force another engagement on the French fleet but without success. When Parliament met in October his management of the fleet was called into question but nothing came of the charge, though Russell found it necessary to explain his movements in detail.

Meanwhile King James, with the full support of the French Court, began intrigues with some of the English noblemen who had been instrumental in bringing William to the throne but had already become disillusioned. These included the Earls of Danby and Shrewsbury and the Duke of Marlborough. Marlborough went so far early in 1691 as to write a letter to the ex-King asking his forgiveness for his defection and holding out the promise of support from many of his friends. Some of the men who now appeared as leaders of a movement for the recall of James had been alienated from William by his neglect to give them high offices, others by his unwillingness to show preference for the Whig Party.

The Stuart Papers, compiled from James's own diaries and correspondence, give the impression that the English fleet was already in secret revolt against William. Subsequent events proved this to be untrue but James was certainly in correspondence with Russell, whom one of his emissaries described as more of a republican than a friend of any monarchy. James also sent Russell a formal declaration of intent in the event of his reassuming the English throne. Russell replied that James had made insufficient provision in his declaration for the freedom of the subject. James then forwarded another declaration, promising, as indeed he had promised at the beginning of his reign, complete religious freedom and a general pardon for political offences.

The suggestion is that Russell was convinced and promised to direct the English fleet away from the path of the French ships bringing James back to England, so that he could have an opportunity of landing troops without opposition. There are many inconsistencies in this account. It is difficult to see how Russell could have changed his opinion so completely in two years. The Prince of Orange had certainly not lived fully up to his promise; the Whig Party still found itself unable to proceed with many of its cherished ideas for reforms. But Russell was not a revolutionary by nature, even though he had been a prime mover in the negotiations with William. It seems very very doubtful whether a man who had always had such friendly relations with Mary as Princess and Queen could have countenanced activity which could only end by her losing the throne. According to one account the Queen knew of the correspondence between James and Russell and asked him to continue it so as to gain James's confidence and persuade him to divulge the detail of his plans in concert with the King of France.

Whatever the explanation, when the French fleet set sail to escort James to England with a strong force to support his re-entry into the country they had every expectation that the English captains would desert or at the very worst would do nothing to impede their voyage or James's landing. Yet Russell had addressed a letter to King William only a few days before, fearing, as he said, that the incidence of war might possibly put it out of his power to see His Majesty again. He stressed that he had cause to complain against the King for his neglect of some of his relatives who had made great sacrifices on his behalf, but added that the King should be at ease and that whatever might be the monarch's pleasure, the King should ever find him "with all faith and duty your obedient subject".

That was written on 10th May. The Battle of La Hogue took place ten days later. The French fleet—men-of-war and transports—was under the command of Admiral Tourville. It met a very different reception from what it had been led to expect. Whatever the temper of the English captains may have been before the action, Admiral Russell took the unheard-of step of calling on the sailors to throw overboard any captain who should be a traitor. The second-in-command, Admiral Carter, when he fell mortally wounded, called on his captain to fight on as long as his ship would float. The English flagship sought out the French flagship and within the framework of a major naval engagement there was a separate single conflict between Admiral Tourville and Admiral Russell. In the end Tourville's ship was towed away hopelessly crippled, many of the French ships were sunk and thousands of the troops being transported were drowned. Before the victory was complete, fog descended on the scene but as soon as it had cleared Russell made a signal to pursue the enemy without quarter. The pursuit continued all the next day and was called off only when the remaining French ships had reached the sanctuary of the French coast.

The striking power of the French Navy was broken by this English victory and the threat that England would fall under French domination was averted for the greater part of a century. Even King James, who sailed back to France while the battle was at its height, is said to have been moved to admiration and to have remarked to his French companions, "*Voilà mes Anglais, comme ils se battent bien!*"

The battle over, Admiral Russell reasonably hoped for the rewards of victory. In one way he was not disappointed. King William, delighted at the discomfiture of the French, made him a gift of £10,000. But he was criticized as well as praised and accused of not using the advantage of victory to sweep the seas of all French ships. He was aggravated, too, by confused orders which he received from the King in the weeks and months following La Hogue. Early in 1693 he was removed from the command of the Navy and appointed Treasurer of the Royal Household but immediately before his retirement from the Navy the Commons voted unanimously on a motion praising his conduct throughout the summer's service and complimenting him on his courage and vitality.

The Navy was again placed under the aegis of a board of commissioners. But the committee satisfied William no better than Russell had done and in the following year he recalled Russell to his former position.

The battle of La Hogue had not apparently discouraged James. No sooner was Russell back in full command of the English navy than he sent an emissary to ask the Admiral if he was willing to give him an opportunity of landing on English soil. Once again astonishingly Russell appears to have expressed his willingness to assist the exile but asked him for a new declaration of policy. The declaration, instead of reconciling the Protestants in England, alienated Catholics abroad. "So," says Wiffen, "by engaging in this intercourse Admiral Russell had wrought as much service to King William as the victory of La Hogue."

Even ever-optimistic James came to the conclusion that Russell's promises of help, active or passive, were not to be relied upon. The voluminous notes made during his exile contain the illuminating comment written about this time, "Russell in all probability do but delude the King by the Prince of Orange's permission." That may well be so. The confidence which the King still reposed in Russell is well shown by his action following the discovery of Sir John Fenwick's plot to assassinate him in 1696. Fenwick accused Russell among others of complicity and produced evidence of Russell's apparently treasonable correspondence with James at the French Court. William, however, was so far from being convinced that he appointed Russell to lay before Parliament the evidence for Sir John's impeachment.

By now, Queen Mary having died prematurely, William was

being compelled to depend more and more on the Whigs, Russell's position was still an extremely strong one and he was still respected by the leaders of the party of reform. William took every possible step to appease him and his friends. Many of the dissidents were reconciled, including the Duke of Marlborough, who realized that Mary's sister Anne was certain to succeed and saw his way through his influence over Anne to obtaining ultimately the highest offices of state.

Shortly after Fenwick's execution Russell was raised to the peerage with the titles Baron Russell of Shengay, Viscount Barfleur, and Earl of Orford. According to Lady Russell, writing to a Mr. Thornton, Edward Russell was not over-keen on the honour: "I believe what the town says, that Admiral Russell did not seek title, but I do not like to say it was crammed down his throat. Marks of good princes' favours should be received with some easiness though our natures do not incline to them, and where there is merit so notorious they cannot be rejected." The new Earl of Orford was treated like a hero; his victory at La Hogue was now seen as a vital blow for English naval supremacy. He was the confidant of the King and one of the most popular men at Court.

In 1699 he asked to be relieved of the office of Treasurer of the Navy. This was assumed to be, and may well have been, due to his consciousness of continued differences with the King's policy. The Parliament elected in 1698 was strongly Tory in character. One of its first acts was to reduce the number of the Standing Army and to reduce the vote for the Navy. The Tories did not share William's fear of France and believed that the Treaty of Ryswick in 1697, one of the provisions of which was that the French King would give no further support to James, had ended at once the threat of French invasion and the equally great fear of the restoration of Roman Catholicism. William, willingly or otherwise, associated himself with the policy of the Tories. Russell and his friends, on the other hand, believed that a strong Navy was essential for the well-being of

England and that any reduction in the vote for its maintenance was a false economy.

In these circumstances Russell had little option, but his resignation was an embarrassment to the King, who was moved to unwonted anger. He was certainly not prepared to use his influence to protect him when he was impeached for alleged malpractices while in the Mediterranean in the summer of 1694, having been sent by William to Spanish waters to support the Spanish Court at a time when a complete blockade of Spanish ports was threatened by the French fleet. The French Admiral retired to Toulon on hearing that Russell had sailed through the Straits of Gibraltar and the latter wintered his fleet at Cadiz. The complaint made against him was that he had failed to join action with the French fleet, now only just recovering from its losses at the Battle of La Hogue, and that he had kept his fleet in foreign waters during the winter when he ought to have sailed back to England.

In fact Russell had achieved the main object of his assignment. The blockade of the Spanish ports was lifted and the piratical activities inspired by the Bey of Algiers were discontinued as soon as the English fleet appeared. The Spanish Court was so well satisfied with the results of its appeal to England that the King of Spain is said to have made a personal present to Admiral Russell of jewels valued at 80,000 crowns. Even that fact was brought up as evidence against him, the implication being that he had sold his services to the Spanish Court without due authority.

The charge hung over his head for nearly two years. He was brought to trial in the House of Lords in 1701 and made a spirited defence, justifying himself in detail. Although his accounts for expenditure had already been approved he submitted them for a fresh examination. "There was not," said his episcopal friend Burnet, "so much as a collar to fix a complaint upon him." He was acquitted without a dissentient voice.

On the principle that where there's smoke there's fire, however, the Earl of Orford's star was in the descendent during the latter years of King William's reign. He retired into private life and although well received by the Court of Queen Anne was not called upon to fill any public offices until 1706, when he was a commissioner for the Union with Scotland. William had foreseen the necessity of uniting the two countries as well as the two crowns. The Scottish Parliament in 1704 had passed an Act of Security, which decreed that after the Queen's death the throne of Scotland should be alienated from the English sovereign unless Scotland enjoyed the commercial privileges which had hitherto belonged to England alone.

The Whigs had promoted the idea of union consistently ever since the accession of William, so that it was natural that when the appointment of commissioners to draw up a treaty of union was discussed the Earl of Orford's name should be considered. This was the time of the ascendancy of John Churchill, Duke of Marlborough, and of the Duchess, formerly Sarah Jennings, who had been a companion of the Queen since Anne was a child. Perhaps in resurrecting the Earl of Orford from his obscurity the Duke had in mind the many common battles which they had fought together—the struggle to place William on the throne, the struggle to persuade William to rule with moderation and introduce reforms. Now Marlborough was the head of a government largely Tory in character, and this was one of the few opportunities he had to use Lord Orford's services. It was an excellent choice, for Lord Orford again showed his competence and enthusiasm and was chiefly responsible for the preparation of a treaty which, contrary to many people's expectations, was accepted with alacrity by the Scottish Parliament in Edinburgh.

The most important clauses of the agreement were that the two kingdoms should be united under the title of Great Britain and should have one Parliament, that all British colonies and ports should be open to Scottish vessels, that the Presbyterian Church of Scotland should be maintained and the Scottish Courts of Law remain unchanged. The treaty was not only acceptable to both countries and all parties but proved lasting. It is to the credit of Edward Russell that the agreement which he was so largely responsible in negotiating with the Scots has persisted so little mutilated to the present day.

One year after the Bill for the Union had passed through both the English and Scottish Parliaments, Russell was invited to succeed the Earl of Pembroke in his old office of Lord High Admiral. He was flattered by the offer and hesitated, but in the end refused. He felt he had suffered enough for the services he had rendered in the past to the Navy. Instead, in 1709 he accepted nomination as First Commissioner of a Naval Board. A year later, when the Duke of Marlborough and other friends in the Ministry were dismissed, he resigned and once more sought the quiet of retirement until on Queen Anne's death in 1714 he was appointed one of the Lords Justices for the charge of public affairs.

The Commission of which Russell was a member invited Prince George of Hanover to assume the throne. He was the symbol of the Protestant succession and welcome to the majority of the nation. Russell was co-opted to the Privy Council immediately on the new King's arrival in England and soon afterwards resumed his appointment as a Commissioner of the Admiralty, a position which he held until his final retirement from public affairs in 1717. He was then 65 years of age but lived in retirement for a further ten years, dying at his house in Covent Garden on 26th November 1727.

Was he a careerist who deserved to be described as selfish and mercenary by his enemies, anxious to "back it both ways", or was he a man of the highest principles as well as of great ability, so devoted to the cause of reform that he was prepared to risk his position and his very life twice over in the course of three years to achieve his objects? Or was he a sailor who was drawn incidentally into politics and in effect a kind of secret agent, in the service of William III?

The answers to these three questions, if they could be found, would be the keys to the enigma of his character. Bishop Burnet, who knew him personally as well as anyone, said that the faults alleged against him and inherent in his make-up were too passionate a disposition, intolerance, and love of pleasure. The first of these three may be inferred from his public career, the last two do not appear from the record of his life of service unless one attributes his various retirements to impatience rather than to principle. Certainly his career was his life. No woman, no other interest, distracted him. Family ties meant nothing to him. He was utterly devoted to his work whether as a naval commander or a politician. On the face of it he was a man of principle and it is hard to credit him with mercenary motives strong enough to overrule his conception of his duty.

The opinion of an anonymous contemporary is preserved among the Birch Papers in the British Museum: "His affection for the service of his country and his zeal to annoy his enemies were remarkable. He never treated his Prince with the arts of flattery, nor by silence and submission when wrong measures were pursued. When the King had been prevailed on to dismiss his friends and attempted to pacify him by declaring he would turn out no more, the reply was 'Your Majesty has none remaining in your service'."

CHAPTER SEVEN

The Russells' London

THE RUSSELL's title is derived from the Woburn estate in Bedfordshire but the wealth of the family from the 16th century was derived equally from the Tavistock estate in Devonshire and the Fenland Thorney estate. The former was by far the more important until the time of the 4th and 5th Earls, who by the part they played in the draining of the Fens enhanced the value of the Thorney estate twentyfold. Yet the wealth of the later Russells was derived from the development of their London estates far more than from their agricultural interests. In London they set their stamp on the metropolis to a greater extent perhaps than any other landowners.

The 1st Earl had a London house. It was expected of a nobleman who was also a courtier that he should be instantly available when the Court was in London and although, as we have seen, Chenies was a remarkably convenient family home, accommodation in London was also essential. This first Russell house was on the south side of the Strand a little to the west of Temple Bar. It was not a large house like Chenies and extraordinarily little is known of it from the Russell papers.

When the family came into possession of the Long Acre and the Covent or Convent Garden, properties of the dissolved Abbey of Westminster, the house near Temple Bar was abandoned and a new house built on the north side of the Strand on the monastic land in a more magnificent idiom. This house may originally have been a manor-house of the Abbey of Westminster enlarged and refurbished for the 2nd Earl. It would certainly have been a gracious and, by the standards of the times, opulent house, bearing comparison with the homes of the bishops and other noblemen, several of whom had built palaces on the south side of the Strand with gardens sloping down to the river.

The Russell's home in the Convent Garden, though scarcely capable of being described as princely, was typical of the larger town houses of the 16th century. The classical ideas of the Renaissance had influenced building in some parts of the country, as in the Countess of Shrewsbury's Hardwick House, but Queen Elizabeth was known to be conservative in her taste, in architecture as well as in every phase of life. The result was that few of the London homes of her courtiers showed much sign of the radical change of fashion represented by the Renaissance. There was no equivalent of Hardwick Hall in London.

Most of the houses were gabled. Almost all the smaller ones were still of wood or half-timbered, although the risk of disastrous fire in the city was even then recognized, as it had been by the Romans in the 1st century A.D., and there were periodic attempts on the part of the sovereigns and their advisers to rebuild London in brick and stone because of their greater resistance to fire. The trouble was that not everyone could afford these materials and London within the limits of the medieval walls was such a crowded city that rebuilding presented as difficult and long-term a problem as it does today. Bedford House, however, and others like it outside the city walls were mainly stone-built, although since the aesthetic success of Wolsey's brick-built Hampton Court more and more houses were wholly or partially of this relatively new building material — new, that is, if we disregard the days of Roman Britain.

However, fashions were changing and with the death of Queen Elizabeth there was a decided swing in taste away from the traditional Gothic forms towards forms that owed more and more to Italian originals. King James I was sympathetic to the new ideas, as presented to him by one of the most consummate

11

artists of the century, Inigo Jones, whose influence in shaping the Russell's London in the 17th century was paramount.

Jones had studied building in Italy for several years. He had made precise copies of many of the Renaissance buildings which had transformed the appearance of Rome and modified that of every other Italian city. He loved Italian art yet he had an original genius appreciated by many Italian artists—for Jones was an artist first and foremost, an architect only by accident, because architecture was an important branch of art. His finest work was in designs for the masques. His principal contribution to building was the elaboration of designs, some-times rather rough, which it was left to the skill and imagination of the master builders to complete.

The year 1615 is one which divides the traditional from the classical in English life, for that was the year when King James I appointed Inigo Jones Surveyor-General, a position in which he was able to exercise a paramount influence on the reconstruction of London right up to the Civil War. As Surveyor-General, he had the responsibility for ensuring that all buildings conformed with government requirements. Consequently hundreds of buildings are described as "attributed to Inigo Jones". in country as well as town, without any real appreciation of what "attributed to" implies. All Jones did was to discuss with the owner the kind of building and to supply a drawing or, as it was said, "make the modell", something he could do in a day or less, something, indeed, which came so naturally to him that he could sit down and sketch out three or four variations on the same theme for the owner's approval.

Jones's training and personal inclinations conforming, as they did, to the personal taste of the sovereign ensured that almost all the "modells" he made were Italianate in design, although he made full allowance for the difference between the climate of England and that of Rome. He did not make the mistake of the monastic orders, which adopted lock, stock and barrel the design of continental abbeys and priories, without realizing that work during the winter in windowless cloisters, even though they were protected by the fabric of the church, was virtually impossible in England.

Jones did, however, make exceptions to the general rule. When the Chapel of Lincoln's Inn needed to be rebuilt he appreciated that a classically designed chapel could not harmonize with the Tudor Gothic work of all the other buildings of the Inn. He made the "modell" for a highly conservative chapel which survives in a largely unaltered form. But the exceptions he made were only in very special circumstances. When the 4th Earl of Bedford conferred with him on the possibility of developing Covent Garden, the area behind his Strand House, as a residential area, he must have been adamant in his insistence on a layout and design conforming to classical ideas.

By then Charles I had succeeded James but retained Jones as his Surveyor-General, for Charles was much more positive in his admiration for the Italian way of life than James had been. He believed that London was an unworthy capital, that it sadly lacked the fine buildings associated with Rome and other European capitals, that it was generations behind its times. Perhaps his enthusiasm was greater than that of his Surveyor-General. It was certainly not less. Moreover Charles deplored the tendency of London to spread out towards Westminster and wished that the rather mean houses which had been built quite illegally on the Bedford estate along Drury Lane and in Long Acre could have been swept away and new ones built in their place, or the land allowed to revert to the pasture land and orchard which it had been a hundred years before. He was responsible for the establishment of a commission for buildings, of which Inigo Jones was a member and in effect the executive officer. The main purpose of the commission was to ensure that haphazard new development did not take place.

The 4th Earl was in no position to argue. As we have seen, he had not always been in royal favour. He had achieved a great deal towards the modernization of the Woburn estate, however, and it was the most natural thing in the world that he should look for ways of developing the Covent Garden estate, which was ideally suited to the needs of the increasing number of people seeking a town house outside the walls of the city but within easy reach of it and of the royal domain of Westminster and Whitehall. He was, of course, on intimate terms with the King and was able to put his plan before him in person. The King's position was ambivalent. While he did not like the idea of new houses being built, especially so near the site of his proposed palace of Whitehall, he liked even less the current appearance of the Strand, still less that of Long Acre. He certainly regarded the Earl's own home as out of date, so that the latter was able to hold out the inducement that the redevelopment of the site would add to the dignity of London. After many consultations the King agreed and issued a licence with many conditions in 1630, leaving the carrying out of the conditions to Inigo Jones.

Thus, although the Earl was by no means a classical scholar and not particularly interested in Renaissance art—he was primarily a man of the country—he found himself willy-nilly committed to a highly modern and Italianate scheme, encouraged by the thought that when it was completed it would increase, as proved to be the case, the revenues of the Bedford estates. And a very fine plan it was, though one wholly strange to the English urban landscape.

It was in effect an Italian piazza, of which one side was formed by the Earl of Bedford's garden wall and the other three by new buildings. The Russell home itself was modified to conform with the new fashion, though not apparently entirely rebuilt. It may have been treated in the same way as so many Elizabethan houses were in the 17th and 18th centuries, with a classical front thrown over a Tudor façade, one of the most interesting sidelights in English social history on the principle of keeping up with the Joneses (one wonders whether the first Jones of all was really Inigo!).

Two sides of the square—the north side facing the Russell garden wall, and the east side—were made up of large houses suitable for people of distinction, with coach houses behind them, that is, towards Long Acre and Drury Lane. The fourth side, the west, was reserved for a church flanked by a residence on each side. The two main blocks of houses on the north and east were fronted by a covered walk or colonnade from which access was gained to the main entrances. They were brick-built (the King had given the Earl a choice between brick and stone) but were covered with stucco to give the appearance of stone, an almost entirely new departure in England. The interior of the houses was beautified by rich panelling of a design as classical as that of the piazza itself.

The whole scheme was completed with remarkable speed, the church being finished in little more than three years after the Earl had received his royal patent. The church one must regard as being wholly the brain-child of Inigo Jones. Indeed, according to Horace Walpole, the Earl was alarmed at the rapidly increasing bill for the development. Ready money was never a strong point of the Russells, or indeed of any other landed proprietors. Their wealth was counted in land values, their income, however large, earmarked for the upkeep of their mansions and for paying pensions to members of the family and old retainers. If ready money needed to be raised over and above the usual outgoings some part of the Bedford estates had to be sold, usually the outlying manors in Devonshire, which were not entailed. However much profit the Earl might see ultimately accruing to him from the Covent Garden development, he would naturally wish to keep the preliminary expenditure within bounds. He may well have asked Jones to build the church without unnecessary ornament and to have it plain "like a barn". To this proposition, according to Walpole, Jones replied, "You shall have the handsomest barn in Europe", and indeed it was!

The striking Tuscan columns at the east end of the church

are a still impressive landmark in the Covent Garden scene, whether as a background for the activities of market porters or as a stage set for the first scene of *Pygmalion*. Curiously, this is not the church which Inigo Jones designed. That building was practically destroyed by fire towards the end of the 18th century and rebuilt brick for brick and stone for stone precisely according to the original plan. People who saw the reconstructed church at the beginning of the 19th century could not remember any difference between it and the original.

One thing which makes the Church of St. Paul more than ordinarily significant is that the magnificent east end is a sham entrance. The real entrance, a far less conspicuous one, is at the west end, where the plain, if not barn-like, appearance of the church is far more noticeable than in the aspect it presents to the square, most of which is now occupied by the 19th-century market house. The row of houses on the east side has disappeared completely, but the north side has been reconstructed in approximately the same idiom. One house in the north-west corner (King Street) was the home of a famous Russell, Edward Russell, Earl of Orford, Lord High Admiral of England. But this was a later addition to the piazza, built towards the end of the century and giving only a rough idea of the appearance of the houses in the original development.

Even the fruit and vegetable market, which has caused fantastic traffic congestion in an area of a square mile for the whole of the 20th century (before the motor-car age as much as since) and is soon to be transferred to a less congested area south of the Thames, is in a sense traditional. Permission was given to a few select traders in fruit and vegetables to offer their wares on the south side of the piazza under the shelter of the garden wall of Bedford House at the very beginning of the scheme, and this permissive trading even then of a specialized nature was the forerunner of a market complementary to the market in fish and flesh of Bloomsbury Square. The conversion of the piazza into Covent Garden market and its abandonment to the market house and the offices and showrooms of the market men was really a matter of assessing priorities. The Russell piazza in the 19th century was no longer a fashionable place of residence but the need for a modern market in fruit and vegetables had increased as fashionable London moved further and further to the west. At the time they were built, however, the Earl found it uncommonly easy to dispose of his newly erected properties, some of which were leased at the very high rental of £150 a year and were the homes of minor noblemen and people of fashion, with a sprinkling of city merchants.

While a Russell was thus at once consolidating the fortunes of the family and setting a new trend in urban design, another nobleman was considering another development on parallel lines less than a mile away. Thomas, Lord Wriothesley, 1st Earl of Southampton, was rewarded in 1545 for his services as Lord Chancellor with the manor of Bloomsbury and some adjoining land, formerly the property of the Carthusian monastery, or Charterhouse, which before the dissolution had been one of the most influential and wealthiest of the many London monasteries. At the time, however, the grant of this land did not seem of special significance. It contained a rather decrepit manor-house, and a number of farm buildings, but was used mostly as grazing ground on lease to several farmers. It was not regarded highly because some of it was boggy. If anyone had forecast that this insignificant parcel of Wriothesley land would become the cornerstone of the Russell fortunes in the following century he would have been thought a promising candidate for Bedlam.

The Earl's London residence was Southampton House, on the south side of Holborn near the boundary with the City of London. He saw no reason to change it. He did, however, obtain by royal grant or purchase land adjoining the Bloomsbury manor towards St. Giles and renewed the grazing rights which had first been granted by the prior of the Charterhouse. The 3rd Earl, a great favourite of King James I, secured a frontage on Holborn for the Bloomsbury estate, of which the western extremity was Tottenham Court Lane. The plot of land linking the manorial estate with Holborn was near the Church of St. Giles-in-the-Fields and formerly part of the endowment of the leper hospital of St. Giles. Its acquisition made it possible for the Earl to think in terms of utilizing the estate for the building of a larger and more fitting residence than the one at Holborn Bars.

It is likely that King Charles I criticized him for the number of unlicensed timber buildings which had appeared on the estate. He may also have suggested that the house at Holborn Bars was no longer fitting for an earl. So the Earl of Southampton was in much the same position as the Earl of Bedford at the same time. Certainly London had flooded over its walls and had nearly surrounded the Earl's house. Anyone looking out of the upper-floor windows would have seen rather mean jerry-built houses in place of green fields.

It is difficult to know on whom to pin the blame for indiscriminate building. In those times it was one thing for the Privy Council to make a rule, quite another to enforce it. The Earl of Southampton did not in the circumstances have much difficulty in obtaining a licence to build a mansion for himself on the Bloomsbury estate. After one or two preliminary skirmishes it was granted in 1640, but the Earl's plans did not mature. With the outbreak of the Civil War he abandoned the idea of building—indeed it might have been difficult or impossible to obtain labour or materials—and was in no position after the war to incur the expenditure involved. He was fined so heavily for his support of the Royalists that he took the line of least resistance and retired to his Titchfield home.

However, by 1657, his fortunes recouped, his feud with Cromwell forgotten, he returned to London and having obtained government approval resumed his plan of operations for a Bloomsbury house, but not at that time for building any other houses on the estate. His mansion was completed in good time for the Restoration. It is described as a long low building in the classical style. It was one of the many mansions which were "attributed to Inigo Jones". Poor Inigo Jones was dead some years before its building started. Even so, the description may not be as inaccurate as it sounds. Just as the Earl of Bedford consulted with Jones and received from him a "modell" so the Privy Council certainly required the Earl of Southampton to have similar consultations when the licence of 1640 was granted. Jones may well have made his "modell", and the house completed nearly twenty years later may easily have been built according to Jones's design.

After the Restoration the Earl was in great favour at Court. He felt confident to proceed with the second part of his plan. He obtained a licence in 1661 for the building of a piazza very similar to the Earl of Bedford's Covent Garden. The houses were on the land immediately to the south of the new mansion, forming a square enclosed by houses on three sides, and the garden of the mansion on the fourth. The arrangement was still referred to as a piazza but very soon, like so many other foreign innovations originally known by an alien word, went native and was referred to as a square. Bloomsbury Square was the first to be known by this name. It was so successful both as a practical proposition and on aesthetic grounds that it proved the prototype of most of the major building schemes of the next hundred years, while other landlords, jealous of the success of Bloomsbury (or Southampton) Square, paid its creator the highest possible compliment, that of imitating him.

If Pepys and Evelyn may be regarded as typical men in the street in reference to the middle and upper classes of society, the success of Lord Southampton's scheme must have been most gratifying to him. Evelyn was not over-enthusiastic about Southampton House but he enthused about the good air and the view from the house to the north, which was unrestricted as far as the heights of Hampstead. Pepys admired the style of the mansion and of the houses being built around the square. Evelyn, with his wonderful ability to hit the nail on the head, pinpointed the real virtue of the scheme. He said it was "a noble square or piazza and a little town". He was quite right. It was indeed a little town, destined to become a very big one. It had all the ingredients necessary for urban life—gracious houses, a quasi-rural atmosphere, a market, and a church nearby. Those were the factors that ensured the success of the suburban development to which the Russell family contributed as much as any landlords in the following centuries, building on the foundation which the Earl of Southampton had laid.

The market was later expelled from Bloomsbury Square and ultimately became a row of shops in a street adjoining it, while other streets contained houses for people less wealthy than those who could afford a site in the square itself. In the case of this first experiment further impetus was given by the Great Fire of 1666, which accelerated of necessity the process of dispersal so far as the city magnates were concerned and by the popularity of the Earl himself, whose friends were eager bidders for a house in his square.

The Earl was not responsible for the building of the houses himself. He leased the land on which they were to be built on 42-year leases, with the provision that the houses should be solid enough in construction and elegant enough in design to grace the square. After 42 years the site and house built on it reverted to the estate, but was usually returned to the lessee or his heir on payment of a substantial fine and increased rent for the renewal of the lease. This was not only a profitable but a very convenient method of development for landowners whose estates were entailed or held in trust. It was followed by the Russell family in their later essays in development, with the exception that the period of the lease was lengthened by stages to the 99 years which was almost universal in the 19th century.

The Earl of Southampton died in 1667, leaving no son, but three daughters who were co-heirs to his estates. The estates were divided into as equal portions as possible and the apportionment of the parts among the daughters was decided by casting lots. The second daughter, Rachel, widow of Francis, Lord Vaughan, who was himself the heir of the Earl of Carbery, obtained the manors of Stratton and Micheldever in Hampshire, Southampton House, and the manors of Bloomsbury and St. Giles. A note of the allotment in her own handwriting has survived. Two years later she remarried. The bridegroom was William Russell, the second son of the 5th Earl of Bedford.

So Bloomsbury and St. Giles became part of the Russell inheritance (and Southampton House became one of the most exciting social and political centres in London). The story of William, Lord Russell, has been told in Chapter 5. He was an ardent reformer, virtually the founder of the Whig philosophy. He was a splendid host, a good husband and a fond father. Lady Vaughan, who abandoned her title and was known as Lady Russell after the death of Francis, Lord Russell, William's elder brother, proved an indomitable support for her husband's ambitions and was able, with the help of the increasing revenues from the Bloomsbury estate, to maintain a style of living which impressed all, friends and enemies alike. A son was born to them and named Wriothesley in memory of her father.

Building continued around the mansion and new streets were laid out, one linking Southampton House with Tottenham Court Lane. More significantly, this new street was named Russell Street and later renamed Great Russell Street when another known as Little Russell Street was constructed. The Russell family was obviously putting an indelible stamp on the growing neighbourhood, for more leases were granted along the new streets, some before the streets were actually constructed, others after. The "little town" was already growing into a major suburb.

On the death of his brother, William became heir to the earldom but did not live to become heir to a dukedom. One fine summer's day in 1683 an emissary of the King arrived at Southampton House and asked to see Lord Russell, who within an hour left the great mansion for ever, in custody on a charge of treason. When he was convicted, the Duke of York pressed for the execution to take place in the square outside the convicted man's house. That was too much for the Privy Council, but to make a great public example the execution was carried out in Lincoln's Inn Fields only three minutes' walk from Southampton House. The scaffold was erected at one end of the open space and the vast hostile crowd that gathered to witness it was held back by troops 100 yards away.

Lord Russell was at once a popular hero and a martyr. Southampton House ceased to be the gay and fashionable place it had been. Rachel never recovered from the shock and sorrow, and even the building which went on inexorably just beyond the confines of the square, as well as in the few remaining empty spaces around the square itself, meant little to her now. For a time the development of Bloomsbury was in the hands of the estate agents. The Earl was as shocked by his son's execution as Rachel was. In any case he was far more interested in the Thorney and Woburn estates than in Bloomsbury. When he was compelled to stay in London he still used Bedford House in the Strand. He visited Southampton House on occasion but there is no record of his having stayed there, even when Rachel was alone in the great house.

She concentrated for the next few years on educating her son. It is on record that she said she did not want to meet anyone except solicitors and the others whom she had to meet in the management of her affairs. Her subsequent life proved that her words were meant to be taken literally. So Southampton House was virtually closed so far as the Russells' old friends and acquaintances were concerned. Without a forceful personality behind the scenes the development of Bloomsbury slowed down, except for filling the empty spaces in the developments which had already been planned.

In 1700 Wriothesley's grandfather, by then created Duke of Bedford, died and Wriothesley succeeded as the 2nd Duke at the age of 20. He had married Elizabeth Howland, heiress of the manors of Streatham and Tooting Bec, when he was 14 and she was 11. After completing his education he had travelled abroad, like so many of his class, and on his succession to the Dukedom had not yet set up house with his wife. In all the circumstances the marriage was a remarkable success and Elizabeth proved an ideal hostess in London, in Woburn and in the manor-house of Streatham, which the young pair often used. Wriothesley was neither a businessman nor a politician. His whole being was concentrated in his passion for art, literature and music. In the eleven years in which he and Elizabeth entertained in London, their guests were of the artistic rather than of the political world.

One great change in Bloomsbury must be attributed to Wriothesley, although it was the work rather of his agents, his part being merely to agree to something which struck him as eminently reasonable. That was the demolition of Bedford House and the passing of the most important link in London with the 4th Earl and Inigo Jones. Even in his eighties the late Duke had used Bedford House and had shown not the slightest interest in the newer and more pretentious home of his widowed daughter-in-law. But the wheel of change had turned full circle. Just as the 1st Earl had been persuaded to build Bedford House on the land of the Abbey of Westminster because the existing Bedford House on the south side of the Strand was old-fashioned and the 4th Earl had been persuaded by Inigo Jones and King Charles to rebuild so as to accord with the new Italianate ideas, so by the time the 1st Duke died Bedford House, even as rebuilt to the design of Inigo Jones, had become woefully old-fashioned. It opened directly on to the Strand, which every year became a busier and noisier thoroughfare, even at night, when drovers were driving their charges to Smithfield and the market in the square at the back of the house was becoming more important as London expanded.

There seemed little point in building a new Bedford House on the site of the old. Southampton House had not yet become

old-fashioned and the young couple had obtained a great deal
of new furniture and tapestries for the walls as soon as they set
up house there. Elizabeth probably felt that she would rather
not cope with the vast organization necessary when a new house
was being fitted out. In any case there was not room between
Covent Garden and the Strand to build a house comparable
with Southampton House. So the Duke or his agents sold all the
contents of Bedford House and it was pulled down, leaving the
site vacant to await the best bidder for a lease. It was a sad
break with the Russell tradition but an inevitable one.

Wriothesley and his wife both died of smallpox contracted
while they were staying at the manor-house in Streatham, a
part of Surrey which for some reason unknown had acquired an
evil reputation for the prevalence of the disease. He died in 1711,
she in 1724. Wriothesley was succeeded by his son, also called
Wriothesley. By the time the latter's mother died, his grandmother Rachel, who had continued to live in Southampton
House, had already died and the great house was utterly
neglected. The Duke and his younger brother, John, lived in
the Streatham manor-house under the care of trustees and
tutors. Both married granddaughters of the redoubtable Sarah,
Duchess of Marlborough, during the next few years, Wriothesley marrying Anne, daughter of the Duke of Bridgewater, and
John Lady Diana Spencer, daughter of the Earl of Sunderland.

Sarah, though crippled with rheumatism, exerted an almost
unbelievable influence on the life of the Russells in London and
on the development of Bloomsbury during the next decade.
The first thing on which she set her heart was the reopening of
Southampton House as a ducal residence. She admired the
place immensely and indeed was not above borrowing some of
its treasures to grace her own numerous houses. Blenheim
Palace and Marlborough House were her background. She
could not see why a granddaughter of hers, married to the head
of one of the wealthiest families in England, should not preside
over a town house which was at least the equal of Marlborough

House, especially as Woburn could not compete with the outrageously sumptuous Blenheim.

In the event she did not persuade Wriothesley to reopen Southampton House. He did not live long enough for her imperious personality to achieve its end. It would have been an embarrassment to do so, for Wriothesley contrived to dispose of most of the ready money available to the estate (no one knows quite how he did it). Just before he died in 1732 there was talk of his leasing Southampton House and the whole of the Bloomsbury and St. Giles's manors.

When Lord John succeeded, Sarah was much more successful. She and Diana were devoted to each other and John proved a far more economical Duke than his brother. He was interested in politics and agriculture, and had good business ability. He saw the advantages of Southampton House both as an aid to his political career and as a gracious place in which to live, and saw the economic possibilities of further development in the Bloomsbury estate. He was even ready to accede to Sarah's suggestion that the house should be renamed Bedford House—and so it was known until, like the two older Bedford Houses, it was demolished.

By 1730 the first phase of Bloomsbury development had come to an end. For the next 20 years the revenues were enhanced far more by increasing the yearly rent when leases fell in than by the laying out of more streets or the building of more houses. This was sound economics. For the time being the demand for town houses had been satisfied. The Earl of Southampton's "little town", even in its currently enlarged form, was relatively compact and contained all the services and amenities which its residents demanded. Further development to the north, it was felt by John and his advisers, would spoil the rural character of this suburb and reduce its value, even if it proved an easy task to sell building leases.

The prospect from the windows of Southampton House and its neighbour in Great Russell Street, Montagu House, the next

largest establishment, was still over green fields to the heights
of Hampstead and Highgate. Scarcely a house in this direction
intervened in the view. No one looking north from the windows
of Southampton House could have imagined that this was a
place within a mile of the most important commercial and
business centre in the world. The market had been removed
from the Square to a point about 300 yards to the south-west,
just north of the street which linked Holborn with St. Giles.
North of the market a broad road had been built, Hart Street,
which was continued as Vernon Street along the south side of
the square. To the east King Street had been continued northward to Southampton Row. Centuries later the latter absorbed
King Street, but at this time Southampton Row was a row in
fact as well as in name, its single line of houses on the east side
looking across the gardens of Southampton House and the open
fields beyond.

King Street was lined with houses on both sides; so was
Great Russell Street as far as its junction with Tottenham Court
Lane, now generally known as Tottenham Court Road, while
the whole area between Great Russell Street and St. Giles and
between St. Giles and Long Acre was criss-crossed with lanes
and alleys and a few paved roads. This was an area in which
a new kind of tenant had appeared, mostly traders and small
businessmen, whose work in many cases was in connexion with
the market in Hart Street.

Southampton or Bloomsbury Square was still the most
fashionable part of the west end but the leases of Southampton
Row were also expensive and attracted a number of wealthy
residents. Many of the new streets had shops but there were few
in this part of the Bloomsbury estate, which catered for people
of fashion. It was all the same to the Russells, for Covent
Garden had become a fashionable shopping centre in its own
right as well as retaining some of its earlier prestige as a residential area.

In startling contrast with the opulence and respectability

of Bloomsbury and Covent Garden the narrow roads to the south of the parish and church of St. Giles, however, had already begun their downward slide. They were already one of the most notorious slum areas in London.

In the early part of the 18th century Henry Flitcroft was the architect who worked most closely with the Dukes of Bedford. He was responsible for much of the new building at Woburn and certainly advised on work under consideration in Bloomsbury, although it must be remembered that much of the responsibility for the new houses at that time was still that of the lease owner. Flitcroft's only influence could be in advising on what form the building directive embodied in the leases should take. He was, however, the architect of the new parish church of St. Giles, and architect meant something different from what it had done in the time of the 4th Earl and Inigo Jones. Architecture as a profession had come into its own and although Flitcroft had no early training in the art and craft of building—he was the son of William III's head gardener—he had by study and experiment become one of the most respected architects of his time. He was imbued with the classical tradition but was blessed with a lively imagination which made his work outstandingly original.

In 1717 the Duke's trustees obtained an Act of Parliament allowing them to rebuild St. Giles-in-the-Fields. This was an undertaking quite separate from the building by the state of the 50 new churches envisaged by the Act of Queen Anne's reign. The Gothic church, once the chapel of the Hospital of St. Giles, was the only medieval building left in the manors of St. Giles and Bloomsbury. Now a fine classical church arose on the site of the old one. It was distinctly conservative in treatment. Flitcroft may well have felt that the innovations he championed in the country might not suit the temper of London. In some ways St. Giles resembles St. Martin's-in-the-Fields, of which the architect was James Gibbs, in others the older St. James's, Piccadilly, one of the minor masterpieces of Sir Christopher

Wren. It is a fine composition and the steeple is better placed at the west end of the temple-like structure than Gibbs's spire in its central position in St. Martin's. The Russells were justly proud of it. Happily it is still possible to see it very much as they saw it, though its surroundings have changed beyond all recognition.

Although the Russell family undertook the building of St. Giles from the estate's resources with the help of subscriptions from parishioners, no criticism had been offered when the commissioners for Queen Anne's 50 churches, designed to relieve the overcrowding in existing churches where suburban development was taking place, proposed that Bloomsbury should become a new parish separate from that of St. Giles. A site was selected after consultations in which the commissioners and managers of the Bedford estates took part between Little Russell Street and Hart Street. Rachel, Lady Russell, and the trustees of the 3rd Duke signed the document allotting the site for the church in 1714.

In this case neither the Duke nor his trustees had any part in selecting the architect. Nicholas Hawksmoor had succeeded James Gibbs as surveyor-in-chief to the Church Commissioners. The new church became the parish church of St. George, Bloomsbury, in 1724. Like St. Giles it remains virtually intact, having escaped the worst attacks of redevelopment and enemy bombardment. It was built to an unusual design, though like St. Giles it was inspired by the form of a classical temple. Considering that it was built under an Act which produced only a few churches notable for beauty rather than economy, it is very successful, the steeple tower a fine landmark in the 20th century, but a far more conspicuous one in the 18th. Much ribald criticism was evoked at the time, and has continued to be expressed at intervals, of the figure which caps the spire; often described as St. George (in keeping with the dedication of the church), it is, to be strictly accurate, a statue of King George I wearing a toga. The thought of that rotund little gentleman wearing a toga may be humorous, the superimposition of the figure on the spire technically unfortunate, the taste of this curious compliment to the Hanoverian dynasty doubtful, but the idea at least was an original one beautifully executed and the church as a whole was worthy of the fashionable residents who worshipped in it.

So much for the changing face of Bloomsbury and St. Giles's. In terms of the estate, what had happened in the fifty years ending in 1730 was that the number of tenants of the estate had trebled, the rent roll doubled. In the next thirty years the rent roll was doubled again, reaching nearly £8,000 a year, from which must be deducted the not inconsiderable expenses of management, road building and repair.

This excellent trading result must owe a great deal to the business acumen of John, the 4th Duke. He and his Duchess moved into Bedford House in 1735. They carried out no major reconstruction but they refurnished and redecorated the house on a grander scale than ever before. Much of the existing furniture and decoration was more than fifty years old. Now with commerce rapidly expanding it was possible to import newly fashionable articles from the Far East as well as from every country in Europe. A great deal of furniture was purchased from China, for it was the beginning of the age in which enthusiasm for the art of the Far East degenerated into an uncritical passion for Chinoiserie.

Changing tastes were reflected, too, by the substitution of wallpaper for tapestries and the addition of landscape paintings to the great number of family portraits that hung on the walls of the chief rooms. The portraits of the Earls and Dukes of Bedford and of Sarah, Duchess of Marlborough, still took pride of place. The Italian painter Canaletto was extremely well represented, with at least 24 Venetian landscapes hung in various rooms. There were, too, paintings by Sir John Thornhill from the cartoons of Raphael in Hampton Court. These were hung in the ballroom and in 1800, when much of the contents of Bedford House came under the hammer, were presented to the Royal Academy.

During the residence of the 4th Duke hot and cold water baths were fitted. Probably there had been some form of cold bath before that time (there was a bathroom at Woburn in the 17th century) but the hot-water bath was an innovation arising from the presence of unlimited piped water. The whole of the Bloomsbury estate was supplied with water by the New River Company but between 1740 and 1745 new pipes—they were still of elm—were laid across Southampton fields to augment the supply and increase the pressure in Bedford House and the neighbouring squares and streets. It is strange to think of an 18th-century house with all mod. con. but Bedford House very nearly achieved that ideal of the 20th century, with water closets as well as piped water.

The New River Company, that brain child of King James I and Sir Hugh Myddelton which had brought water from the springs of Amwell in Hertfordshire to supply the needs of a growing London, did more to "modernize" the way of life of Bloomsbury people than any other single body or individual, but the Duke's relations with the Company were not always cordial. Nor was the Duke in his later years a man to mince his words. He wrote to the directors some time in 1763 telling them that he was going to renew the paving of Great Russell Street, "Observing," he said, "that the pipes belonging to you are continually breaking and that the pavement when taken up to mend the pipes is always laid down in a very bad manner. I give you this notice in order that you may direct the pipes to be made good that lie under the street I am going to repave." He further requested them in none too courteous terms to make sure that whenever occasion arose to take up the pavement they should ensure that the pavement be laid down again upon a level with the rest. He added that he would regret the necessity of taking any measure that might be disagreeable to the Company!

In this second heyday of the Bloomsbury mansion it approached the brief splendour of the time when Lord William and his wife had entertained the leading Whig politicians of the day. The society entertained in the middle of the 18th century was still predominantly a Whig one but the Whig party had grown to maturity and was accepted as the party of progress and reform rather than of revolution. There are records of magnificent balls and receptions and of the entertainment of ambassadors and members of the royal houses of European countries. One of the most magnificent of all the occasions in the history of Bedford House was in 1762, when Lady Caroline, the Duke's favourite daughter, was married in the chapel of Bedford House to George, Duke of Marlborough, the great-grandson of the 1st Duke and Sarah, Duchess of Marlborough, thus forging yet another link between the Russell and Churchill families.

The Russells' London horizon was not wholly limited by Covent Garden and Bloomsbury. From their home in the midst of London's new West End they looked out across the seas to distant lands. The story, which in a strange way echoes that of the merchant adventurers of Weymouth who had founded the Russell line, began, like so many other parts of the Russell saga, with the dissolution of the monasteries. When the Thames-side lands on the Surrey bank belonging to the Abbey of Bermondsey were divided, one small part came into the possession by gift or purchase of the Howland family, whose final heir, Elizabeth, was the wife of the 2nd Duke. The 1st Duke, however tired he was of business and however unwilling to enter into new commitments in the latter part of his life, had seen the possibilities of this desolate stretch of marsh-land. He urged development, and soon first a dry dock and later a wet dock were built.

The venture was a success from the beginning. The dry dock became the yard of a famous firm of shipbuilders, the brothers Wells, while the wet dock was leased to the East India Company

and the South Sea Company, which had "taken over" the
Greenland Company, which at one time had a virtual monop-
oly of the whaling trade. As the rental paid by the South
Sea Company was more than £500 a year and that paid by the
East India Company rather more, it will be seen that this
inspiration of the 1st Duke, fostered and improved upon by the
4th Duke, was a money spinner. Incidentally, it was productive
of enhanced prestige at a time when London society was
becoming increasingly mercantile. The City of London, long
the strongest force in the kingdom, stronger even than the
sovereign, was now in a position to dictate to Parliament in
much the same way as it had in the past to the sovereign. Wise
noblemen made certain that they had City connexions.

The Russells' interest in the Rotherhithe docks was by no
means confined to leasing them to operating companies. They
shared the risk with the companies concerned, importing and
exporting valuable cargoes, and in the time of the 4th Duke
owning at least an eighth interest in some of the ships. An
account dated 4 February 1761 shows that the dividend on a
voyage of the *Duke of Bedford*, when that ship caught a whale
and a half in 1760, was £124 9s. 6d. After all expenses were
paid, the balance paid to the Duke was less than £40. Ten
years earlier the net profit on such voyages was considerably
higher, reflecting the decline of the whaling industry about this
time. The *Duke of Bedford* sailed no more after 1761 and the
Rotherhithe dock was used almost exclusively by the East
India Company, which, like the South Sea Company, named
many of its ships after the Russells. By judicious management
the Russells ensured a good profit for the shipbuilding company
in the dry dock by prevailing on the lessees of the wet dock to
commission them to build their ships. The *Bedford*, the *Russell*
and the *Tavistock* were all built in Wells' shipyard.

The 1st Duke's enterprise in this respect had far-reaching
effects, for the Rotherhithe dock was the first enclosed wet dock
to be constructed in England. It was thus the prototype of the

vast system of docks through which the traffic passing today is greater than that of any other port in the world. The *Bedford* was captured by French privateers, and many other ships were captured or foundered in high seas. On the longer voyages there were considerable delays, goods ordered in eastern ports failed to be delivered, and merchants to whom goods were being consigned disappeared. The trade was accompanied by many risks but it was a profitable one and the 4th Duke in particular had every reason to be grateful for the revenue derived from it.

The principal export handled by the ships in which the Duke had an interest was woollen cloth, much of it manufactured from the fleeces of sheep grazing on the ancestral estates of Tavistock. Imports included furniture, draperies and ornaments, some of which the Duke used himself in Bedford House, and commodities such as snuff, for which there was a ready market on the Bloomsbury estate and in Covent Garden, where it was retailed by some of the shops on the ducal property. The East Indiamen were the ships in which the Duke imported the Chinese furniture, wallpaper and ornaments with which he decorated Bedford House and Woburn Abbey, while other noblemen and the *nouveaux riches*, too, falling in line with the new taste, commissioned the Duke's agents to arrange for the import of similar goods. In just the same way Stephen Russell must have arranged for the import and distribution of wine carried from Bordeaux by his ships to the port of Weymouth.

The building over of the Bloomsbury estate to the north of Bedford House was deferred until after the 4th Duke's death. There was little further expansion in any part of London between 1735 and the Peace of Paris in 1763. The times were too uncertain for speculative building on the grand scale and the policy of consolidation followed by the Duke of Bedford was paralleled by the policies adopted by other landowners in London's West End.

In 1755, however, an event had taken place that was to have

more far-reaching consequences than the circumstances appeared to warrant. The event was the decision of Parliament to construct London's very first by-pass road, the New Road. It was planned to link the Edgware Road with Islington, thus permitting drovers and the drivers of heavy commercial wagons to reach the City markets, especially Smithfield, without using the Oxford Road or Holborn, in which residents complained bitterly not only of the intolerable congestion of traffic but of the incessant noise—not surprisingly, since most of the houses rose directly from the roadway without the intervention of a forecourt or a front garden, and the roads were so narrow that the houses on either side of them acted as sounding-boards and intensified the nuisance.

When drovers and wagoners had the bright idea of avoiding the congestion of St. Giles by travelling through Bloomsbury Square and Great Russell Street there was a tremendous to-do. Petitions were addressed to the Duke's agent and suggestions were repeatedly made of raising the matter in Parliament. The gravamen of the residents' complaint was that "the peace and quiet of His Majesty's subjects are disturbed, their pavements damaged and the expense of repairing them according to law much increased". The Duke did what he could to avoid unnecessary disturbance, although he was powerless to prevent the passage of the wagons along Great Russell Street, nor did Parliament take any action. But when new roads were built on the estate he emphasized that they were private roads, and barred them with a locked gate to which a key was supplied only to residents and their friends on application. Needless to say, the scheme did not work well for very long, any more than thousands of other schemes adopted by landlords of that and subsequent periods to deter the public from taking the shortest distance between two points, whether or not there is evidence of a public right of way.

The New Road did not run through the Bedford estate but was cut in a straight line, precisely the line of the modern

Euston Road, the name which it ultimately acquired, at varying distances from the irregular north side of the Bloomsbury estate. In spite of the fact that the road was a respectable distance away, residents complained bitterly that the dust from passing traffic made it impossible to keep their houses clean. The farmers who still leased Southampton fields for grazing declared that the dust destroyed the value of the pasture land. The Duke of Bedford, however, took a slightly different view. Unperturbed by the threat of dust he saw a possibility of making a short cut on his numerous travels to Woburn and prolonged Southampton Row to a junction with the New Road (at the spot where St. Pancras Church stands), the final portion being built after much argument and negotiation over the land of the Duke of Grafton, owner of the neighbouring estate.

The importance of the New Road to the Bedford estate, however, was that it facilitated the development of Southampton fields and all the open ground lying between the gardens of Montagu House and Bedford House on the south and the boundary of the estate on the north. Montagu House had ceased to be a private residence. It was taken over as the home of the British Museum in 1753 and the Duke conceived the idea of building another "little town" on the same lines as the Earl of Southampton's original "little town" to the north of it, and called it Bedford Square. He died before the scheme came to fruition but his widow, Gertrude, with a character as positive as that of any of the Russell wives, was fully competent to press forward with the late Duke's scheme during the minority of her grandson Francis, who was six years old when he succeeded to the dukedom. She replaced many of the older members of the management staff and overruled if she did not persuade the trustees acting on behalf of the Duke.

Bedford Square was begun in 1774. The late Duke thought rather fancifully, perhaps, of this urban paradise as a replica of the King's Circus in Bath, to which he had been a frequent visitor and which he admired. This was a very much greater

speculation than the Russells had attempted before. Not only
the planning, as before, but the building was the responsibility
of the estate. The chief confidant and adviser of the Dowager
Duchess was Robert Palmer, now the agent of the estate. He
not only carried out the detail of the scheme but invested his
own money in it. The outbreak of the war with America in 1775
like a bolt from the blue produced at once an economic depression and an increase in costs, making what was always a bold
speculation a very risky business indeed. However, all turned
out for the best. The square was completed and tenants quickly
found. It proved one of the most profitable of the Russell
ventures and provoked a great new spate of building which in
the course of forty years engulfed the whole of the rest of the
estate.

Bedford Square was in many ways the most attractive part
of this last stage of development. Its architect is unknown but
it can quite fairly be described as in the Adam style. It shows
the first signs of mass production of columns and mouldings,
especially in the Coade stone elaboration of the doorways.

The managers of the Bedford estate were not alone at this
time in extending the area of urban development. The Foundling estate pressed northward with a programme including
Mecklenburgh Square, which is almost parallel with Bedford
Square and was virtually a copy of the latter, not so much in
point of architecture as in the idea lying behind it, that of a
little town independent of surrounding neighbourhoods, with
large houses for the wealthy and smaller ones for the less well-
off. The executive of the Foundling plan was a master builder
and architect, James Burton. He succeeded Palmer as development manager for the Bedford estate.

In 1800 the 5th Duke was granted by Act of Parliament a
licence to proceed with the scheme which included the demolition of Bedford House. It was a sad day for the Russells'
London but, like the demolition of the second Bedford House in
the Strand, inevitable in the changing circumstances. Burton

probably acted as contractor to the 5th Duke, either sharing the risk or taking the whole risk of the new speculation. In place of Bedford House there appeared the north façade of Bloomsbury Square (it remains much as it was designed). To the north of that, Russell Square took shape between 1805 and 1814, a rather poor relation of Bedford Square. Tavistock Square followed, although Burton completed only the east side and the roads connecting Russell Square with Tavistock Square and with Bloomsbury Square. Then there was a pause.

By now Euston Square, on an adjoining estate, was being built astride the New Road and the way was open for a continuous development on the Russell estate to meet it. Burton certainly made a fortune from his work and retired to conquer fresh fields on the Sussex coast. His place as speculator-in-chief in Bloomsbury was taken by Thomas Cubitt. He had a number of workmen in constant employment and specialized in purchasing leases of land, building on it and then either selling the leases of individual houses or letting them. He was just the man for whom the Bedford estate managers were looking, although the arrangement with him precluded the Russell family from having any direct influence on this, the last stage of building Bloomsbury.

Cubitt started on the work about 1822. To him must be credited Tavistock Square (except the east side, which, as we have seen, was the work of Burton), Gordon Square, Woburn Square, and the adjoining roads. The houses he built were fine ones, well designed and uncommonly well built, as serviceable today as they were more than a century ago. Early in his operations Cubitt designed Woburn Walk, then known as Woburn Buildings, as a shopping centre to serve the new estate. Here was another little town on a rather larger scale than those of the earlier ones in Bloomsbury.

So the Russells' London was completed, a magnificent design which had a positive unity, in spite of the long period separating the construction of different parts. Its story since the early

part of the 19th century has been one of change and substitution, some of it necessitated by the building of wider roads,
some dictated by the changing requirements of commerce and
the decline of Bloomsbury as a fashionable residential area.
But the Russells' London lives on. Bedford House is no more,
the piazza of Covent Garden is hardly remembered, but so
much survives of the squares and handsome streets linking them
that one can reconstruct the whole in imagination. Significantly,
too, the very first contribution of the Russell family to London,
St. Paul's Church in Covent Garden, which also marks the most
southerly point of the Russell stake in London, survives, having
been rebuilt brick by brick after severe damage by fire; so does
Woburn Walk, beautifully reconstructed in recent years, marking the last phase of the Russell contribution and also the
extreme northerly limit of the estate.

CHAPTER EIGHT

Constitutional Reformers

THE PATTERN of Russell political and social thought had been set by the end of the 17th century. The creation of the Dukedom was an accolade which encouraged future holders of the title to imagine that the Russell way of thought had the stamp of universal approval. By the time Queen Anne came to the throne the Russells were established as one of the greatest Whig families in the country as well as one of the wealthiest and most influential. And Whig the family remained without a break for two hundred years. As the term Whig began to fall into decline, if not disrepute, the Russells remained liberal in thought, though no longer concerned with party politics. The present Duke's mild conservatism marks a distinct break with tradition.

Whereas some of the Russells before the end of the 17th century had been frankly revolutionary, now that the English Constitution was on a firm basis they became constitutional reformers, always with an eye to the rights of the individual, a passionate regard for freedom of speech as of opinion. They were often outspoken in their criticism of the Crown but always acted in accordance with the practice laid down by law. They were generally in advance of their times, probing further and further towards the modern conception of government. They were indefatigable in working for the wider representation of the people in Parliament and were leaders always of progressive thought. Recent Dukes have been in the forefront of the movement to abolish the hereditary qualification for the

House of Lords. They achieved a great deal, partly by determined perseverance, partly by virtue of the honoured name which they bore.

English people have always tended to trust the Dukes of Bedford because it was exceptional for a family of great landowners to be concerned with the advancement of popular government and to be prepared to sacrifice their position of privilege if the voice of the people could be made more representative. Yet that is precisely what they proved to be willing and anxious to do time and time again.

In the 18th century Francis, 5th Duke of Bedford, stands out as the embodiment of progress. In the 19th century the distinction passed to a younger son, Lord John Russell, whose conviction of the rightness of and necessity for parliamentary reform did more than anything else to pave the way towards universal adult suffrage. Although these two are most prominent in the pages of history, many other Russells have contributed a generous share to political change as well as to improvement in the relations between landlord and tenant, and to the better social organization of the counrtyside, an aim probably just as important for a landed family as political success.

The 1st Duke was succeeded by his grandson Wriothesley, born in 1680, who was educated privately and at Oxford University, which he entered at the beginning of 1696. Here he developed a taste for classical literature and a preoccupation with art which remained with him all his life. One of his minor contributions to cultural advancement was the financing of a magnificent edition of the Poems of Pindar, one of his favourite classical authors. After Oxford he toured Europe and, as the heir to the recently created Dukedom, was received with marked respect in almost every court.

Wriothesley did not, however, run true to form. He was far more interested in art and horticulture than in politics and built up what was one of the finest libraries in England. He did, however, take part in a number of debates in the House of

Lords with considerable effect and in accordance with what
one might reasonably call the family tradition. In 1703 he
spoke in favour of the Bill against occasional conformity, which
he thought would weaken the position of the Church of
England. In 1710 he came forward in support of the Whig
government when he cast his vote against Dr. Sacheverell, who
was impeached by the Whigs after he had preached sermons
attacking the Ministry. He was in the majority but the judgment of the Whigs in prosecuting this fiery divine was shown to
have been poor, for his conviction provoked a reaction in
favour of the Tories. In 1711 Wriothesley supported the Earl
of Galway when the latter was criticized for his conduct in the
war with Spain. Just as he was beginning to earn a fine parliamentary reputation he died of smallpox in May 1711.

He was succeeded by his son, also christened Wriothesley,
who was then only three years old. He shared his father's
interest in art and the portrait painter Whood was a protegé of
his resident at Woburn Abbey. But his health was poor and by
the time he came of age he was in no position to take part in
politics. He died in 1732 at the age of 24. He had contracted
very large debts of honour on the Continent but as he had not
succeeded in repaying them, the final settlement was left to
the 4th Duke, his younger brother, who was a very different
kind of a man.

Strong, able and determined, John, the fourth Duke, combined an active participation in politics through two reigns
(he was generally out of sympathy with the sovereign) with progressive and enlightened management of the Russell estates. He
is rather an enigma, for contemporary writers are unanimous in
describing him as more fond of sport than of politics—a "merry
little Duke", as Horace Walpole saw him. Certainly he was
small of stature and gay in manner.

His life was in the best Russell tradition. He enhanced the
family reputation. He had a background of university education and travel abroad and in his early twenties developed the

ambition to take an important part in political life, which he believed his rank and fortune demanded. In his travels he saw at first hand the strengths and weakness of the governments of most of the European countries and used this experience to good advantage in the following years.

He was only 22 when he succeeded to the Dukedom and within a year was taking part in the debates of the House of Lords. Sir Robert Walpole at this time was the head of a Whig Ministry which had a highly successful record, both in scotching the revolutionary activities of partisans of the Pretender and in rationalizing the machinery of the government. He was not popular and was opposed by a strange coalition of Jacobites, Tories and disaffected Whigs, who accused him of seizing autocratic power in a constitution designed to be democratic.

Pulteney was the brilliant leader of a rebellious section of Whig opinion and quickly won the support of the Duke of Bedford. He was a persistent and outspoken critic of Walpole until the latter was defeated in 1742 and resigned his office. By then the Duke of Bedford's stature in Parliament had increased and his friends were probably right in judging that his influence was a powerful factor in bringing about the fall of the Walpole Ministry.

In the circumstances it is not surprising that Sir Robert Walpole's son Horace is astringent in the extreme in his recollections of the Russell family in general and the 4th Duke in particular. The Duke did not endear himself to King George II, either, when in 1743 he spoke effectively against the proposal that sixteen thousand of the King's Hanoverian troops should be absorbed in the English army.

The Duke was also instrumental, partly by logic, partly by sentiment, in the rejection of the Bill to extend the penalties for high treason to the heirs of those convicted. The Bill was directed at those convicted of corresponding with the Pretender but after speaking several times in a long debate Russell made a strong case for rejection by allusion to the melancholy history

ve left, Hastings, 9th Duke of Bedford, was responsible for many improvements
the Woburn estate and for the building of the present parish church; *above right*,
lliam, 8th Duke of Bedford, took little interest in the Russell estates, which were
ministered by his cousin Hastings; *bottom left*, Lord John Russell ... a long and
entful political career in which he formed two ministries; *bottom right*, Francis, 7th
ke of Bedford, eldest son of the 6th Duke and a close friend of his youngest
ther, Lord John Russell, was a man of great personal charm and popular
with all ranks

Sackville, 10th Duke of Bedford, was able to make little contribution to the Russell heritage, living only two years after succeeding to the title

Herbrand, 11th Duke of Bedford, witnessed but refused to accept the dramatic social changes of the first half of the twentieth century of his own family. He justified the part which Lord William had taken under an arbitrary government, mentioning the part of the Russells in calling the House of Orange to the throne, and warned his fellow peers against permitting a Bill to become law which would "lay prostrate the lives and properties of descendants if corrupt and tyrannical times like those of Charles I or James II should again by any chance return and call for another renovating revolution". John, 4th Duke of Bedford, might act strictly in accordance with the Constitution but he could contemplate the possibility of a "renovating revolution". Times had not changed much.

In the following year he accepted an offer to join the "Broad Bottom" Government, the coalition formed by Henry Pelham and his brother, the Duke of Newcastle. He was appointed First Lord of the Admiralty, with the Earl of Sandwich, a great personal friend, acting as his deputy. The country was in a near panic owing to the disastrous course of the war with France and the progress being made by the Young Pretender in Scotland. The Duke was the first nobleman to raise at his own cost a regiment for the defence of the country. His example in raising and paying the wages of a thousand men was followed by many other peers, giving a renewed sense of confidence to a country badly shaken.

The Duke was a great success as First Lord, showing vast energy in arranging for the repair and refitting of obsolete men-of-war and improvement of the defences of the south-coast ports. He was nominally responsible for the organization of the expedition which captured Louisburg and the Island of Cape Breton at the mouth of the St. Lawrence. He was rewarded for his good work by the largely honorary appointment of Warden of the New Forest. Then in February 1748 he was transferred from the Admiralty and appointed Secretary of State with special responsibility for the northern counties, a key appointment in view of the danger of insurrection in Scotland. He recommended the Earl of Sandwich as plenipotentiary in

13

the conduct of negotiations which led to the Peace of Aix-la-Chapelle, while the Duke himself undertook negotiations for the commercial treaty with Spain, which was signed in 1749 and which had the result of placing English traders on the same footing in Spain as they had been in the reign of Charles II. This agreement, known as the Treaty of Madrid, was a considerable triumph for the Duke's diplomacy. It was welcomed in the Commons by members of all parties, including the rising William Pitt, and the vote sanctioning the treaty was carried by 203 to 74. The best comment on the treaty is that 35 years passed before it was called into question by either country.

During this period in his political career, though there was still no personal liking between him and the King, he strengthened his position at Court by increasingly cordial relations with the Duke of Cumberland, who was as much at loggerheads with the Duke of Newcastle and at variance with the policy of Newcastle's brother Henry Pelham as Prime Minister as Bedford was himself.

It is difficult to see how the Pelham administration maintained itself against so much opposition, or for that matter how the Broad Bottom Ministry, which depended on an uneasy truce between warring political parties, achieved the good results it did. It was certainly a critical time for the government when, through the Duke of Cumberland's influence, the Duke of Bedford was appointed one of the Lords Justices to carry on the sovereign's work while King George was abroad. The Duke concerned himself most with foreign policy and inspired successful negotiations with France, which had approved landings in Tobago, an island that counted as an English possession. The French Government under threat of retaliatory action, withdrew the occupying forces.

One incident illustrates clearly the strange relationship between Pelham and the Duke of Bedford. The former negotiated a commercial treaty with Bavaria—a treaty that proved to be of little real importance. The crux of the matter was that the treaty was signed before Pelham laid it before the Lords Justices for their approval. The Duke of Bedford made a vigorous complaint to Pelham and declined to attend the deliberations of the council when, as he maintained, points to be discussed were irrevocably settled beforehand. He left London for a time and threw himself into the work of the Woburn estate.

Many expected the Pelham administration to fall but it somehow weathered the storm. Suggestions were made by Pelham's friends that the Duke had neglected his duties as a member of the council of the Lords Justices. The King refused to take any part in the argument. When he returned to England in January 1751 he refused a request from Pelham that the Duke should be removed from office, saying that he would consider no change at present and that whoever should "importune him on the subject" would incur his displeasure.

In April the Duke applied for the position of Lord-Lieutenant of Devonshire and was duly appointed. In this office he became an unofficial adviser to the King on foreign affairs, with an overall responsibility for the work of the ambassadors in France and Spain. His position in the government had become untenable, partly owing to the death of the Prince of Wales, who had always been a firm ally of his, like the Duke of Cumberland, partly because Pelham had turned against his friend and associate, Lord Sandwich. He resigned but it is said the King was very uneasy and offered him the position of President of the Council, which he refused.

For the next few years he was out of politics. With the death of Henry Pelham the Duke of Newcastle became Prime Minister, but in 1755 Henry Fox was created Secretary of State in another coalition government and asked the Duke to join the government. This he refused to do but showed his friendship for Fox by permitting some of his associates in opposition to join the administration and later acting as mediator between Fox and Pitt.

The King had made an abortive effort to reconcile the differences between these two statesmen which was stultifying English operations in the war with France. That the Duke succeeded was uncommonly welcome to the King, who was sincerely grateful for his help given and probably for the first time he recognized him as a true patriot, however uncompromising. He rewarded him with the Lord-Lieutenancy of Ireland and was relieved when the Duke accepted the appointment, the Duke of Newcastle promising, and actually giving, every possible assistance to make the government of Ireland relatively easy during the Duke's term. Support was promised by Pitt and Fox and gratitude expressed by the King.

In his work in Ireland the Duke of Bedford had the opportunity to show his real calibre. He was a great success and with constant support from the home government achieved more than any other Lord-Lieutenant of the century. Ireland was in a sorry state when he opened the Irish Parliament on 11th October 1757. The bulk of the population was then, as it has always been, Roman Catholic but the policy of recent governments had been to deny Roman Catholics not only any part in the government but even freedom of religious worship. The Protestant Lords and Commoners elected to the Irish Parliament passed penal legislation which, although happily it could not always be enforced, had built up an intolerable resentment among the Irish people at large. There were also disastrous feuds between the Protestant landowners themselves. The element of Presbyterianism which had been introduced into Ulster through the Scottish plantations provided yet another warring faction.

The history of Ireland during most of the 18th century reads as though it existed solely for the benefit of Protestant landowners, who fought bitterly among themselves for the privileges which the English Government could give them. Religion bulked large in all their transactions. Intolerance was rampant. To add to the unhappiness of the country, the population was increasing rapidly and with only primitive methods of agriculture the amount of food being produced was in many years insufficient for the people, of whom more than a million were permanently on the verge of starvation. For a man whose home policies had shown fear and horror of "Popery" the Duke of Bedford showed remarkable tolerance in his management of Irish religious affairs. He incurred criticism from many members of the English Government on this account, though the success of his regime was sufficient to negative the criticism and to ensure that when his term was over he laid down his office with honour.

The two most influential, and at the same time most troublesome, leaders of Irish opinion were the Primate, the Archbishop of Armagh, and Lord Kildare. It was a tribute to the Duke that he was able to steer a course of apparently perfect impartiality between the factions led by these two statesmen. It was only natural that he should be welcomed by the Presbyterians and by the powerful Society of Friends. The aim of his policy, stated for the first time when he opened Parliament and re-stated at each opening of Parliament, was to achieve compromise between all the elements of Irish society, so that the country might be prepared in the case of invasion by a foreign power. That was the point he stressed again and again. And it was a point that the Irish noblemen with their stake in the land could and did appreciate. It was known to the English Court that the French were preparing an invasion of Ireland, or at least planning one.

The Duke won popularity with the Irish Lords and Commons by opposing vehemently Pitt's repeated demands for the transfer of units of the Irish army in order to build up the English forces. He also asked for authority to act on his own initiative in an emergency without reference to the English Government and was granted this additional power on the understanding that it would only be used if communications were cut. He was successful in promoting and passing through the Irish Parliament a Bill transferring to the management of a

Revenue Board the detail of raising revenue, so that this should never again be subject to party politics. He appointed an Irishman, Sir Richard Cox, as Controller, making in this respect a complete break with tradition, but the King accepted his recommendation.

By the Autumn of 1758 he was able to report to the Privy Council that England could depend on the Irish people in the case of war, and that numbers of Catholics would support the Crown if a French invasion took place. Nothing ever arose to falsify this prediction. He pointed out to the Government that additional highly trained troops were necessary for the protection of the distant provinces and that the garrisons in Cork, Waterford and Limerick must be increased. To this the Duke of Newcastle and Pitt agreed reluctantly.

In 1759 the threat of French invasion became more imminent. Reliable reports were received of an invasion fleet at Havre and Brest, and it was at this point that the Duke renewed his efforts to ensure Catholic support. He pointed out to the Privy Council that the penal code directed against Roman Catholics had been enforced "with a severity and perseverance disgraceful to the very name of British rule". Even the Catholic nobility were in fear of their lives. He said that he would not be satisfied in the discharge of his office if the maxims of exclusion and intolerance were not abandoned. His views became known in Ireland and Catholic clergy began to preach obedience to their flocks, invoking the divine blessing on a governor who gave them hope for the mitigation of the penal laws. The Duke allowed a Registry Bill to be introduced for the registration of Roman Catholic clergy. He argued vigorously in favour of it before the Privy Council, saying that Christianity and good policy alike required that the Irish people should be allowed free expression of their faith. He pointed out that earlier governors had connived at the activities of Catholic priests and that it had proved impossible to enforce the penal laws, which many Catholics held in contempt. Such

people were more dangerous to the government than a regis-
tered Popish clergy.

Unhappily his arguments did not prevail against the passion
of the Archbishop of Armagh, who described the measure as
repugnant to Protestant noblemen, who were unwilling that
there should be legal recognition of that "proscribed and hated
sect". The Bill was killed, but the sympathy of the Irish people
for the Duke of Bedford was assured.

Without his intervention in Irish affairs, it is probable that a
revolution would have taken place, as promised to the French
by Irish Catholic expatriates. Instead, all, or almost all, the
Catholic nobility offered their support for the defence of the
country. In practice the invasion did not take place, since most
of the French ships were destroyed by the English fleet or forced
back by adverse weather. Only one detachment of the fleet
arrived off the coast of Ireland, after sailing round North
Scotland, and attacked Carrickfergus, but sailed away when
the strength of the forces which the Duke of Bedford could
deploy against them was realized.

The only major incident while the Duke was in Ireland was
a serious riot in Dublin, caused by a completely unfounded
rumour that an early union of the two countries was intended.
Doubtless the rumour was started by French agents, for it
coincided with the sailing of the French fleet on its ill-fated
expedition. The Duke authorized the use of cavalry to disperse
the rioters when the Mayor of Dublin refused to take effective
action but he wisely instructed the troops not to fire on the
people, but to disperse them by intimidation. He received the
formal thanks of both Houses of Parliament for his handling of
the crisis. The extraordinary progress made during the Duke's
period as Lord-Lieutenant towards pacifying the country is
shown by the peaceful nature of the general elections held after
he had dissolved Parliament by proclamation following the
death of George II in the autumn of 1760.

The Duke retired from the Lord-Lieutenancy of Ireland, as

required by the Constitution, on the King's death and held no office in the first ministry of George III's reign, but was summoned to the council by the King. He threw his weight into the cause of making an honourable peace with France before further inroads were made on English resources and was ultimately given extraordinary powers for negotiating the terms of the Treaty of Paris in 1763. The conclusion of this treaty between England, France, Spain and Portugal was due largely to the Duke's firmness and persistence and, above all, patience. Again and again he continued negotiations when agreement seemed impossible and ended by securing for his country all England's conquests in America, including Canada, and a number of the West Indian islands.

Immediately he had signed the treaty in June 1763 he was replaced at his own request by an ambassador at the Court of Versailles. He brought home with him a magnificent set of Sèvres china presented to the Duchess by the French King and a letter to George III from Louis, expressing admiration for the zeal and talent which he had brought to the accomplishment of his task. Writing to Lord Bute, the Duke said, "The French ministers have great confidence in me, as they know I am incapable of being the instrument of ill faith". That was literally the truth.

On his return he was drawn once more into the maelstrom of politics. The administration of Lord Bute was vastly unpopular and, failing to obtain the support of the Duke of Bedford, Bute resigned and was succeeded by George Grenville as Prime Minister. At the King's own suggestion the Duke was appointed President of the Council in this government. The coalition between Bedford and Grenville has become known as the Bedford Ministry. It was a Whig ministry but opposed by some of the most influential of the Whigs, including Pitt. Among the Acts it passed was one imposing customs duties on the American colonies and the iniquitous Stamp Act of 1765, which became law in spite of the strong protests of the American colonies. The ministry foundered on the shoals of the Regency Bill, Grenville's insistence on the exclusion of the King's mother from the Regency Council arousing so much opposition that he was forced to call on Lord Rockingham to form a ministry. "I am glad, my dear Lord," wrote the Duke to Lord Sandwich, "that the farce is at last at an end". And for the Duke it was the end.

During his retirement he received many honours, including the position of Chancellor of Dublin University in succession to the Duke of Cumberland. He was approached by Pitt (the Earl of Chatham) to join the Grafton Ministry in 1766 but declined. In the following year he was severely shocked by the death of his son Francis, who was killed in a hunting accident, and by that of his widowed daughter-in-law, who died a year later.

His last years as a statesman were clouded by the implacable enmity between him and Lord Bute. He had taken office after the Peace of Paris only on condition that Lord Bute was excluded from the government. The Duke's main objection to him was that he had not supported him with adequate vigour when he was negotiating the terms of the peace. Apart from that they had disagreed on almost every political topic.

The Duke's eyesight was now failing and in the two or three years before his death in 1771 he took no part in public life. His finest hours were undoubtedly as Lord-Lieutenant, or rather Viceroy, in Ireland but his parliamentary career was a distinguished one and he held together a strong body of Whig opinion for more than two decades. He was too uncompromising to be popular either with the King or with his colleagues in coalition but he had all the Russell talent as a negotiator and all the Russell desire for the prosperity of the country and the interests of the common man.

He was succeeded by his grandson, Francis, who was only six years of age when he succeeded to the Dukedom. Directly he took his seat in Parliament (his minority terminated in 1786) he showed that his ambition was to follow in his grandfather's footsteps.

He had a formal education at Westminster and Trinity College, Cambridge, and followed this with extended travel abroad. But he was not a bookman in any sense of the term and his command of English was limited. Yet by sheer determination he was known by the age of 26 as one of the most effective speakers in the House of Lords.

Francis was a close friend of the Prince of Wales, later Prince Regent, and acted virtually as "best man" at his wedding. In politics he followed the Whig tradition and was a staunch supporter of Charles James Fox, vociferously opposing the war with France in 1793. Edmund Burke's published opinion of him as "the Leviathan among the creatures of the Crown—huge as he is, he is still a creature" is unfair. It was coloured by indignation at the Duke's opposition to a proposal to grant him a pension! In fact, although always cordially received at Court, he showed considerable independence in judgment and sometimes alarmed the Prince of Wales with his advanced views.

Francis died suddenly in March 1802, still unmarried. With another twenty years of experience in parliamentary procedure he might have equalled or exceeded the achievements of the 4th Duke. Certainly in his brief period of public life he was a bulwark of Whig tradition and showed enormous promise of things to come. It was his misfortune that the Whig movement was at a low ebb during his parliamentary career.

His brother John, who succeeded him as 6th Duke, made an equally early start on a political career and was elected Member of Parliament for the borough of Tavistock in 1788, continuing to represent Tavistock until he took his seat in the House of Lords on his brother's death.

By the time he became Duke he already had three sons: Francis, who was born in 1788 and succeeded to the dukedom; William, who was born in 1790; and John (Lord John Russell, later 1st Earl Russell), born in 1792, all destined to have distinguished careers. He took up residence at Woburn and spent a great deal of his time there. He was instrumental in making several significant contributions to the science of agriculture, and concentrated on rearing a breed of sheep with the object of a greater weight and quality of wool. He was also an inveterate traveller, in Britain as well as abroad, an activity which in the 19th century was still open to the wealthy. It was characteristic of the Duke and his wife that minor hardships counted for nothing provided they could see and learn, visit friends and relations in distant parts of the country. They rode through the growing towns of the Midlands and North-west—Northampton, Leicester and Manchester—stayed for some time in the Lake District, and carried on into Scotland, where they entertained Walter Scott at Selkirk, travelled to Hamilton in the Clyde valley, and so by Stirling to Perth, to the Trossachs, and across the mountains to Speyside. Inverness was the furthest point they reached. They returned to Woburn after three months' absence. This journey was in effect a fact-finding mission, an effort to evaluate the conditions of the people in many parts of Britain. It had a great influence on Lord John, who accompanied them.

The Duke carried on faithfully the Whig traditions of the family. It was his misfortune, as it had been of Francis, that the Whig Party was out of office during much of his life, especially from 1807 onwards. Otherwise he would surely have been a leading member of the government. He was described by his contemporaries as a plain unpretending man who talked well in private life but was reserved in society. He was a great patron of the fine arts and one of the best farmers in England.

When the coalition "Ministry of All the Talents" was formed by Fox and Grenville in 1806 on the death of William Pitt, he was appointed Viceroy of Ireland and although his tenure of office was brief he made a start, however small a one, on mitigating the over-severe penal code which was one of the chief causes of Irish resentment then and later.

The Act of Union had only been passed six years before. The problem of relieving the disabilities of the Catholic people had been tackled by William Pitt immediately after the Act of Union but his proposal was greeted with cries of "No Popery", the traditional cry of English Protestants from the time of the Reformation until well into the 19th century. The result of Pitt's effort was merely to aggravate Parliament and offend the King.

When the Duke of Bedford arrived at Phoenix Park, the Vice-regal Lodge on the outskirts of Dublin, he soon had visual demonstration of the intense feeling among the Catholic population. He had the sensitivity to discern the people's distress and to disregard the synthetic gaiety of the English colony in Dublin. He realized that little could be done to improve the lot of the Irish people but he also foresaw that unless some religious freedom was granted the inevitable result would be insurrection or civil war.

Fox died in September of 1806, when the administration reverted to Lord Grenville. The ministry was concerned almost entirely with war; indeed the only important civil legislation carried out by this government was the passing of the Act for the Abolition of the Slave Trade. The news in the autumn of 1806 was of the defeat of the Prussians at the Battle of Jena and the Berlin Decrees issued by Napoleon which, if they could have been carried out, would have spelt the doom of British international trade. Lord Grenville's answer to the Berlin Decrees was an order in council prohibiting trade with French ports.

In view of these stirring events Ireland slipped into the background of public consciousness. Even so, Lord Grenville felt obliged to give some attention to the Duke of Bedford's Irish despatches. In these the Duke was true to his conscience as Viceroy, to the policy of the Whig Party and to the traditions of his family. He informed Lord Grenville that it was essential on the grounds of humanity and utility to make an immediate start on solving the Catholic problem by admitting Catholics into the British Army and by employing Catholics as sheriffs in Ireland. The former was the more difficult of these suggestions. Before the Union an act had been passed allowing Roman Catholics to hold commissions in the Irish Army and Militia but the act forbidding them to hold commissions in the British Army was still in force. Since the Union, Irish contingents were liable to be transferred. The Duke of Bedford's contention, which had been urged on him again and again by Irishmen, was that a Roman Catholic officer serving in accordance with the law in an Irish regiment would be liable to penalties if his regiment were posted to England.

Lord Grenville duly presented to Parliament a bill relieving Catholic officers from these disabilities. The Tory argument was that by the Mutiny Act a Catholic officer was compelled to perform his duty as an officer wherever he might be serving and this protected him from legal penalties if he were serving in England. There was clearly a majority against the bill in the House of Commons. The King, who still wielded a major influence, expressed his displeasure. The bill was defeated but Grenville refused to give an undertaking that the Irish Catholic question would not be raised again. "The Ministry of All the Talents" therefore resigned and the appointment of the Duke of Portland as Prime Minister began a period of exclusively Tory government which lasted for twenty years.

The Duke, in accordance with precedent, resigned on the fall of the government. He returned to Woburn in a mood of frustration and disappointment, leaving Irish people grateful for his efforts on their behalf but more determined than ever to persevere with their efforts to win justice from the British government.

That proved to be the end of the Duke's political career. He remained a powerful figure in the Whig Party, inevitably so because of his wealth and personal influence, but he rarely spoke in the House of Lords and concentrated on the development of the Woburn estate, and to a lesser degree on that of the family property in London and Devonshire. Indirectly his influence was greatest in the enthusiasm which he kindled in his son, Lord John, and the pride he took in the latter's skill as a speaker and success as a budding statesman.

He finally renounced a political career in 1827, when to his great sorrow he found himself politically divided for the first time from his youngest son. A crisis had arisen when Lord Liverpool, who had been Prime Minister without a break since 1812 and whose ministry had been returned at the general election in the autumn of 1826, had a severe stroke and resigned. The King thereupon asked Canning to form a ministry, but the selection was unpopular; among many leading Tories the Duke of Wellington declined to serve under him. Canning thereupon turned to the Whigs. Although many notable Whigs were against the scheme, he succeeded in forming a mixed ministry with the support of some influential members of the Whig Party. This emphasized the inherent differences in the Party. The strength of the Ministry was never seriously put to the test, for at the end of the first session of Parliament Canning died suddenly.

The short-lived Canning ministry, however, had not only emphasized the divergence of views among leading Whigs but had also brought to light a serious difference within the Russell family. While the Duke was strongly opposed to Whig co-operation with Canning, both his sons then sitting in Parliament, Lord Tavistock and Lord John Russell (who incidentally was now representing the Irish constituency of Bandon Bridge) threw in their lot with Canning. Though neither took office in his ministry both supported him to the full, Lord John going so far as to say publicly that he was very happy to see Canning in office without the restrictions of traditional Tory policy.

The Duke's feelings are clear from letters he wrote to Lord John and quoted in Spencer Walpole's *Life of Lord John Russell*. In August he wrote, "It is my misfortune to differ from you and I hate differing from those I love." Earlier, in April, he had written, "All I hear upon politics so disgusts and dispirits me that I almost wish to hear nothing further on so painful a subject. I consider the hope of carrying the Catholic bill as now at an end." (The removal of some of the disabilities of Irish Catholics had always been one of the main planks of the Duke's political ambitions.) Finally he wrote once again to his son in the following May, "I have closed my political book and will content myself with assuring you that I have no feelings either of bitterness or displeasure. Literary subjects are far pleasanter than those connected with politics."

The Duke had resigned himself to playing little part in politics after his resignation as Viceroy of Ireland. But this deep-felt disagreement with his sons, and particularly with Lord John was too much. He not only took no further part in politics but showed no further interest. It was the beginning of the end for one of the most conscientious and conventional Dukes of Bedford. He had done much to improve the living conditions of his tenants. He had shown himself alive to the paramount need for parliamentary reform. He had made few enemies and many friends, and had upheld all the traditions of his party and his family. Yet circumstances conspired to frustrate his every ambition. He had a stroke in 1835 while in Scotland and never completely recovered. He died four years later.

CHAPTER NINE

Farming Reformers

EVEN THOUGH the Russell family has taken a less active part in politics since the early part of the 19th century, it has achieved as much success in agricultural reform as earlier members did in public affairs. The Woburn and Thorney estates were ideal, because of their size, position and soils, for large-scale experiment in improved methods of farming. In a century and a half, during which slump has followed boom, and boom, slump, in rapid succession, the Dukes have led the way in making the best of available resources and in gradual rationalization of farming. They have introduced and tested many new crops and new ways of working the land, with the accent during the last fifty years on farm mechanization. They were for generations pioneers in breeding improved strains of sheep. Though today Thorney is no longer a Russell estate, Woburn continues to be a model of large-scale farming.

They have had the capital to finance experiments on a far more ambitious scale than most landowners and have had the interest to watch progress with a critical eye, employing consultants (especially in the 19th century when farming became for the first time a science) drawn from the ranks of brilliant men who needed only support of landowners such as the Dukes of Bedford to make a significant contribution to the rural economy.

The Russells' interest in agriculture goes back, of course, much further than the beginning of the 19th century. Every Earl and Duke in one sense has been a farmer. The management of the estates was a major preoccupation even with men

ings, 12th Duke of Bed-
father of the present
, succeeded during the
nd World War when
urn Abbey had been
1 over by the Govern-
ment

Bertrand Russell, 3rd Earl
Russell, philosopher and reformer, possesses many of
the characteristics which
have distinguished the
Russell family through
nearly six centuries

John, 13th Duke of Bedford, maintains family traditions by "selling Woburn to the world"

such as the 4th Duke, whom most people think of as a statesman. He was essentially a countryman, in spite of the distinction
he achieved in politics. He made Woburn a true counterpart of
Bedford House in Bloomsbury and used it for extensive entertaining, delighting his guests with the wonderful collection of
furniture and decorations which he imported from India and
China. He also had the gardens remodelled, adding gazebos and
classical temples, the fashionable foibles of the 18th century,
combining business with pleasure when he walked and talked
with his political guests in these agreeable surroundings.

But his chief interest was in the management of the estates.
He read widely on agriculture and employed in a consultative
capacity some of the most forward-thinking of 18th-century
agriculturists, personally supervising all the experiments that
were made. He also extended the Woburn estate by purchase,
recognizing, as the 1st Duke had done, that the larger an estate
the more chance it had of being run on an economic basis. Both
were pioneers of rationalization in land usage, both remarkably
successful for their times.

The policy of expansion, linked closely with the idea of
better utilization of the land, had been carried on vigorously
in the years following the death of the 1st Duke, as laid down
in his will, but the 4th Duke did far more than carry out what
he was required to do. He took every opportunity to extend the
Woburn estate even if, as sometimes happened, this meant
selling land in Devonshire, where the Russell estate was not
nearly so closely knit as in Bedfordshire, or for that matter as the
Fenland estate of Thorney, and did not offer the same opportunities for improvement. By the end of the 19th century the
Thorney estate approached 20,000 acres in extent and the
Woburn estate, excluding Woburn Park, exceeded 30,000 acres.

The revival of arable farming in the 17th century certainly
derived in part from the Elizabethan interest in gardening,
which became a major preoccupation among wealthy people
during the following century. Like architecture, horticulture

14

was still not the exclusive province of the professional. Much of the impetus which lay behind intensive cultivation sprang from the creation of private gardens and the introduction of new fruits and vegetables from the Continent. It is interesting to recall that the potato, the very staple of rural life in later centuries, was a luxury crop confined almost exclusively to the gardens of the wealthy at the beginning of the 17th century and had not even made its bow as a farm crop.

The 3rd Earl came into possession of Moor Park in Hertford-shire and with the Countess made it his home; its gardens were almost his only interest for the last ten years of his life. The Moor Park gardens in their maturity won the highest possible praise. They followed in many ways a formal plan based on Italian originals but apart from the usual terraces and grottoes, fountains and statuary they contained a great number of rare English and continental plants. It is significant that the Italian horticulturist Castel Vetri dedicated to the Countess his treatise on fruit and vegetables that were then cultivated for the table in his own country. The Moor Park gardens were a model which was copied in great houses for more than fifty years. Their real significance lay in the proof they gave that non-native plants, fruits and vegetables could be cultivated by intensive methods on English soil.

The prominent part which the 4th Earl and the 1st Duke took in the grandiose scheme of draining the Fens has been described in a previous chapter. Carving out a great estate from the Fenlands, however, was one thing. Ensuring its profitable use was another. The 5th Earl during his long residence at Thorney made a most valuable contribution to the progress of English farming methods. At first people thought of the re-claimed Fens as good pasture-land and nothing else. The Earl and his agricultural advisers recognized that it included some of the richest land in England and transformed a great deal of it into arable fields.

There had still been little research, and none on a national scale, into farming as opposed to horticulture. Much of the success of the Thorney estate was due to the influence of Walloon families that settled there as tenants and brought with them the inherited skill of the Low Countries, especially in corn cultivation and the rearing of sheep. The new land won from the Fens was not subject to the archaic system of cultivation which derived from the open-field system of the Anglo-Saxons and still bedevilled farming activity in the midland counties. Enclosure could be and was carried out immediately and this showed the great advantage of enclosure allied with the outlawing of the "privilege" of village farmers to pasture their flocks on the stubble fields. This custom made sowing of spring crops worthless, since the cattle and sheep consumed the sown crop. On the Thorney estate clover was commonly under-sown, while experiments showed that this made it quite necessary to leave fields fallow in alternate years, and supplied a valuable additional source of fodder.

So successful had this new method of arable farming proved before the 1st Duke died that its principle was extended as rapidly as possible to the Woburn estate. Its success accelerated, if it did not originate, the great work of Georgian enclosure of the common fields and waste land.

Wriothesley, the 2nd Duke, maintained the Russell tradition so well set by his grandfather. He had only recently come of age when he succeeded and survived for only nine years, but in that short time he earned a sparkling reputation as a husbandman and horticulturist. When the Earl of Orford visited him in the autumn of 1708 he was impressed by the improvements which had been made to the park and grounds at Woburn. Writing to the Duke's mother, he said, "Your son busies himself with improving his park and grounds and has the reputation of a great husbandman", and implied that the Duke was so absorbed in supervising the work on the estate that he could not tear himself away even for a short visit to the Earl's home at Chippenham.

Wriothesley certainly made further courageous experiments in domesticating foreign plants and often tried to persuade Sir Hans Sloane to inspect his work at Woburn. Writing in 1709 to Sir Hans, he said he was about to receive "a great collection of rarities and particularly a large collection of Ranunculae from Candia such as was never before seen in England". Of all the 18th-century Dukes he was the most passionately fond of the country and most sincere in his interest in farming for profit as well as for pleasure.

Even so, John, the 4th Duke, made more solid progress towards the ideal of transforming the Woburn farm-lands into one of the most productive and well-managed estates in England. His lifetime was pre-eminently one of transition in agriculture throughout the country. During the latter half of the 18th century the first changes which ultimately became known as the industrial revolution were already affecting the balance between rural and urban life. The towns were growing, the population was increasing, and there was an urgent national as well as local need for farmers to produce larger quantities of food to feed the people of the towns.

This made apparent the equally urgent need for agricultural research. The time was long past when overworked land could be abandoned and new fields ploughed. The scientific rotation of crops had already been seen as a partial remedy for the wastage of land. However, there was no consensus of opinion about the way in which land should be treated to avoid exhausting it. Many farmers, especially in remote areas, continued to follow the conservative methods which had proved to be inadequate. Some of the greater landowners were apathetic, either because their main interest was not in the land or because they could see no need for reform at a time when agriculture was booming. In bad years a poor farmer could make a good living, since the price of corn became so high that many townspeople were reduced to the point of starvation.

John recognized that reform in farming was just as much in

the national interest as reform in government. He determined
to make the Woburn estate an example which others would
follow, just as they had followed the horticultural example set
by his ancestors. He instituted with his private resources a
programme of research which in later generations became the
province of the government. He was quick to see the far-reaching possibilities of the rotation methods proposed by Lord
Townshend ("Turnip" Townshend), of Norfolk, who was the
first to popularize turnip cultivation. Turnips had been grown
in many gardens for decades, almost certainly in the gardens of
Woburn and Thorney, but as in the case of the potato, commercial cultivation had lagged far behind. By 1750 almost the
whole of the arable land on the Bedford estates had been turned
over to the four-year rotation—corn, clover, turnips, fallow.

This made all and every difference to the rural economy. It
is not an exaggeration to say that it doubled food production
in a quarter of a century. The four-year rotation at one swoop
reduced the non-productive acreage by 25 per cent, since a
field would be fallow only three times in twelve years instead of
four. It increased the possibility of working the same land
continuously for long periods, partly through the beneficial
effect of grass and clovers on the soil and partly by the greater
availability of manure from the larger number of livestock it
was possible to maintain by using the turnip crop as winter feed.

The 4th Duke was also a pioneer in scientific forestry. By the
beginning of the 18th century few additions had been made
since the later middle ages to the number of useful trees,
although a great number of exotics had been imported for
beautifying park-lands. The English forests of oak had declined
with the building of a strong navy in the 16th century—to be
more precise, the demands made on the surviving forests at the
beginning of that century were more than they could sustain.
The timber of the Weald of Kent and Sussex, for instance, had
been depleted to feed the medieval iron furnaces. Everywhere
timber had been used for building when, as usual in the forest

area, no suitable sources of local stone existed. Commentators like John Evelyn had complained bitterly of the changing face of England due to deforestation.

It was a problem too big for ordinary landowners to tackle. In fact it was never tackled conclusively until forestry became a government province. But the Duke of Bedford at least started the series of experiments on which 20th-century forestry is based. In 1743 he personally supervised the planting of a wood known as the Evergreens. This wood contained numerous species of pines and firs for purposes of comparing their rate of growth and the value of the timber yielded. He was assisted by Philip Miller, previously the gardener of the Company of Apothecaries at Chelsea, who became one of the most respected as well as one of the most forward-looking "men of trees" in the 18th century.

The 11th Duke records a characteristic anecdote of his forebear, who was determined to use his own methods in nurturing his beloved evergreens. When the plantation needed thinning he instructed the head gardener on the extent of the thinning required. The gardener protested, "Your Grace, I cannot possibly do what you desire. It would destroy the plantation and injure my reputation as a planter." John always a slightly imperious person, said, "Do what I tell you and then I will take care of your reputation." That is precisely what he did. Evergreens was thinned, and incidentally badly damaged, but a board was nailed to a post facing the road, carrying the inscription, "This plantation has been thinned by John, Duke of Bedford, contrary to the advice and opinion of his gardener."

The landowners of the 18th century, and still more of the first half of the 19th century, were proud to be farmers. In spite of the rumblings of the industrial revolution agriculture was still Britain's most important industry. Until recently it had been its only industry. The great landowners felt it their duty as well as their pleasure to lead the way in reform. C. S. Orwin makes the interesting point that the noble landlords of the period were so proud of the improved strains of livestock which they were instrumental in breeding that people like the Duke of Bedford and the Earl of Leicester (Coke of Norfolk) were "well content to be portrayed as adjuncts to their prize stock and in farmyard scenes" by artists such as Stubbs and James Ward.

The 4th Duke also left his mark on the countryside of Bedfordshire and Cambridgeshire by the amount of new building he inspired, for by the latter half of the 18th century, partly no doubt owing to the drift of workers from country to town, there was a growing consciousness of the need to improve farm workers' cottages and the homes of the tenant farmers. The number of Georgian farmhouses and cottages on the Woburn estate and to a lesser extent on the Thorney estate (many of which were rebuilt again during the 19th century) are testimony to the interest which the 4th Duke and his successor took in the welfare of the men and women working with them on their estates. This was, of course, in accordance with the precedent set when the 2nd Earl endowed a free school at Woburn.

The boom in farming continued almost without a break right up to the end of the Napoleonic Wars. In spite of the lavish expenditure necessitated by modernization the estates were showing a good profit, most of which was ploughed back into the land. Charity in a sense begins at home and it was the 4th Duke who was responsible for the rebuilding of Woburn Abbey. Until 1745 considerable parts of the medieval building had survived, while the Elizabethan mansion which had been built on the site of the abbey and incorporated some of the fabric of the monastic buildings had been little altered. The cloisters of the abbey were in use as stables.

In 1746 John made a clean sweep. The cloisters and the surviving parts of the monastic church were demolished and the conventual buildings which were in use as farm buildings were rebuilt. The Elizabethan mansion was replaced by a new house, substantially the house that stands today, designed by Henry

Flitcroft in an unusually restrained style for the period. It was smaller and plainer than several other 18th century ducal residences, but was in keeping with the character of the 4th Duke, who in spite of the fact that the Russell wealth was probably in real terms as great as at any time, always discouraged wasteful extravagance of any kind.

The town of Woburn had been badly damaged by fire in 1724. It was a place that had grown up at the gates of the medieval abbey and became a fairly prosperous market centre under the auspices of the Earls and Dukes of Bedford. It was rebuilt piecemeal but much of it dates from the lifetime of the 4th Duke and includes many fine houses and groups of Georgian cottages far in advance of village and small town homes in many parts of midland England.

Francis, the 5th Duke, was just as much an enthusiast for agricultural experiment as the 4th Duke. He was the eldest grandson of the 4th Duke, his father, also christened Francis, having been killed in a hunting accident when the future Duke was only two years old. His mother died a year later, it is said of a broken heart. He had two brothers, John, a year younger, and William, who was born after his father died. Francis was only six years old when he succeeded to the title in 1771.

In the years that he was responsible for the management of the Bedford estates—he came of age in 1786 and lived until 1802—he laid the foundations of another "bloodless revolution" at Woburn, though what he did followed naturally, perhaps inevitably, from the pioneer work of his predecessors. He is best known for three phases of his work, each of which was designed to have a major influence on the developing of farming. He inaugurated the Woburn sheep-shearings, he founded a local agricultural society and started a model farm of 300 acres devoted entirely to the growing of experimental crops and the use of experimental methods of fortifying the soil.

This for the end of the 18th century represented research on the grand scale. The Woburn model farm became the prototype of experimental farms established in the 19th and 20th centuries. The Woburn agricultural society was the forerunner of the Royal Agricultural Society, while the Woburn sheep-shearings became the principal centre of agricultural interest in the Midlands. The sheep-shearings were the equivalent of the agricultural shows which today are held in almost every county. They provided a stimulus for the development of breeding, infusing the spirit of competition. Many hundreds of exhibitors attended Woburn each year and although sheep-breeding was given pride of place at the festival, there were competitions and prizes for cattle and horses, and also for ploughing.

The tenants of the Bedford estate, of course, took an active part and were encouraged by the Duke to concentrate on breeding improved strains, often with his direct financial assistance. It was a time when many of the traditional farming implements had become out of date and an important function of the annual meetings was the introduction of new types of implements, especially ploughs. Robert Salmon, who was surveyor to the Dukes of Bedford from 1790 to 1821, was responsible himself for many improved implements which were first publicized at the Woburn sheep-shearings.

Perhaps the greatest tribute to the advanced methods of Duke Francis is that he initiated a prolonged series of experiments in the growing of new and improved species of grass in 1797. A hundred years later these experiments were still being continued by the Royal Agricultural Society on the Woburn estate.

The first sheep-shearing was held in June 1797. Subsequent meetings were held in the same month every year until as Arthur Young, the Secretary of the Board of Agriculture and one of the greatest protagonists of innovation in farming, said, "It became by far the most respectable agricultural meeting ever seen in England, that is, in the whole world, attended by nobility, gentry, farmers and graziers from various parts of the three kingdoms, from many countries in Europe, and also from

America." It was Arthur Young, too, who attributed to Francis, the 5th Duke, who from its foundation was President of the Smithfield Club, "singular skill and high success in ameliorating the breeds of livestock". He was utterly sincere when he wrote, "The agricultural world never sustained a greater individual loss than the husbandry of this empire has suffered by the death of the Duke of Bedford."

One claim often made for the Woburn sheep-shearings is that they were the first festivals of their kind in Britain. It is a justified claim so far as a truly international gathering is concerned but Sir John Sinclair, the first President of the Board of Agriculture, was instrumental in arranging a local sheep-shearing festival at Queensferry on the Forth in 1791, six years before the Woburn festival was inaugurated.

Francis was never married but he showed little of the indifference to his surroundings that one associates with the true bachelor. Guided by Lady Maynard—the famous Nancy Parsons before her marriage to Viscount Maynard—who acted as housekeeper for him for many years, he transformed the interior of the new Woburn Abbey into a far more comfortable and elegant home than it had been in the time of the 4th Duke. Much of the present decoration of the Abbey is due to his genius and that of Henry Holland, one of the finest architects of the age, who collaborated with him.

John, the 6th Duke, brother and, as we have seen, near contemporary of Francis, held Woburn and Thorney during one of the most critical periods in English agricultural history, 1802–39. Though he may have lacked some of the enthusiasm of Duke Francis, he at least maintained a keen interest throughout his life and continued with all the experimental work that Francis had initiated. He succeeded his brother as President of the Smithfield Club but resigned in 1821 over differences of policy. The Duke took the view that the main object of the Club in publicizing methods for improving the strains of beef cattle had been achieved and that it no longer served a useful purpose.

He also discontinued the Woburn sheep-shearings, partly because the management of this festival had become extremely difficult owing to the number of exhibitors and the crowds of interested people who were attracted to it at a time when shortage of accommodation was acute. The sheep-shearing festival had indeed achieved a great deal both on a national and international scale and had been responsible directly for the formation of a number of agricultural societies based on the Woburn local society. It was a tribute to the esteem in which the Duke was held as a farmer that he was invited to become a Governor of the Royal Agricultural Society in 1838 and was elected Vice-President.

The years in which he was responsible for the management of the Russell estates were made notable by the final and highly successful assault on the remaining commons and wastes. What the Georgian commissioners and innumerable Acts of Parliament for enclosure during the 18th century had failed to achieve was made good. A great deal of the Woburn estate consists of sandy soil. Where it approaches the summit of the ridge it was unsuitable for intensive agriculture until the science of soil improvement revolutionized the scene in the early part of the 19th century.

By the time Duke Francis died virtually every acre capable of being cultivated by the new methods had been enclosed. It paid dividends, too, in contrast with many of the commons enclosed in this period in the south country, such as Bromley Common, which never repaid the work of improving them after enclosure in terms of corn or meat but became residential areas all too soon covered in bricks and mortar. The improved land on the Woburn estate soon made a worthwhile contribution to the aggregate of food produced and has continued to do so to the present day.

The first decades of the 19th century were, in fact, one of the high spots in the history of the Woburn estates and the Duke, who carried on the family policy of purchasing farms and even cottages in the areas adjacent to the original Woburn estate, became probably as influential as any single landowner in Midland England.

Francis, the 7th Duke, spanned the period 1839–61. Although many expected the repeal of the Corn Laws in 1846 to lead to a decline in English farming, the fear was not immediately realized and these two decades were marked by a resilience in agriculture that has rarely been matched. It was in a sense the swan song of agriculture based on the ideal of English farmers producing food for the English people. For several fortuitous reasons foreign competition did not become as severe as was expected. The importation of foreign wheat relieved the possibility of famine but did not unduly depress the prices paid to English farmers, or at least not to such an extent that they were unable, as later, to compete. This was partly because many mechanical and chemical aids were available to them before they were to their competitors. Canadian agriculture was only in its infancy and desperately short of manpower, while many of the railways which later made the transport of imported grain easy and inexpensive were still in the stage of projection when the Corn Laws were repealed.

So with rents relatively high and the tenant farmers prosperous, the Woburn and Thorney estates enjoyed a considerable surplus of revenue which the 7th Duke employed for the most part in still further improving the estates. He was one of the first to pioneer new methods to combat under-drainage, in particular the cylindrical clay pipe which was invented in 1843 and which replaced the rather primitive drains which were previously popular and consisted of underground conduits for surplus water made only with the help of stones and brushwood buried about 2ft. under the surface.

Amazingly it took more than a decade for the new principle to be adopted on a wide scale. The encouraging result achieved in Bedfordshire was one of the deciding factors leading to the general adoption of a rational form of land drainage. The cost, of course, was high and the pioneers were necessarily the great landowners such as the Duke of Bedford. However, the cost was quickly seen to be repaid many times over and the work of the Duke of Bedford and a few others led to the formation of Land Drainage and Improvement Companies which advanced the necessary capital to landlords who could not meet the cost out of their own resources.

The Duke was a Governor of the Royal Agricultural Society from his accession until his death. In his official capacity and from his personal interest in agriculture he was closely associated with Dr. Gilbert in the latter's investigations into improved methods of fattening cattle. He put at the disposal of the Society and of Dr. Gilbert the whole resources of Woburn Park farm, giving financial as well as advisory assistance in a series of successful experiments.

William, the 8th Duke, was a semi-invalid and unable to take an active part in the management of the estates, which he delegated to his cousin Hastings Russell, who on his death succeeded him as 9th Duke of Bedford. He, and Herbrand the 11th Duke after him (the 10th Duke, Sackville, lived only two years after the accession to the title), were responsible for the management of the estates during a period in which the whole character of English farming changed from a state of thriving boom to one of neglect and almost fatal depression. It was a tribute to both that the Russell land in Bedfordshire survived the ordeal and was ready to play its full part in averting the food crisis of the two world wars of the 20th century. The cost of maintaining it in terms of capital depletion was considerable, all the more so because monetary reserves had not been built up in the years of the plenty but diverted, as we have already seen, to the improvement of the land and the welfare of tenants.

This policy was followed by Duke Hastings on a scale at least equal to that adopted by his predecessors. A contemporary expert, Dr. Voelcker, described him as "possessed with the best knowledge of the details of farming of any nobleman in the country". That is probably true but he is remembered most clearly by his unswerving work to improve social life on the estates. He was a great builder and supporter of schools and churches. On the Woburn estate expenditure exceeded £8,000 on these two objects alone in every year between 1865 and 1869, reaching £16,000 in 1867 and £23,000 in 1868, and exceeding £11,000 again in 1877. These are terrific sums when allowance is made for the fall in value of money during the last hundred years. The modern equivalent would be more nearly ten times greater.

The 11th Duke said at the end of the century, "The Bedford system of land management has not been carried on with gain as the principal object, which has been to realize among the agricultural population such a standard of moral and of physical wellbeing as would have been unobtainable by strict adherence to commercial lines of administration." No one could quarrel with his summing up of the situation.

Before the Education Act of 1870, which introduced the School Board system, there was no legal obligation for landlords to educate the children of agricultural workers but the social obligation to do so was accepted as one of the conditions of ownership. After 1870 the social obligation no longer existed but the charitable work of the 9th Duke continued without pause. He believed that the minds of children were affected by their physical environment and regarded it as a personal responsibility to ensure that they had healthy conditions in their schoolrooms as well as in their homes. When the Education Act was passed he made over no less than 24 school-houses to the authorities at a nominal rent of 10s. each and the estate continued to keep all these schools in repair. During his tenure of the Bedford estates more than £16,000 was spent on schools in Bedfordshire and Buckinghamshire, and nearly £3,000 on the Thorney estate.

Many of the village churches on the estates were restored and enlarged at his expense. One of the most outstanding and still present tributes to the social work of the Russells in the latter part of the 19th century is the parish church of Woburn, which was erected in 1868 at a cost of £35,000. It is one of the more successful small churches in the style of the Victorian Gothic revival, its vaulted stone roof in keeping with its 13th-century design.

The real break came between 1875 and 1880. A world-wide economic depression was accompanied in England by a series of years in which the weather was adverse to farming—far worse than at any time within living memory—culminating in 1879 in a summer which had greater rainfall than usual and a remarkable deficiency of sunshine. The harvest was a failure, even by the standards of those times, when harvest home was a very genuine thanksgiving. In 1879 the yield of corn on many of the Bedford estate farms was reduced by more than 25 per cent. In some parts of the Midlands and eastern England the yield was reduced by as much as 50 per cent.

Inevitably rebates of rent had to be granted. Even so, many farmers failed and new tenants were sometimes difficult to find. This in turn led to a reduction of the land under plough and a corresponding increase in permanent pasture. The change was accelerated by a rapid increase in the supplies of wheat available from Canada.

Just as Duke Hastings was not persuaded by the passing of the Education Act to cease his work for education, so this period of rural depression did not deter him or his successors from pressing on with their schemes for land improvement, even though the cost of the work had to be met from capital rather than from revenue.

The measure of the crisis on the Bedford estates is well illustrated by the remissions of rent which were granted to tenants on the Thorney estate after 1879. In no year until the end of the century was the nominal rent charged. In 1879, 1887 and 1894 the remission was 50 per cent. In most other years it was more than 25 per cent. In 1881 all the farms on the estate were revalued and the nominal rents reduced by an average of 10 per cent.

Figures have been published which give the net income of both the Woburn estate and the Thorney estate between 1816 and 1895. In 1816 the net income from the former was £23,000, reaching a peak of more than £25,000 in 1840. By 1866 it had fallen to £4,000 and there were deficits in the following two years, with recovery only in 1877. From then until 1895 there was a deficit in six years which amounted to more than £12,000 in 1879 and nearly £10,000 in 1894. The story of the Thorney estate is similar. The net income in 1820 was between £12,000 and £13,000, reaching a maximum of £15,000 in 1851. This was converted into a deficit of more than £2,000 in 1879 and nearly £5,000 in 1881. Actually during the whole of the 19th century the average net income derived from the Woburn estate (excluding expenditure on Woburn and its park) amounted to rather less than one per cent of the capital outlay in the same period on new works and permanent improvements. Perhaps the 11th Duke was right in saying that the landowner was the greatest loser of all the classes interested in agriculture by the mere fact of responsible possession. One can see quite clearly the considerations that led him to sanction the disposal of the Thorney estate.

Two major schemes of research complete the story of the Russells as agricultural reformers. The Woburn experimental farm was founded in 1875 after the passing of the Agricultural Holdings Act, which provided for compensation for outgoing tenants on the unexhausted value of soil enrichment which they had carried out at their own expense. This brought into sharp focus the inadequate knowledge of the long-term effects of fertilizers—knowledge which was essential if the arbitration tribunals established under the Act was to function efficiently and fairly. The council of the Royal Agricultural Society, after long deliberation, decided that it could not afford a grant for an experimental station, whereupon the Duke agreed to assume the whole cost of the undertaking, which was directed by a committee of the Royal Agricultural Society. What was intended as a temporary undertaking became a long-standing one which progressed from the object of evaluating various manures to comprehensive experiments with the enormous number of new fertilizers that came on the market.

The other experiment was begun in 1895, when the Woburn research farm was already twenty years old. This was an experimental fruit-farm designed to investigate in a scientific manner all matters related to fruit growing, both of practical and of scientific interest. At the end of the 19th century no similar station existed in England apart from the Chiswick gardens of the Royal Horticultural Society. It was yet one more example of a private individual filling a long-felt want in the absence of state intervention. Today, although government intervention on a national scale in farming has become a reality not envisaged in the first decade of the present century, the Woburn estate still includes scores of farms which can reasonably claim to be the equal of any comparable farms in Britain.

CHAPTER TEN

Victorian Statesman

THE DUKES OF BEDFORD took a less active part in political life during the 19th century but the traditions of the family were maintained by Lord John Russell, who was the third son of the 6th Duke and the first Russell to become Prime Minister. His career was a projection of the lives of his father and his brother Francis, the 7th Duke. Although there were at least two occasions in his political life on which he and his father were in disagreement, the 6th Duke was intensely proud of him, helped him in his early career with every means at his disposal, and shared with him in his triumphs and disappointments. He and his brother, the 7th Duke, were firm friends for most of their lives. When Francis was a Member of Parliament before succeeding to the dukedom he and John were almost invariably at one in politics as in their personal relationship, while after his succession Francis took over the role of elder brother.

Lord John, who became Earl Russell, was essentially a Russell—a Whig and a protagonist of parliamentary reform and of religious toleration and a strong supporter of the cause of the Irish people. The family hero was for him, as for all the later Russells, William, Lord Russell, on whom he wrote an elaborate memoir. But Lord John was never a rebel, as some of his ancestors had been. He was a man who strove to achieve his political ends by parliamentary action. He became more and more conventional as he grew older. Before then he had carved for himself a permanent niche in English history as the originator of the first reform bill, a tremendous achievement in the face of the opposition from members of his own party as well as from the Tories.

Like every Russell, Lord John was born to greatness. The paramount influence of the landowners, among whom the Duke of Bedford was counted one of the most influential, is difficult to realize in the 20th century. The family's wealth—for it was still one of the richest families in the country—was also a great help, though Lord John was not himself a wealthy man by the standards of the time. The mere fact of being one of the Duke of Bedford's sons assured him a place in Parliament and marked him out for rapid promotion if he showed ability and integrity. Lord John had both of these qualities in full measure, so his success as a politician was a foregone conclusion.

The problems of government at the beginning of the 19th century were enough to dim any lesser man's enthusiasm. The root of the trouble, which came very near to provoking civil war and did, in fact, lead to some bloodshed, was that Parliament failed to keep pace with the changing temper of the people. A majority in the House of Commons could be assured by the landed proprietors. By no stretch of the imagination could Parliament be said to represent the people. Although King George III and King George IV were constitutional monarchs, they wielded sufficient influence to be able to negative reform measures which were distasteful to them. Even Queen Victoria, though she recognized far more clearly than either of the last two Georges the responsibilities as well as the privileges of a constitutional sovereign, still had considerable influence on the general tenor of legislation.

In the early years of the 19th century at least three hundred members of the House of Commons were "nominated" by landed proprietors. Indeed the return of these three hundred members was dependent on the whim of not more than 150 landowners. Many "rotten boroughs" were entitled to return two members to Parliament, although there was either one effective elector or only a handful. The classical example was

Old Sarum, which had not a single inhabitant (though it retained substantial ruins of its medieval walls) but had the right to return two members to Parliament. At the other end of the scale the growing industrial towns, such as Manchester and Birmingham, were without representation. Corruption was commonplace, in the sense that many aspiring politicians purchased nomination. Alternatively their families purchased whole boroughs at a price out of proportion to their real value.

While nothing was done to remedy the nonsense that this state of affairs made of representative government, political consciousness was growing, especially in the manufacturing towns, in which a well-educated middle class had already made its appearance. Several abortive attempts at reform had been made in the 18th century but every one had been overruled in Parliament with the approval of the King. In 1785 William Pitt, at the height of his ministerial reputation, brought forward a motion by which it was proposed to disenfranchise 36 of the rotten boroughs and to transfer their representation to the counties and to London. This was a mild enough measure, yet it was defeated by 248 to 174 and might well have caused Pitt's downfall. Then in 1793, while Pitt was still Prime Minister, Lord Grey proposed a rather more sweeping measure of parliamentary reform but was defeated by 232 to 41.

After that nothing was attempted, let alone achieved, until Lord John made reform his primary objective. Even the enlightened politicians who had been sympathetic to Pitt's measure and that of Lord Grey became alarmed by the spread of Radicalism. While what was called the spirit of anarchy was abroad it seemed to them inopportune, in Pitt's own words, to make hazardous experiments. No one in authority paid any heed to the increasing number of Hampden clubs pledged to use every possible means to ensure a wider representation of the people. The memory of the French Revolution was still fresh. Many feared that any concessions to popular feeling might encourage revolutionary action. It is difficult to follow the logic of this position but it is one that was made many times in Parliament. In any case, Parliament was increasingly concerned with war. This tended to relegate domestic issues to the background, while the victories of the Duke of Wellington resulted in great personal influence for a man who was a diehard Tory.

Another matter of vital importance to England at the beginning of the 19th century was the threatening position in Ireland. The Act for the Union of Great Britain and Ireland had come into effect in 1800. It meant nothing to the majority of the Irish people. A repetition of the rebellion of 1798 which ended in the bloody defeat of the rebels at Vinegar Hill was a distinct and ever present possibility. The Irish problem was linked with the Catholic problem but all proposals to relieve the Catholics of their disabilities came to nothing. A recommendation by the Duke of Bedford as Viceroy of Ireland to relieve Irish Roman Catholic officers from the disability of the law that prevented Catholics from holding commissions in the English army led, as described in the previous chapter, to the fall of Lord Grenville's ministry.

In the light of the vast changes that have taken place in less than a century and a half, it is easy to say that the leaders of English society were doing their utmost to cut their own throats. Yet the ruling class of England, and incidentally of Ireland, the landowners, believed as sincerely in their right to govern as medieval kings believed in their divine right. The fact remains that there was no denouement in England comparable with the French Revolution. Without the work of Lord John Russell and a few of his forward-looking colleagues the result might have been very different.

The year 1792, in which Lord John was born, was the year of the storming of the Tuileries and the September massacres in Paris. It was a year on which he looked back long afterwards as typifying the ruthless slaughter that would follow in England if the opponents of reform refused to see reason. When his father succeeded to the Dukedom in 1802 the family moved to Woburn, which Lord John found far more congenial than the homes in which he had spent his early years. He was always described as a frail boy, inheriting his mother's chronic ill health. Poor health again and again in later years half persuaded him to give up a political life for a literary one. But he was always capable of rising to an occasion and his constitution must have been excellent, seeing that he lived well into the eighties in complete control of his faculties.

He was enrolled at Westminster School in the autumn of 1803. His diary entry for the first day of school, Friday, 23rd September, reads, "Coldish. The boys play at hoops, peg-tops and peashooters." His entry for Monday, 10th October: "Cold. I was flogged for the first time today." Clearly even at the age of eleven he was prepared to take everything in his stride. Lord John, looking back on his comparatively brief stay at Westminster, remarked on the physical strength which boys needed to hold their own. Truthfulness and courage were regarded as of paramount importance but one can see what led Lord John's grandson Bertrand to reach the conclusion that conventional school training was designed to teach boys to be bellicose. He recalls that if boys were "engaged to fight", the masters allowed the fights to take place in school hours and gave permission to any other boys who wanted to see the fight to be absent from class.

The pace proved too hot for him; at least his father thought so, and he was removed from Westminster. For a time he had a private tutor at Woburn, then was sent to a private school in Kent, where he remained until 1808. That was virtually the end of his formal schooling.

While his father was Viceroy of Ireland in 1806–7 he paid two visits there in school holidays. He was also a frequent guest at Holland House in Kensington, a famous meeting place of Whig politicians. He was a great favourite with the Hollands themselves, where he met people of the calibre of Sydney Smith. Already the interests which he maintained throughout his life were formed—in literature and the theatre. He was an eager and rapid reader and amused himself by writing a great deal of verse, notable rather for the enthusiasm of the author than for any inherent poetical value.

He impressed the Hollands so much that they persuaded the Duke to allow them to take Lord John with them on a journey to Spain in 1808–9. The Spanish journey was a great event in his life, a journey not without danger and certainly one that required stamina. Spain had revolted against the French occupation and Sir Arthur Wellesley, later the Duke of Wellington, had been despatched to Portugal at the head of a sizeable English army with the avowed purpose of driving the French from the Peninsula.

Lord John's experiences in Spain made a great impression on him. He admired Spanish people. He developed a youthful hatred for the "unholy tyrant" Napoleon. In his comments recorded in his diary, scrappy though it was, he showed a remarkably mature approach to the privations of the Spanish people and appreciation of the brave fights they had made to preserve their country. This prolonged visit (he was in the Peninsula for more than a year in all) did more perhaps than his earlier association with Whig thinkers to stabilize his conviction that freedom, whether of a nation or of an individual, was an inalienable right.

"I take the liberty of informing you and your Opposition friends," he wrote to his father in April 1809, "that the French have not conquered the whole of Spain!" That was just what English parliamentarians were saying most insistently. Lord John was only 16 years old at the time.

He had no definite plans for a political career at that time but one can see how his mind was influenced by the injustices of the Napoleonic conquests. Already in his teens, he was beginning to show impatience with the traditional theorizing of Whig thought. He became vastly indignant at what he regarded as the inane vaporizings of Whig politicians in Parliament on the subject of the Peninsular War. He attacked impartially the government and the opposition in letters to his father. He accused the government of stultifying the efforts "of a people who had risen in the most glorious manner". He was just as indignant at the Whigs who maintained that England should have taken no part in the war and were urging the end of hostilities on the ground that Spain was effectively conquered. In reference to a speech made by Lord Grey, one of the leaders of the opposition, he wrote, "It appears to me a declaration against the liberty of the people's right to depose an infamous despot."

When he returned to England Lord John enrolled at Edinburgh University, which had won a great reputation for its progressive thought. He was persuaded to go to Edinburgh against his will by his father and the Hollands, but once he was installed he became absorbed in his studies. Then, if ever, Edinburgh deserved to be known as the modern Athens. Lord John became president of the Speculative Society. In its debates he associated himself with the need for providing legal and educational facilities for poor people.

His work as a statesman of Reform was foreshadowed during his three years at Edinburgh. In one article published in the Whig Register series he argued the case for Parliamentary reform with surprising clarity, maintaining that the power of the Crown could be diminished most effectively by the reform of the House of Commons, first by a bill for the abolition of rotten boroughs, then by a bill for the extension of representation to the industrial towns and the gradual extension of the franchise.

Whatever Lord John may have lacked at this time in physical strength, he always found the stamina to undertake what appear to 20th-century eyes to be the most hair-raising and arduous of journeys. In the autumn of 1812 he set out once more with two friends for a tour intended to include Sicily, Greece and Egypt. He did not go much further than Spain, where he insisted on his companions leaving him while he travelled alone in this still war-wracked country, in imminent peril of being captured by French soldiers or being caught in a hostile ambush.

He was the rather unwelcome guest of the Duke of Wellington at his headquarters in Burgos, where he came under enemy shellfire. He spent some time with his brother William, who had been appointed to Wellington's staff, and arrived in Madrid just two days after the French had evacuated it. His friends regarded him as foolhardy and his father was so worried that he decided on a drastic step to halt his son's intrepid journeys. The Duke in fact wrote to Lord John to tell him that he had nominated him to a vacant Parliamentary seat at Tavistock. Lord John hurried home and arrived to find that he had already been elected. He took his place in the House of Commons in the autumn of 1813.

If the Duke supposed that arranging for Lord John's return to Parliament would change his way of life at a single stroke, he was much mistaken. Lord John spoke seldom in the Commons during the next few years—and with little distinction. He pleaded ill health as a reason for his absence from important debates. In fact he was so discouraged by the conduct of the apparently invincible Tory government and so disillusioned by the lethargy of the Whig opposition that he felt he could achieve nothing.

He spent many months in Italy and Germany during 1814 and 1815. When he went to Italy, Wellington had achieved his final and decisive victories over the French army, the first Peace of Paris had been signed and Napoleon had gone into exile on the island of Elba. While in Italy, Lord John arranged to sail to Elba and there sought and obtained an interview with the man who had held absolute authority over France for fifteen years and had come so near to the conquest of all Europe.

It must have been an exciting adventure to come face to face with the man whom he had come to think of as a monster—the tyrant and despot threatening human civilization. He was not the first—nor the last—to be disillusioned. They talked of the Duke of Bedford, of the Duke of Wellington, of conditions in France and Spain. Napoleon, said Lord John, was affable and anxious to please, but he found his conversation trivial. He was not overawed, rather contemptuous. As he says in his diary, "He appears very short which is partly owing to his being very fat. He has fat cheeks and a turn-up nose. He has a dusky grey eye which would be called vicious in a horse. He asks a number of questions without object and shows ignorance of the most common facts."

The social crisis of 1816 evoked Lord John's first important speech in the Commons. The Government brought in a Bill to suspend temporarily the Habeas Corpus Act, so that citizens could be arrested and held in prison on suspicion of being concerned in acts of sedition. Lord John spoke strongly against the proposal which, he said, constituted a denial of the most sacred rights of Englishmen. It was of no avail. The Bill was passed by a large majority. Lord John again retired into the country. But it was a turning-point in his political career. Travel and authorship, especially the writing of the biography of his ancestor, William, Lord Russell, were still as important to him as ever, but he began to hope, if not to expect, that the reactionary social attitude of the Tories might be modified.

The inexorable course of events urged him on. England, socially, was going from bad to worse. That was no vain opposition lament. It was stark fact which no one, Whig or Tory, could dispute. The end of the Napoleonic war with the signature of the second Peace of Paris brought lasting peace, but not the rewards which many believed would be the fruits of victory. Far from it. The war had been fought on borrowed capital. The reckoning was a hard one for landowner and working man alike. Demand slackened; labourers were dismissed indiscriminately; there was a slump in agriculture and in industry. Thousands of the armed forces were released at the end of the war. There were no jobs or them in town or country. They roamed from one town to another in search of work . . . and food. Frustrated, they were fine material for the agitator looking for vocal support.

Bloody riots were commonplace. The Corn Law of 1815 prohibited the import of grain until the price had reached a prohibitive level. The result was hunger for hundreds of thousands of low-paid workers and starvation for the unemployed. Members of the Luddite movement restarted their campaign to destroy the North-Country machinery which they blamed for their distress. Workers banded together to protect their interests. The Government reacted by prohibiting "Combinations" and treating any public assembly of workers as an act of sedition.

In December 1816 a crowd of artisans and journeymen met on Spa Fields, Bermondsey. The Yeomanry was ordered to deal with the trouble, but before the rioters were dispersed a number of shops had been wrecked, the Royal Exchange had been damaged and many of the people taking part in the demonstration were injured. It is significant that the Common Council of London on this and other occasions gave its support to the demand for reform. A petition was sent to the Prince Regent by the Council, describing the distress of manufacturers and artisans as insupportable.

During 1817 and 1818 unrest spread to the Midlands and the North. Armed clashes were reported between rioters and Yeomanry in Derbyshire, Nottinghamshire and Lancashire. Manchester was a hotbed of revolutionary ideas. The climax came in 1819 when some thousands—eighty thousand according to one account—of demonstrators met in St. Peter's Fields in Manchester. The Yeomanry charged with drawn swords; a small number of people were killed, a much larger number injured either with sword wounds or by being trampled underfoot. It was a shameful day, but not so bloody as tradition has made it appear. It became known—and still is known to many —as the Peterloo Massacre.

In the General Election of 1818 Lord John had been "re-elected" for Tavistock. Lord Tavistock (his elder brother) sat for Bedfordshire, Lord William for Bedford and the other Lord William, Lord John's uncle, was returned with him for Tavistock. The election virtually by a single man, the Duke of Bedford, of three sons and a brother to the House of Commons was an apt commentary on the electoral procedure of the time. At the next General Election only two years later after the death of King George III, Lord John, at the request of the yeoman of the county, offered himself as candidate for Huntingdonshire and was duly elected. Thereafter he could take his place in the House of Commons as a member chosen on his own merits.

The 14th December 1819 was the day on which he proposed in the House a modest measure for Reform. He urged the Government to abolish the representation of boroughs in which corruption was proved and to transfer the seats to industrial towns or counties. He said, "I desire only to revert to the wholesome practice of enlarging the basis of representation which continued until the end of the reign of King Charles II."

He had friends among his political adversaries. The official view was that a bill to disenfranchise a specific rotten borough would not be opposed. Lord Castlereagh said that Lord John had argued his case so well that he had "disposed his mind to make any practicable conversion". High praise indeed. It looked as if the House might take a first step, however faltering, towards righting acknowledged electoral abuses. Then came news of the Cato Street Conspiracy, a plot by radical extremists to murder the whole Cabinet. Ministers were so shocked that there was renewed opposition to concessions, however slight, to popular demand. Lord John's bill was dead for the time being.

When the new Parliament met, Lord John returned to the attack. In 1821 he reintroduced his proposal for the disenfranchisement of Grampound. To the surprise of many and the consternation of a few the bill passed both Houses of Parliament and became law. According to Lord Eldon it was "the first turn of the helm towards the whirlpool of democracy". And Lord Eldon was a man of normally moderate views!

Lord John's reputation was enhanced by his handling of this bill. He was satisfied to have achieved *something*, even though the representation of Grampound was transferred to Yorkshire, instead of, as he wished, to one of the still unrepresented northern towns. He won respect too by joining with the opponents of the new King's proposed measures to humiliate his Queen Caroline, especially the bill "of pains and penalties" against the Queen, sponsored by Lord Liverpool as Prime Minister. Ultimately the measure was dropped and Lord John, identified as he was with the "Queen's Party" and with the movement for electoral reform, began to assume the role of hero of the people. He was regarded with cautious approval even by the radical reformers, though he was not one of them and at no time showed the least sign of changing his Whig principles to conform with what he believed to be impractical extremism.

Lord John was the first effective champion of the middle class. He swore to abolish electoral corruption but he had no fault to find with privilege as such. He took it for granted. He worked long and hard to widen the basis of representation, to supplant members of Parliament returned for the "boroughs" of the past by members representing the big and growing "new" towns; he fought for the lowering of the property qualification for the vote, but he never by word or deed supported the idea of universal suffrage. That, he thought, was the first stage on the way to anarchy.

Those facts do not belittle what he achieved nor lessen the importance of his achievements in averting revolution and in mitigating the unhappy lot of those who had no stake in the land or in industry. He struggled on through many disappointments. Between 1822 and 1826 he introduced five measures to give representation to the new towns and to lessen corruption. All were defeated or withdrawn when it was certain that they had no chance of success.

It seemed as though the diehards had entrenched themselves behind last ditch defences, determined to stand their ground or perish in the attempt. Tories like Lord Liverpool were unable to recognize the peril that was at hand or to realize that modifications of the constitution which they resisted so strongly were nothing, positively nothing, compared with the destructive forces that would be unleashed if some move were not made quickly to placate the people. All over the country isolated instances of violence were occurring almost every day. If communication had been easier between one district and another, almost certainly there would have been revolution. As it was, industry and commerce were being impeded and the middle classes could not shut their eyes any longer to the danger at their doors.

That is probably why, when Lord Liverpool was compelled by illness to resign, Canning was chosen to form an administration. Canning was only by courtesy a Tory, in fact he was a distinguished statesman, liberal in many of his views. His appointment split both the Tory and the Whig Parties, for some leading Tories refused to join his government, while he was supported by a number of Whigs. After only five months Canning died. Attempts were made to re-form a coalition government but they failed. Then the Duke of Wellington became Prime Minister, with Sir Robert Peel as Leader of the House of Commons. The Tory machine was back in full working order.

Only one event stands out in the career of Lord John during this interlude. He introduced a motion for the disenfranchisement of Penrhyn and the transfer of its members to Manchester. Penrhyn was notoriously a corrupt borough and the bill was passed through the House of Commons only to be cast out in the Lords. One might well say of the Tories at this time, "When will they ever learn?" The rejection of this proposal so incensed middle-class opinion that from that day onwards a large measure of reform was assured and ultimately a decline in the power of the Upper House. However, the Duke of Wellington and his friends still had a few years in which to carry on their rearguard action, though it became a more and more difficult operation.

Lord John triumphed in his campaign for the repeal of the Test Acts, which compelled all who were appointed to office of profit under the Crown to take the sacrament according to the rites of the Church of England. In his own words: "It was the custom of persons to be waiting in taverns and houses near the church, not going in until service was over. The ceremony used to be called qualifying for office and an appointed person called out 'those who want to be qualified will please to step up this way.'" It may have been the only time they took the sacrament, possibly the only time they entered a church.

It is said that Lord John was surprised when his proposal was approved by the Commons. His handling of the matter was praised by members of both parties. Now people began to regard him as a possible future leader of the Whigs.

This measure did nothing to help Roman Catholics, who were still precluded from any office. The persecution of Irish Catholics was a standing rebuke to the government. It was not Lord John himself but Sir Robert Peel, with Lord John's active support, who introduced a bill for the partial emancipation of the Catholics in 1829, this single Act possibly preventing the outbreak of civil war in Ireland.

The general election of 1830 showed a swing in favour of the reforming parties. There was, however, still a majority for the Duke of Wellington's government. The Duke promptly committed political suicide. On the debate following the King's Speech he said that he would not bring forward or support any measure for reform: "I shall always feel it my duty to resist such measures if they are proposed." With a slender majority and many of the Tories convinced that something must be done, Wellington could not sustain office and was succeeded by Lord Grey at the head of a coalition government pledged to reform.

For the first time Lord John took office. He was offered and accepted the post of Paymaster-General. The office gave him prestige, and made it reasonable for Lord Grey to ask him to be the spokesman for the government on reform in the Commons. Typically Lord John was rather sarcastic about the office: "The work was all done by the cashiers and the only official act of any consequence that I performed was the giving of allotments of garden ground to seventy old soldiers." And very proud of those gardens he was, often revisiting Chelsea Hospital to see what the pensioners had made of the waste ground he had allotted to them.

His remark about his office was only an example of his slightly pedantic humour. In fact he worked hard, too hard many of his friends believed, on the reform bill. At Lord Grey's request he introduced a proposal for sweeping changes on 1st March 1831. This was not a proposal to disenfranchise a few nomination boroughs. It was a bill to change the whole basis of representation, to take power from the privileged aristocracy and give it to the business magnates and middle class. In his speech of introduction he recalled all the old arguments for reform. "What would a foreigner think," he said, "if he were taken to a green mound and told that it sent two members to the British Parliament." All boroughs with less than two thousand inhabitants were to lose the franchise. Forty-seven others with populations of less than four thousand which returned two members were to have their representation halved. The seats thus made vacant were to be distributed among the growing towns, including five Irish and eight Scottish boroughs, and among the counties of industrial importance. The property or rental qualification for the vote was to be reduced.

The proposal was a bombshell, going much further than most Members of Parliament had expected. Inevitably there was last ditch opposition to it. But it was carried. Its most important effect was that electors were increased from one per cent of the total population to about three per cent and that the new middle class would have as powerful a voice in electing the Lower House of Parliament as the landed proprietors.

Before the bill could become law Parliament was dissolved by King William IV. After a general election the new Parliament was still more strongly committed to reform and Lord John was given a seat in the Cabinet. He immediately introduced his bill for a second time and it was passed by the House of Commons only to be rejected by the Lords. That was the sign for renewed rioting in places as far apart as Nottingham, Bristol and Leeds. Even in London the windows of the Duke of Wellington's house were broken, a signal insult to a statesman who had been hailed only a few years before as the saviour of the country.

In December 1831 Lord John once more moved the Reform Bill and strong pressure was brought on the King to create enough new peers to ensure that the bill would be passed by the Lords. This the King refused to do. Lord Grey resigned. The King asked the Duke of Wellington to form a government. The Duke reported that he could not do so. Lord Grey resumed office. And now the King saw that further protest was useless but instead of creating new peers he wrote to every member of the House of Lords asking that the course of the bill should not be obstructed. So in June the Reform Bill passed into the Statute Book and early in 1833 the first reformed Parliament met.

That undoubtedly was Lord John's finest hour. Political success was assured to him, but he never regained, not even as Prime Minister, the accolade of well-deserved triumph, the triumph of justice over privilege, that he had achieved in 1832. His skill in debate did not diminish for many years. He was responsible for many other useful bills, but he was, after all, an aristocrat. He believed that his great Reform Bill made further reform unnecessary. Where others pressed forward he lagged behind. Before he became Prime Minister his image was that of an elder statesman. His erstwhile Radical supporters, pressing for more and more reform, nicknamed him "Finality Jack", a description which stayed with him for the rest of his career. It

16

was not long before workers in towns and country were disillusioned. The Reform Bill, in which mysteriously they had had so much faith as a means of relieving their material distress, did nothing to help them. The idea of universal suffrage, of the people's charter, was as far away as ever.

For a time Lord John made Ireland his special concern, though he despaired of achieving justice for Irish Roman Catholics. "In England," he wrote, "I hope it may be true that there is no wrong without a remedy. In Ireland all is wrong and nothing a remedy." He did, however, achieve one major reform, the passage of an act reforming the Irish Church, which had the effect of making part of the revenue from tithes previously paid by a Roman Catholic majority for the endowment of the Anglican Church available for public welfare.

Lord Grey's resignation was caused by the conflict over Irish affairs. He was succeeded by Lord Melbourne, who nominated Lord John Leader of the Commons. Lord John accepted, although he was conscious of the difficulty he faced in attempting to weld such a heterogeneous assortment of statesman as composed the administration. He is quoted as saying: "If I were offered the command of the Channel Fleet and thought it my duty to accept, I should not refuse it." That epitomized his whole attitude to public service.

King William, opposed to progressive thought like his predecessors on the throne, refused to approve the appointment. This was a lethal step to take so far as Melbourne's government was concerned. It was also another case of political suicide, for although King William did not live to reap the whirlwind, his successors did. Acts such as this quite fatuous gesture of his caused the nation to veer more rapidly towards the modern idea of the function of a constitutional sovereign. In the event, Lord Melbourne resigned and the King asked Sir Robert Peel to form an administration. This, too, inevitably was short-lived and Lord Melbourne resumed office in 1835, continuing as Prime Minister for the next six years.

Lord John was appointed Home Secretary in this government, and a very fine Home Secretary he proved himself. In the first session he steered the Municipal Reform Act through Parliament. By this act municipal affairs were placed in the hands of ratepayers instead of a small number of freemen who could not pretend to represent the people. The ratepayers elected the councillors and these councillors elected the aldermen and the mayor. Seniority became by tradition the qualification for the higher echelons of municipal service. A similar bill for Ireland passed the Commons but was thrown out by the Lords.

The next few years were relatively quiet ones in Lord John's career. He was fully established as a Parliamentarian. As long as Lord Melbourne was Prime Minister he was one of the chief props of the government. The combination of Lord Melbourne and Lord John Russell was not, however, one to provoke legislative fireworks. Both were conscious of the need to revise the government's attitude to Ireland but neither succeeded in penetrating effectively the barrage of opposition sustained by the House of Lords.

The fiery Daniel O'Connell was the undisputed leader of the Irish movement but the majority of Irish members regarded him as a revolutionary. For a time he was mistrusted also by the Young Ireland Party, which called consistently for more extreme action than the peaceful measures of protest encouraged by O'Connell. Lord John had spent so much time in Ireland that he was well aware of the problems of the Irish people. Although O'Connell tended to distrust all Whig statesmen on principle, he and Lord John reached a mutual understanding. If this could have been maintained through the disastrous years of the forties, Ireland might have been saved much bloodshed and untold distress.

That Lord John was in advance of his time in his attitude to the problem of overseas territories was shown when he became colonial secretary in 1839. He had, of course, the usual 19th-century conviction that British rule could do nothing but benefit colonial territories; he could scarcely conceive that the people of Australia, for instance, or for that matter Ireland, might be better off without the protection of England. The idea of an Irish Republic was unthinkable. Not even Irish champions like O'Connell dreamt of such a thing. But Lord John was sympathetic to the idea of self government, though his interpretation of the term was a limited one.

By 1841 the Melbourne Cabinet was divided on many issues. The final crisis came when in response to the increasing pressure of the Anti Corn Law League a measure was introduced which in effect reduced the duty on wheat, though not admitting it free. The government was defeated. This was a personal disaster for Lord John. He had introduced and supported eloquently the proposed measure. It was a complete reversal of the omens which heralded the session—when the Duke of Bedford wrote to Lord John, "You and your colleagues may march into Parliament with colours flying and drums beating."

In the election that followed, the Whigs lost further ground. An administration was formed by Sir Robert Peel, and Lord John found himself out of office with the unenviable duty of acting as Leader of the Opposition. He had, however, by then achieved one of his greatest ambitions. He had agreed to contest the City of London and was returned by a good majority.

In opposition Lord John was as consistently painstaking as he had been while a member of the government. Sir Robert Peel was not nearly as conservative in his policy as many had imagined, or as some of his supporters wished him to be. At a time when the "party line" was not so rigorously enforced as in the 20th century Lord John was often able to support measures proposed by the government, and over the Irish question in particular found himself in the strange position of being respected both by the conservative government and by the radical O'Connell.

The arrest of O'Connell and his trial in Dublin for sedition focused Dublin attention on Ireland more than ever before. It was Lord John who in 1844 proposed a motion asking for a committee of the whole house to consider the affairs of Ireland. How near he was to the root of the Irish trouble was proved, if proof were needed, by the words with which he introduced the motion: "We have before us the notorious fact that Ireland is filled with troops, and that the barracks in which these troops are posted have been fortified. Preparations have been made as if the government were hourly in expectation of civil war. In England the government is a government of opinion. The government of Ireland is notoriously a government of force." He urged Parliament to put Catholics, Protestants and Presbyterians on a footing of perfect equality and the Irish people on a footing of equality with the English.

The speech was well received. The Whig members cheered O'Connell when after his acquittal in Dublin he resumed his seat in the House and Lord John shook hands with him. It was a tribute to both men. O'Connell was generous enough to say that the speech had made up to the Irish much of what they had suffered before. Unhappily Lord John's motion was defeated after nine days of debate, largely owing to the opposition of English Nonconformists and Scottish Presbyterians. O'Connell and Lord John between them—two such dissimilar characters— were powerful enough in harmony, but not quite powerful enough.

As compensation, Peel himself introduced in 1845 measures which went some way, though not far enough, towards the pacification of Ireland. His proposals increased the endowments of Maynooth College, the main centre of education for the Catholic priesthood, foreshadowed the foundation of three colleges, the Queen's Colleges, for higher education in Irish towns and gave greater security to Irish tenants. It is significant that although the measure was passed, Sir Robert failed to secure a majority of his own party. It was the support of Lord John and his Whig colleagues that ensured the success of the bill.

Later in the same year Peel introduced a bill for the partial repeal of the Corn Laws, spurred on by a cold, wet summer which caused an unusually poor harvest, and the first sign of the potato blight in Ireland which threatened the very existence of the Irish people. This was not enough, said Lord John; the logic of events demanded that the tax on imported corn should be removed entirely.

Sir Robert resigned. Inevitably it was Lord John who was summoned by Queen Victoria and entrusted with the task of forming a new administration. This he was unable to do and Sir Robert resumed office, but only for a short period. Now he proposed that the Corn Laws should be repealed gradually so that Free Trade became a reality in three years' time. The compromise passed safely through both Houses of Parliament. It alienated a large number of Peel's own supporters, many of them landowners who saw in Free Trade the ruin of their agricultural prosperity. When Peel introduced a measure to give extraordinary powers to the government of Ireland to quell sedition he lacked the Whig support which he had for the repeal of the Corn Laws and was defeated.

Lord John was the architect of the fall of the Peel Ministry. It was appropriate that he should again be asked to be Prime Minister. Now the increasing political gloom was on his side and he had no difficulty in forming a government which, in the main was a coalition of all the liberal forces in the House. He took office on 6th July 1846 after more than thirty years of unselfish and often enlightened public service.

He was unfortunate in being called on to direct the government at a time when circumstances made it necessary for him to solve two problems which were virtually insoluble, the problem of Ireland and that of civil discontent in an expanding economy. That he failed on both counts is not necessarily an indictment of his ability or his character. He had to contend with established precedent and carry with him a parliament that was still not representative. None of his contemporaries suggested that Lord John was anything but well meaning, though his political opponents were numerous and his handling of affairs was criticized widely. "Reformer John" had given way to "Finality Jack". It was a case of a liberal-minded politician who had achieved many of his original objects being called on to direct a still immature democracy in coping with problems to which not only Lord John, but many of his successors, failed to find a satisfactory answer.

If his failures as Prime Minister are remembered most vividly by historians, it is only fair to credit him with the social measures for which he found parliamentary time during those six years in which crisis followed crisis and the temptation to defer social legislation must have been great. While he was Prime Minister a bill became law which had the effect of advancing the cause of popular education. Thus Lord John built on the foundations which had been laid by the Melbourne administration, by increasing grants payable to schools which passed government inspection, and by increasing the pay of teachers. A factory bill reduced the number of hours which children and women could work in manufacturing industries. The Poor Law Commission became a ministerial department. Even if none of these measures went far enough to satisfy popular clamour for major reform, they were all useful measures which improved the conditions in which working men and women lived.

At the very first opportunity, too, the new Prime Minister passed through both Houses of Parliament a measure repealing the Corn Laws in their entirety. This Act was of great importance to a people impoverished by a temporary decline in trade and the high cost of essential foodstuffs.

Yet all these things are often overlooked, since the great events and great tragedies of these years were centred in Ireland. Paradoxically, Lord John, who had consistently shown himself to be an ardent supporter of religious toleration, came to be regarded as the enemy of Roman Catholicism, chiefly through his own stupidity or thoughtlessness.

Dissension in Ireland, of course, was no new thing. It had existed before the Union. It had grown more vocal since the Union. How far the oppressive measures of the landlords, mostly English and many absentee, created the temper of the people can never be known. What is certain is that the treatment of the Irish peasants by the landlords in the early part of the 19th century was inexcusable by any standard of judgment. The people were literally treated as slaves to be evicted when it pleased the landlords. To uncertainty and poverty was added in 1845 the spectre of famine, intensified after the failure of the potato crop for the second time in 1846. The gravamen of the Irish complaint against the English was that since Ireland was united with England it was the job of the English government to take effective measures to relieve the distress. Lord John admitted it but either he did not realize the gravity of the position or he lacked the courage to take the massive relief measures which alone might have saved the situation. It was a case in which even the slightest delay was bound to be fatal.

In the event large grants were made for public works to relieve Irish unemployment. It was made easier for Irishmen to emigrate because Lord John saw, rightly, that there were more people living in Ireland than the soil could be expected to sustain, and generous relief was offered on a voluntary basis when the famine was at its height. But it was not enough. There were real difficulties of transport and distribution and the help when it arrived was often too late.

Lord Bessborough, an Irish landlord of more liberal views than most, was Viceroy in 1846. He did all he could to keep the government informed and to expedite the work of relief. Probably one in ten of the population—some estimates put the figure much higher—died from starvation. Hundreds of thousands of others suffered privations from which they never recovered. If Lord John had had the advice of Daniel O'Connell, much more might have been done but unhappily O'Connell was desperately ill and had ceased to take an active part in politics. The Young Ireland Party would have no dealings either with the Viceroy or with the English government. Even the most hidebound Presbyterians in Ireland admired the work of Roman Catholic priests, among them the famous Father Mathew, in helping their flocks. Good intention was everywhere, but effective action sadly lacking. The result was even greater bitterness on the part of the Irish people, leading to more and more serious acts of violence. Smith O'Brien and his followers talked openly now of an Irish republic.

Lord Clarendon, who succeeded Lord Bessborough as Viceroy, reported to the Prime Minister that no Englishman was safe, that the landlords' homes were being fired in every part of the country, and that assassinations were no longer regarded as murders but as executions. Many who presided over inquests on famine victims brought in verdicts of murder against Lord John Russell. Lord Clarendon asked for special powers. Reluctantly Lord John persuaded Parliament to grant these powers by the Treason Felony Act, which made it a crime punishable with penal servitude for life to speak or write against the Crown.

Smith O'Brien was convicted and transported. The fire of "rebellion" was beaten out into smouldering embers but no effort was made to remove the cause. With some justice Lord John was accused of giving his support to the very acts of coercion which had caused the downfall of Sir Robert Peel. Disorders continued, especially in Clare and Tipperary.

At home Lord John was faced with a crisis almost as soon as he took office. A giant Chartist demonstration was arranged for 10th April 1848. The Chartist movement sprang from the discontent felt throughout the country at the failure of the Reform Bill to bring any great improvement in social conditions. The cardinal claims of the people's charter, which had been adopted ten years before, were, first, universal suffrage, second, vote by ballot, third, annual parliaments, fourth, the payment of Members of Parliament, fifth, the abolition of property qualifications for Members, and sixth, the division of the country into equal electoral districts. A hundred years later all the ideas embodied in the charter except annual parliaments had been adopted. But in 1848 the proposals were considered subversive. The people of London and other towns feared that this rally of Chartist supporters on Kennington Common, where 150,000 were expected, and the planned march from Kennington to deliver a petition to the Houses of Parliament might be the prelude to civil war. Troops and special constables paraded the central districts of London. Artillery covered strategic points. All shops were shuttered and scarcely any civilians except the special constables ventured abroad.

Lord John was responsible for the security precautions. He did not believe in the threat of civil war and was careful to maintain the right of people to congregate at meetings. In that he acted wisely. The attack never materialized. Drenching rain proved a stronger defence than military force. The meeting dispersed and the petition was brought to the Houses of Parliament in a hansom cab. London breathed again. And for a time Lord John's reputation was enhanced.

But not for very long. One of the difficulties which he inherited was the position of Lord Palmerston as Foreign Secretary. The latter contrived to remain at the Foreign Office continuously for a period of twenty years. He had grown to know the rulers of most European countries and had certainly made them all aware of the power of England. Replacement of the Foreign Secretary was out of the question. Unhappily Palmerston made frequent mistakes in the next few years and Lord John was blamed for them.

After the *coup d'état* in Paris on 2nd December 1851 (when Louis Napoleon, on reaching the end of his term as President, dismissed the Assembly which refused to amend the constitution so that a President might be eligible for a second term) Lord Palmerston, without the authority of the Prime Minister or of the Queen, expressed the view to the French Ambassador that the *coup* had England's full approval. This was in direct conflict with the official policy of neutrality. Lord John immediately dismissed Lord Palmerston. This action, however necessary as it may have been, seriously weakened the government. Lord Palmerston still had an influential following.

About the same time the ministry was seriously embarrassed by Lord John's personal intervention in a religious dispute which in retrospect seems rather meaningless, though at the time it was regarded with all seriousness. It arose from the action of Pope Pius IX in 1850 issuing a Bull creating an Archbishopric of Westminster, with Dr. Wiseman as the first Cardinal Archbishop, and twelve sees with territorial titles. The reason underlying this reassertion of the spiritual leadership of the Pope was that tens of thousands of immigrants, especially Irishmen, of the Roman Catholic faith were, with the government's full authority, receiving religious guidance in England from Roman Catholic priests. Englishmen in general, and members of the government in particular, and indeed the Queen herself, misunderstood Pope Pius's intentions. They regarded the Papal Bull as making England once more a province of the Roman Catholic Church. There was much talk about Papal aggression.

Even so, had it not been for Lord John's inability to comprehend the real issues at stake he might have followed the advise of Dr. Pusey, the leader of the Oxford Movement, to issue only a very moderate protest to Rome. But Lord John was a Protestant of the old school, with Puritan leanings. He was as Prime Minister as much distressed by the High Church tendency fostered by the Oxford Movement as by a reintroduction of Papal authority. It is only in that context that the letter which he wrote to the Bishop of Durham, and which was published in all newspapers, can be understood. In this he deplored what he called the assumption of power made by the Pope, regarding it as inconsistent with the Queen's supremacy. With almost incredible stupidity he included in this document a strong attack on the High Church movement, saying that High Church clergymen alarmed him much more than the aggression of a foreign sovereign, quoting as typical of the High Church movement the holding of confession and the administration of penance and absolution. "I have little hope that the framers of these innovations will desist from their insiduous course but I rely with confidence on the great mass of a nation which looks with contempt at the endeavours which are being made to enslave the soul."

The Durham Letter achieved no single purpose which Lord John intended. "No Popery" signs appeared on walls and in windows. On Guy Fawkes Day effigies of the Pope were carried through the streets of London and other cities and burnt in the traditional bonfires. Roman Catholics were incensed, High Churchmen were equally indignant, while the Protestants, of whom Lord John was most sincerely one, were angry because he had not done anything more positive than write a letter to stamp out the activities of the High Church or of the Roman Catholics.

The end of Lord John's tenure of office was at hand. He had become so unpopular that he could not have maintained his ministry for much longer in any case. The actual end, however, was unexpected. He proposed a measure for the strengthening of the militia, an entirely routine measure. Lord Palmerston rose to propose an amendment and this was carried against the government. Lord John duly resigned. An apt commentary on these unhappy events was provided in a letter from Lord Palmerston to his brother: "I have had my tit for tat with Lord Russell and I turned him out on Friday last." And so indeed he had, but the real author of the ministry's downfall was Lord John himself.

Lord John remained in politics for some years. He held office on several occasions, was briefly Prime Minister again, but although he outlived his unpopularity and no voice was ever raised against his integrity or his desire to serve the country, he never regained the old authority. He was an experienced Parliamentarian and still a fine debater, imbued with the ideals of public service, a little more cautious after the débâcle of the Durham letter but still rather too prone to errors of judgment to deserve the name of greatness. His closing years in Parliament were an anti-climax.

He was succeeded as Prime Minister by Lord Derby, who was compelled to resign in 1853 when the budget proposals presented by Mr. Disraeli were defeated. Lord Derby in turn was succeeded by Lord Aberdeen, who formed a coalition ministry consisting of the majority of the Whigs and the still numerous members who had looked to Sir Robert Peel as their leader. After much heart-burning Lord John took office in this ministry as Foreign Secretary, while Lord Palmerston was at the Home Office.

The ministry so formed won the Queen's approval but scarcely satisfied anyone else. The division of views between its members was too great. It is said that there was an unwritten agreement between Lord John and Lord Aberdeen for Lord John to take over the office of Prime Minister at an early date. In fact that was not possible because other members of the government were not prepared to accept him. However, he did a good job at the Foreign Office for a time and it was not until the threat of the Crimean War loomed on the horizon that he once more failed to grapple with a difficult situation. This time, however, it was not conceivably his fault. If he had been Prime Minister the Crimean War might never have occurred. The origin of the war lay in the determination of the Russian Czar Nicholas to break the power of Turkey. As head of the Eastern Church the Czar had some ground for intervening in Turkish affairs because of the acknowledged persecution of Christians by the Sultan's government. British policy, however, was to maintain Turkey as an independent state, the thought being that the conquest of Turkey by Russia would open the way to India. "If we do not defend ourselves on the Danube," said

Lord John, "we shall be compelled to do so on the Indus.'
Lord Aberdeen could not be persuaded that Russia would go to
war and pursued a familiar policy of appeasement, while Lord
John again and again in public and in private urged a show of
firmness.

Lord John twice offered to resign but retained his position
on the appeal of the Queen and the Prime Minister. Then
during the winter of 1854–5 when war had broken out, the
troops in the Crimea were dying at the rate of hundreds a week
through lack of supplies. Lord John, who had repeatedly
called for reorganization of the departments concerned with
supply, could bear it no longer and asked Lord Aberdeen to
submit his resignation to the Queen.

This in effect meant the end of the Aberdeen ministry. Lord
Palmerston, one of the few statesmen in whom the bulk of the
country had confidence, became Prime Minister after Lord
John had found it impossible to form an administration. In
Lord Palmerston's ministry Lord John held the office of
Colonial Secretary and represented British interests at the
Second Congress of Vienna, where the great powers, including
Russia, Turkey, France and Great Britain explored every
possible way of achieving peace with honour. Lord John ac-
cepted one of the plans put forward but the solution was not
acceptable to Lord Palmerston. After a censure motion
initiated by Disraeli, Lord John resigned again.

When the Peace of Paris was signed early in 1856 the general
opinion was that Lord John would not seek re-election. The
pundits were wrong. Lord John did offer himself for re-election
by the City of London and was returned in the general election
of 1857. For the next three years, however, he took little part in
politics. When Lord Palmerston again became Prime Minister
in the latter part of 1859, he accepted the Prime Minister's offer
of the Foreign Office and remained Foreign Secretary
throughout the administration.

It was an arrangement that worked remarkably well. Lord

John's old feud with Palmerston was forgotten. It had never existed except on the stage of politics, for there was a strong mutual respect between the two men. Moreover, Palmerston, who for so long had directed the course of British foreign policy, knew his man well enough to realize that Lord John's attitude was not dissimilar to his own where foreign affairs were concerned. He therefore left this vitally important part of the administration during the next few years to Lord John, who proved to be an excellent Foreign Secretary. It was his ill fortune yet again to hold office at a time when no clear-cut policy was possible. He encouraged Italian nationalism. He was instrumental in maintaining Britain's neutrality at a time when it might easily have been drawn into war on the Continent. With much greater difficulty he preserved British neutrality throughout the American Civil War when a lesser, or less experienced, man might easily have led the country into a disastrous war.

The only important infringement of neutrality was the *Alabama* Affair, as it is still known to historians. The *Alabama* was a man-of-war built in a British yard to the order of the Confederate States which sailed on its mission of destruction after Lord John's attention had been brought to its intended use. In this case caution proved the Foreign Secretary's undoing. He thought it right to consult legal authorities, but before the consultations had ended the ship had sailed. This error ultimately cost Britain £9,000,000 in compensation to the United States and brought the country very near to war, but Lord John cannot be blamed for an ultra-careful approach to a most delicate problem.

In his last years of office Lord John returned to his first interest, parliamentary reform. Though Lord Palmerston and most of the Whigs were apathetic, he proposed a moderate reform bill with the support of Gladstone. The bill was withdrawn, however, when it was obvious that it did not have the support of the majority of the House. Before it could be reintroduced Lord Palmerston died. By then Lord John had been rewarded for his fine career of service with an earldom and was again believed to be on the point of retirement.

Lord Palmerston's death changed the picture completely. The Queen wrote to Lord John, saying, "The Queen can turn to no other than Lord Russell, an old and tried friend of hers, to undertake the arduous duties of Prime Minister, and to carry on the government." Lord John could not refuse, especially as Gladstone was willing to serve under him, and most of the men who had been in the Palmerston cabinet were also agreeable to do so. So it happened rather surprisingly that Lord Russell took office as Prime Minister for a second time, at the age of seventy-four.

The reform bill introduced in this second Russell ministry, as put forward by Gladstone in the House of Commons, was a major step towards giving ordinary people a voice in shaping the government. It decreased the qualification for franchise both in the counties and boroughs, and brought into the voting category all householders and tenants in composite households paying £10 rent a year or more. The measure would have added nearly half a million to the electorate and for the first time included the upper fringe of the artisan class. It was also proposed to disenfranchise further small boroughs, reduce the representation of others, and increase the representation of the industrial towns and counties, such as the West Riding of Yorkshire. It was a good measure, very much on the lines of Lord John's first reform bill, varied to suit the changing times. However, an amendment to substitute rating for rental as the qualification for the vote was passed against the government and Lord John resigned after only a few months in office.

That was the end of his active political life. He had the wry satisfaction of seeing Lord Derby's ministry, which succeeded his, pass a much more radical reform bill than he had proposed in response to frantic popular demonstrations. He continued to speak in the Lords occasionally, especially on Ireland at the time of the Fenian outrages. Then he was still urging the course he had advocated all his life—to win the respect of Irish people by redressing their wrongs. He lived also to see the disestablishment of the Irish Church and the Elementary Education Act of 1870, bringing into effect most of the reforms in education which he had urged.

Most of his time was spent with his family at Pembroke Lodge, a house on the edge of Richmond Park which had been presented to him for life by the Queen. He had always been a family man and was regarded with deep respect and affection by all his children, the two daughters born to him by his first wife, the widow of the 2nd Lord Ribblesdale whom he married in 1835, and the three sons and one daughter by his second wife, the daughter of the 2nd Earl of Minto, whom he married in 1841 after the death of his first wife. He felt deeply the death of his brother, the Duke of Bedford, with whom he had been on intimate terms throughout his life. His eldest son also predeceased him and the last years of his life were given lustre only by the presence in his household of his grandchildren.

He died in 1878, content in the belief that he had contributed to progress, political and social, and in the knowledge that he had always done his duty to Queen and country.

CHAPTER ELEVEN

A Pen Mightier than the Sword

BERTRAND RUSSELL, the 3rd Earl Russell and grandson of Lord John Russell, the 1st Earl, has exerted a powerful influence on 20th-century thought, not only in Britain but in almost all the countries of the western world. This he has achieved mainly by writing, with some help from lecturing and broadcasting. He has entered also the arena of national and international politics, with varying success, it is true, but always contributing in some degree to the changing social pattern.

Until he was over forty, until it seemed to many of his academic colleagues that his career had already reached its peak, Bertrand Russell was a mathematician and a philosopher. Primarily a logician, he regarded mathematics and logic as two parts of a single whole. His mind turned only fleetingly towards the application of philosophy to moral and political issues. He himself had implied more recently that he was not conscious of a link between his philosophy and his attitude to everyday affairs. A link, however, certainly exists. His philosophical conclusions led naturally to the championship of the individual against the state, his scepticism to his passionate attacks on outworn shibboleths, his perseverance in certain philosophic truths to his unremitting energy in putting forward points of view, however unpopular, and maintaining them against all opposition.

In a sense his philosophy and his political activities represent two sides of Russell's character, two facets of character which are complementary. In philosophical writing and conversation he has always been precise and rational. Whether his inferences have been accepted or rejected, or whether he has, as so often, found good reason to vary them, he has always been logical and unemotional. Every cause he has championed has been upheld with passionate sincerity. Even when he had passed his ninetieth birthday he was still an influence not to be disregarded, still striving with might and main to set right the problems of the world, to outlaw suffering, to increase the sum total of happiness. Because everyone knew that he had no ulterior motive there has always been a sympathetic audience for his appeals, however misguided or misdirected some people might believe them to be.

In order to understand the immense and rather surprising influence of this scholar turned man of action, whom T. S. Eliot once described as permanently precocious, it is necessary to appreciate the influences in childhood and young manhood that moulded his character. He was born in 1872, when the aftermath of the industrial revolution had not yet brought material change to the lives of the aristocracy, and was brought up in a household in which the name of his grandfather was sacred, He never forgot the loneliness of his childhood; his father and mother, Viscount and Viscountess Amberley, were both dead by the time he was four. He had an elder brother Frank, who became the 2nd Earl Russell on his grandfather's death, and a sister who died before his character had matured.

Viscount Amberley, the 1st Earl Russell's son, who carried on the family tradition of rebellion against conventional ways of life, was a militant atheist. At that time the profession of atheism required courage of a special kind. So it is not surprising that the Viscount named two well-known atheists as guardians of his children. Nor is it surprising that his will was set aside in the Courts and all three children were declared Wards of Court, with the provision that they should be brought up by their grandparents, the now ageing 1st Earl and his much younger and more vigorous wife. So Bertie Russell went to live at Pembroke Lodge, his elder brother his only companion of even approximately the same age.

Life at Pembroke Lodge was peaceful and comfortable, but highly unsatisfactory for a boy of Bertrand's age, especially as Lady Russell was opposed in principle to public school education, and Bertrand never had the advantages of a boarding-school or of mixing on terms of equality with large numbers of other boys until he was past sixteen. Earl Russell himself had little influence but Bertrand had a great admiration for him and for his work for reform. The Liberal tradition at least was unquestioned in the boy's mind. Though in later years he showed unusual mental abilities and an unswerving determination to reach the truth, his political thought was always Liberal or to the left of Liberalism.

Lady Russell exerted a far more potent influence. She was a strange mixture, a member of a Scottish Presbyterian family who retained her Puritan attitude to many facets of life yet held Radical views far less moderate than those of her husband in his later years. She campaigned for Irish Home Rule and for many other causes which only the most extreme Radicals espoused in public. But she was conservative in her views of the appropriate code of conduct in trivial as well as important matters. Bertrand perforce acted in accordance with his grandmother's ideas of what was right and proper for a growing boy to do.

That was the beginning of his questioning attitude. He was told what to do, he wanted to know why he should do it, but no answer was forthcoming except the inevitable "because it's right". "How do I know it's right?" Bertrand must have asked himself on numerous occasions. And that is the very question he continued to ask throughout his days as a student and philosopher. "How can I recognize the truth?" "What is the truth behind the phenomena of daily life?" He was asking the same questions seventy or more years later, but unlike many philosophers he had by then provided answers to many of the questions, and some of the answers had been accepted by a large number of people.

In this backwater of Victorian England Bertrand grew shy and reserved. Lady Russell brought in young friends to amuse him but it was a small coterie. His chief companions were the birds that nested in the gardens of Pembroke Lodge and the animals whose home was in the plantations and thickets of Richmond Park. As he grew older one of his chief pleasures was to walk for miles across the bracken-covered expanse of the park. He developed a real sympathy for nature which he never lost, and his active young mind grappled with problems very different from those which occupied the minds of most boys.

Alan Wood, in his *Bertrand Russell, the Passionate Sceptic*, records two charming but wonderfully illustrative anecdotes of his early life. At the age of five, when told that the earth was round, he started to dig a big hole in the garden, hoping to come out the other side of the world and so prove that it really was round. At the age of eleven he was questioning the hypotheses of geometry, when his brother Frank introduced him to the mysteries of Euclid. Bertrand wanted to know how it could be proved that two things which are equal to the same thing are equal to one another. Frank's reply is said to have been, "If you don't accept the axioms we can't go on." With the practical sense that he was to show so often in later years, Bertrand accepted the position and went on to master Euclid in a remarkably short space of time. But he still questioned the validity of the axioms.

By the age of sixteen he was questioning the axioms of religion, for religious creeds and moral codes came to some extent into the same category as Euclid. They involve axioms which have to be taken on trust. They involve, in effect, an act of faith, and faith had little part in Bertrand's psychological make-up, although by a paradox which is surprisingly common he showed infinite faith in later years in his own beliefs, while admitting publicly that he could not prove them, not even the axiom that suffering is bad. He hated admitting, however, that the proposition was equivalent to "I believe that suffering is bad".

John Stuart Mill was the philosopher who exerted most influence on the boy's thought. His own theories of morals in later years showed the influence of Mill's Utilitarianism, in effect, that the *summum bonum*, that *ignis fatuus* of philosophy, is the greatest good of the greatest number.

When Russell was 16 he went to a private tutoring establishment to bring his classics to university entrance level. He disliked intensely many of his fellow students who were destined for an army career, regarding them as bumptious and ridiculously militant, but his quick wit overcame the difficulties of Latin and Greek to such good effect that he won a scholarship to Trinity College, Cambridge, and took up residence there in 1890.

His youth was over. The transition from the environment of a private school to that of a university which then ranked among the foremost in Europe for its philosophical studies gave him enormous pleasure. He quickly began to spread his wings among other young men of comparable intellectual capacity. And a very remarkable group of friends he acquired, some of them lifelong friends and fellow philosophers, each stimulating the wit of the others, however different their conclusions might be. Among them were George Trevelyan, his elder brother Charles, later a leading member of the Labour Party, who frequently visited George at Cambridge, and Charles Sanger, one of the finest of Cambridge mathematicians and later a famous lawyer. The firmest friend, and one who influenced his future life most of all, was, however, not an undergraduate but a Fellow and tutor, A. N. Whitehead, who regarded Russell as the most brilliant pupil of his year and was happy to collaborate with him after graduation in the preparation of the *Principia Mathematica*.

The years that Russell spent at Cambridge have been

described many times as marking the end of an epoch. The Victorian way of life was dying but was not yet dead; 20th-century ideas of "equality" were not yet apparent. Education beyond the primary stage was virtually reserved for the well-to-do, who still represented a leisured class, their preserves increasingly invaded by the middle class of prosperous businessmen. Between 1890 and 1894 the majority of Russell's fellow students belonged to the traditional aristocratic families. Few of them regarded their term of residence at Cambridge as a stepping-stone to earning a living. They all, or almost all, were bent on a career, but their careers were not estimated in terms of material rewards. Teaching at University level was regarded more as a dedication to duty than as a means to an end. Many of the undergraduates would manage family estates; others would enter politics, at that time not only an unpaid career but a very expensive one. The aim was to be a good mathematician, a good philosopher, a good historian.

This picture may seem uncommonly dated more than halfway through the 20th century. Yet something of it persisted at least until the 1920's, in spite of the complete change in the nation's attitude to education. It is a fact that has to be borne in mind when considering the development of students like Russell and his many distinguished contemporaries. They did not necessarily waste their time. Far from it. But the curriculum of formal study was entirely secondary to the exchange of ideas between fellow students. And here again the position had not changed much thirty years later. It was still possible to spend four years in Oxford, and probably in Cambridge, too, and obtain a good honours degree without attending more than a few lectures of one's own choice and a weekly or bi-weekly tutorial.

So Russell and his friends spent much of their time talking together, either in small groups in their rooms, or as members of the many societies that enlivened Cambridge life. Russell had every opportunity to pursue his early questionings further and to hear what young people of far greater intellectual capacity than any he had known in earlier years had to propose as answers to his questions. He became far more interested in philosophy and in particular in the philosophy of mathematics than in mathematics as such. He obtained a good, but not outstandingly good, degree after three years, and spent his fourth year wholly on logic and philosophy. He laid the foundations on which his future international reputation as a philosopher was built, a reputation, incidentally, that gave him the authority to propound theories relating to moral and political conduct, even though these subjects were in a very different field from that in which he had specialized.

The twenty years that elapsed between his leaving Cambridge in 1894 and the outbreak of the First World War were years of consolidation for him, years of hard work and of great achievement in the narrow world of intellectual endeavour. It is no exaggeration to say that by 1914 he had established a reputation in Germany and the United States, as well as in his own country, as one of the greatest of living philosophers. But his audiences, with few exceptions, consisted of other philosophers and of a relatively small number of well-educated people who were interested in philosophy. His appeal to the mass of the people came later and was only made possible by radical reform of the educational system, with the result that a vastly greater number of people could understand what people like Russell were endeavouring to tell them.

He contracted the first of his four marriages in December 1894. His bride was Alys Smith, a member of a leading Pennsylvania Quaker family. It seemed strange to many of his intimates, not least to his grandmother, that the marriage ceremony was held in the Friends' Meeting House in London. The marriage was a happy one, at least for a few years, and as both the bride and bridegroom had small private incomes the matter of earning a living never arose, any more than it had at Cambridge. Russell's wife provided him with a settled domestic background for his study and writing, and even when romance became a thing of the past this background continued until his reputation was firmly established.

In those early days he was still Liberal in politics but his Radical tendencies were shown by his joining the Fabian Society, of which he was an active member for many years. With his wife he made two visits to Germany, chiefly for the purpose of studying German Socialism, which was then considered the most advanced form of political doctrine in Western Europe. Many German Socialists were in fact Marxists; in Germany the seeds of international Communism had shown vigorous growth, when in Russia they were only just germinating.

On the strength of these visits he wrote his first published book, *German Social Democracy*, in which he forecast with remarkable accuracy the future of the struggle between capital and labour. He said, in effect, that the tactics employed by German Socialists were mistaken and self-destructive. If they persisted in their doctrine of class war they were bound to alienate the ever-increasing middle class of skilled workers and technicians. The latter, he said, would become united with the capitalists. He criticized the Socialists for refusing to work with moderate reformers who before the advent of Marxism had been striving for universal suffrage and the relief of distress in the working class, as prevalent in Germany as in Great Britain and other industrial countries. That, of course, is precisely what happened. In his book of 1896 Russell could not look forward to the future except in general terms but he might well have foreseen the ultimate disaster of National Socialism as springing indirectly from the mistakes of the 19th century.

Russell was far more percipient than any of his contemporaries when in a lecture to the Fabian Society, following his visit to Germany, he said that the progressive Liberal in that country was virtually non-existent and the tyranny of the government was tolerated because of the spectre of Marxism, to which most Germans would prefer a military dictatorship.

He was particularly well received at the Johns Hopkins University, where he gave a series of lectures on the foundations of geometry, bringing logic and mathematics, which had always been considered separate studies, far closer to each other. In these years of study the chief influences in his life were the Webbs, later Lord and Lady Passfield, on the political front, and A. N. Whitehead on the mathematical and philosophical front. After more than ten years intensive work he published in 1910 the *Principia Mathematica* in collaboration with A. N. Whitehead, and thereby once for all established his reputation as a philosopher.

His first book to sell beyond the "closed shop" of professional mathematicians and philosophers was *Problems of Philosophy*. This was published in 1912 and because of its singularly lucid style remained for many years the most popular introduction to the subject for beginners. In a sense *Problems of Philosophy* was an embarrassment to Russell because many of his conclusions had been varied in substance as well as in detail while the book was still in print. By then he had made his debut in public life, not with any striking success, but with sufficient distinction to establish him as a coming man in Radical politics.

It was his belief then that if one accepted the evolution of the race one must also accept evolution in thought. He regarded religion as a facet of life belonging to an earlier period of evolution and included Communism in his mental list of religions. He looked on Conservatism as a clinging to outworn ideas by people who had not the wit to keep pace with the evolution of thought. In the same way he consigned current ideas about sex and education to the same category as religion. He refused to accept the existence of knowledge other than that derived from experience. These were the most important conclusions that guided the philosopher's attitude to morals and politics, allied with a deep humanitarian outlook which caused him to regard human suffering as the greatest of all evils.

His first essay in party politics was in 1907, when he was a candidate at a Wimbledon by-election. He was not an official Liberal candidate but stood against the Conservative candidate with Liberal support. It is said that he was persuaded to become a candidate because of the campaign which had been initiated by Joseph Chamberlain in 1903 against Free Trade. Although the general election of 1906 resulted in an overwhelming defeat of the Conservatives, and incidentally the return for the first time of more than fifty members of the Labour Party to Parliament, Russell in his election campaign found that Free Trade was still a suitable principle to serve as a political platform. "I am a Liberal and Free Trade is an essential part of Liberalism." The only thing which divided him from conventional Liberalism at that time was his support of women's suffrage. This was not quite such an unthinkable topic for Liberals as protection but he was in advance of his times, like so many other Russells in history. He found little support for such a minority view and was defeated.

Three years later, at the general election of 1910, he sought adoption as an official Liberal candidate. His dual theme was still Free Trade and women's suffrage but, alas, Russell was fated not to enjoy for a second time the diversions of the hustings. There were to be no more occasions like the famous one in 1907, when hecklers had released a number of mice, or according to some accounts, rats, in a hall in which there were numerous women in the audience! Unfortunately the committee was informed that Russell was an atheist. This was a heresy far greater than claiming votes for women. Russell's adoption had been considered certain, but, uncompromising as ever, he refused the committee's suggestion that he should attend church occasionally for appearance sake. He was not adopted.

Although by 1914 he had resigned from the Fabian Society because of his unswerving devotion to Free Trade, he was rapidly becoming more Socialist, less Liberal, in outlook. For a time his interest in the wider world of politics waned after his failure to be adopted in 1910. Later that year he was appointed lecturer in logic and mathematics at Trinity College, his old Cambridge College, and found genuine pleasure in returning to a place where the atmosphere had not changed very much since his undergraduate days. Though his audiences were necessarily small, they included many who later became distinguished philosophers or mathematicians. Apart from the pleasure he took in teaching, Russell was happy in the society of his fellow dons. He was specially gratified by an invitation to give a series of lectures at Harvard, U.S.A., where one of his pupils was T. S. Eliot. Thus began a long association of friendship and mutual respect. Russell was in one sense a poet, Eliot equally a philosopher. Each influenced the other enormously.

After the outbreak of the First World War he became a public figure revered by some, despised or hated by others. He was in those years a person whose influence could not be belittled, whose words and deeds were regarded as inspired by a cross-section of society which needed above all a leader to guide its footsteps and a voice to sound its protests.

As a don he had been celebrated for his pungent wit. One witticism rather doubtfully attributed to him was made at a meeting of dons with a strong religious bias. He happened to pick up an examination paper in which there were ten questions of which the students were required to answer only six. "Just like the Ten Commandments," he said, "no one is expected to attempt more than six." On another occasion, the story goes (like Oxford's Dr. Spooner, Russell attracted to his name a vast number of jokes of which he was not the author), he was speaking of a student who had been coached for an examination in Scripture and had painstakingly learned the names of the Kings of Judah and Israel. When faced with the question in his examination "How are the minor and major prophets distinguished?" the boy made a start to his reply by writing: "Far be it from me to make an invidious distinction between major and minor prophets. Rather let us enumerate the Kings of Judah and Israel.''

That is almost certainly an apocryphal story so far as Russell is concerned, but he always had a fund of amusing anecdotes. From 1914 onwards he became far more serious. Although he was not always in agreement with Socialist thinkers, he ceased to be a Liberal, because he believed that the conflict of capital caused wars and incidentally had caused the First World War with its flaming trail of young death and injury which Russell abhorred.

It is difficult to re-create the atmosphere in Britain after the outbreak of war. There had been talk of a possible war with Germany for many years but it was talk that did not reach the man in the street and was certainly not taken seriously by him. So Britain was utterly unprepared for the tragic events of 1914–18, a war that remains by far the bloodiest in the history of the world, a hundred times more lethal than the Second World War. Many European nations, including Germany and France, had something approaching a people's army. Compulsory service for a limited period was accepted without question. Not so in Britain. There was a small regular army—small, that is, by comparison with those of continental powers—and a powerful and wholly professional navy. Liberals and Conservatives alike had always set their faces against conscription. That is why in the early years of the war Britain still depended on voluntary service, surprising as it must seem to the people who did not live through that gruesome period of history. "Your King and Country need you" was the slogan used on posters to encourage young men to join the army. And thousands did so, hundreds and hundreds of thousands, until by 1915 Kitchener's army of civilian recruits was nearly two million strong.

Russell's position was never orthodox, He was not a conscientious objector in the sense in which the term was ordinarily used, to describe people whose conscience would not allow them to take part in *any* war. Yet he was closely associated with the conscientious objection movement and a member of the committee of the N.C.F. (No Conscription Fellowship). He believed at this time that some wars might be justifiable, but not this one, which he regarded as a war of prestige between the capitalist forces of two nations, a war that could only be compared with two dogs fighting in the street. He was appalled by what he thought was the fruitless waste of young lives. He was even more appalled at the belligerence of British people and at the enjoyment which so many seemed to take in all the gory details of the hostilities.

So from the beginning he appealed for an end to a war that ought never to have begun and a negotiated peace. He never swerved from this point of view, writing innumerable articles and addressing innumerable meetings. He convinced many hundreds of thousands of the rightness of his attitude but never made such an impact on the nation as to lessen the determination to see the war through to its bitter end and the surrender of the enemy. He was never pro-German, as he was often accused of being. He did, however, believe that it would be better to incur the risk of becoming a province of Germany than face the certainty of mass annihilation if the war continued.

It cost him dearly to take this stand, for although five thousand objectors by the end of the war had preferred imprisonment or forced labour to conscription, the protagonists of a negotiated peace were the object of ridicule and animosity by the vast majority of British people. It was all the more difficult for Russell because the majority of his fellow dons at Trinity supported the government in its determination to continue the war, an attitude endorsed by the vast majority of people on the home front. There were severe food shortages, but people in munition factories and other occupations useful to the war effort were better paid than ever before. Women took the place of men in many industries and enjoyed the experience.

The danger of heavy bombardment from the air was never a threat in the sense it was during the Second World War. Morale on the whole was high and Russell was espousing a lost cause as well as a highly unpopular one.

When conscription was finally introduced he was over age (although later the maximum age for conscription was raised and included Russell). He won some respect for his propaganda campaigns against conscription by reason of this very fact. It was obvious that he was disinterested. But for the most part he was in the Russell tradition "going it alone". The climax came in June 1916, when he was prosecuted for making statements likely to prejudice the discipline of H.M. Forces after writing a leaflet distributed through the N.C.F. concerning a conscientious objector who in spite of his objection was drafted into the Army and then sentenced to two years' hard labour for indiscipline. He was convicted and fined.

So far, so good, from the pacifists' point of view. The case had given far greater publicity to Russell's arguments than the necessarily limited distribution of the leaflets could possibly have done. But for Russell himself it spelt tragedy and disillusion, for as an immediate consequence of the case he was dismissed from his lectureship by the governing body of Trinity College. He felt the dismissal deeply. His colleagues at Trinity had paid so much lip service to the right of free expression before the war that he could scarcely bring himself to believe that they had been unanimous in condemning him for thus following his conscience.

Nevertheless, undaunted, he redoubled his propaganda efforts, writing and lecturing. Lytton Strachey, who heard one of these lectures, put it on record that he believed there was no one quite so formidable as Russell "to be found just now upon this earth". Moreover Russell found a sympathetic publisher who produced his *Principles of Social Reconstruction*. This had a remarkably large sale and continued to do so when the war was over, in foreign countries as much as at home. Like his *Problems of Philosophy* it was a book for the layman. Though based on principles derived from philosophy, it was entirely practical in its approach to the problems of the day, not only war but education, sex and international relations. It was, in effect, the Russell bible, which influenced post-war generations and was the inspiration of many other books produced by writers who derived their attitudes from Russell.

From that time onwards he was most concerned with the problems of reconstruction, although he continued to work with the pacifists so effectively that according to Lloyd George, then Prime Minister, his speeches interfered with the prosecution of the war. One of the media of propaganda which he used most often was *The Tribunal*, the weekly journal published by the N.C.F. He wrote an article for it early in 1918, in which he said, "Unless peace comes soon there will be starvation throughout Europe. Men will fight each other for possession of the bare necessities of life." He also held out the prospect that American troops would occupy England and France and would be used to intimidate strikers if they succeeded in defeating the Germans. In another paragraph, with characteristic impudence, he said, "I do not see that these thoughts are in the minds of the government. All the evidence tends to show that there are no thoughts whatever in their minds."

He was prosecuted and, rather surprisingly, sentenced to six months' imprisonment, a sentence which was upheld on appeal. The magistrate, in passing sentence, said that Russell had insulted the army of a great nation and he described the offence as a despicable one. Russell spent his time in prison writing and reading and was treated with special consideration. Even so, the prison made a deep impression on him. He said himself that there were many things he missed but, above all, talk. "I never knew how one could hunger for it."

That was the end of his war effort. When he was released a number of his friends and sympathisers contributed to a fund for employing him as a lecturer (it was necessary that he should rank as a teacher in order to be exempted from the call-up to which the alternative was almost certain imprisonment). Among the friends who contributed were Charles Trevelyan, J. M. Keynes and Siegfried Sassoon. He clearly did not lose all his influential or cultured friends! When the war ended the fund was closed and its beneficiary, no longer having a large enough private income on which to live in comfort, set about earning a living as a writer and lecturer.

In the years between the two wars his interests became more and more political and social, less and less concerned with philosophy. He was, however, a frequent reviewer of books on philosophy and also undertook a number of lecture tours, especially to the United States. But the bulk of his writing—and a very large bulk it was—was directed to the layman. There was a ready market, and a receptive audience for his books and articles. As he himself said, "I do not mind pot-boiling. I have no lofty feelings."

This was the time at which his influence on the common man was greatest. Although he might regard some of his books as pot-boilers and his innumerable articles as means of earning a living, the people who read them tended to regard them with special respect because they came from the pen of a philosopher of high reputation. Even a comparatively minor figure like C. E. M. Joad later in this period wielded considerable influence. How, then, could a far cleverer man, or far more facile writer like Russell have failed to cast a spell on untutored minds so that what he wrote became a sort of bible to hundreds of thousands of people, a bible, incidentally, which replaced the Holy Bible?

The main themes of his social and political conclusions appear over and over again in his books, especially in *Principles of Social Reconstruction*, to which reference has already been made, and *Sceptical Essays in Religion and Science*. *Sceptical Essays*, which was completed halfway through the twenty years of uneasy peace, gave what appeared to be philosophical and scientific

18

reasons for an undogmatic attitude in all spheres of knowledge. The scepticism that led him sometimes to describe himself as an agnostic rather than an atheist was to him more real, perhaps, than any other facet of life. It did not, however, deter him from maintaining and sometimes preaching conclusions which offended many progressive people as well as the traditionalists. All his conclusions were bound up in one way or another with his desire for peace and the promotion of happiness which, like most philosophers, he equated with pleasure. Always he was a passionate advocate of peace, a passionate opponent of war. That fact alone predisposed many of his listeners to accept other far more debatable conclusions.

In politics his ultimate aim was internationalism, which alone he believed could prevent a recurrence of war. He saw the threat to peace always as the conflict between two great world powers and clearly forecast almost before anyone else the conflict which was bound to arise between Russia and the United States. If there were only one major power in the world governing every other nation with benevolent despotism there would, he thought, be no cause for war.

Until the outbreak of the Second World War he maintained his position of active pacifism. He saw the desire for power as one of the greatest evils and recognized that unlimited power, whether derived from Russian or American ideology, was equally destructive. Moreover, in the years between the two wars he was far less an admirer of Russia than most Socialists.

In this attitude he was influenced by personal observation during a visit to Russia in 1920. He was dismayed by the bellicose attitude of Trotsky and Lenin. It is recorded that, during an interview with Lenin, Russell suggested that Socialism might be achieved in Great Britain without a bloody war and that Lenin described the suggestion as fantastic. Russell saw unerringly the perils of a dictatorship in Russia, with the religion of Marxism replacing Christianity as an excuse for persecution comparable with the Spanish Inquisition.

The basis of his moral teaching was that creative instincts should be encouraged, possessive ones discouraged. The logical course of action was to work for the greatest pleasure of the greatest number. Another corner-stone derived partly from Freud was that repression of natural instincts in children leads to a bellicose attitude in later life. To this cause he thought could be ascribed the willingness of young men to take part in a war and the positive enjoyment which some obtained from shooting down another man in flames. This conclusion led him to attack the educational system as a whole and the conventional attitude to sex in particular.

These two facets of his thought always obtained greatest publicity. Some of the popularity of his beliefs was no doubt due to the fact that most people are susceptible to any doctrine which makes self-control unnecessary. The influence which his thought had on social life in the twenties and thirties cannot be denied. Many critics who are still loyal to their faith find this influence inexplicable. The solution of the enigma lies in the social conditions which prevailed between 1918 and 1939. The rigid code of Victorian times, rigid, that is, so far as the middle class was concerned, had been slow a-dying. A strict convention in conduct and manners was still observed by millions of people in 1914.

The war brought a wider outlook to many who escaped death or serious injury. Compared with the horrors of war in the trenches, scarcely anything seemed important. Reaction from the years of privation engendered a desire for liberty, which all too often was a synonym for licence, not only then but in other crises in the history of western civilization. The war, after all, had been fought for freedom, the freedom of the individual, and the individual must be free to choose his own way of life unencumbered by outworn traditions and conventions.

Another important thing happened in those few years of conflict. Women had achieved a far better status in the community. They were said to have earned the vote by reason of their help in winning the war. That is nonsense. The suffragette movement, if war had not broken out at the psychological moment, would almost certainly have resulted in the consummation of the long struggle to give women the vote. The war did, however, bring from their homes into office and factories and even into the Armed Forces hundreds of thousands of women who otherwise would never have escaped from parental control. They worked side by side with men and some of the mystery of the relationship between the sexes was dispersed.

Another factor was that after the war there was a surplus of two million women in Great Britain, the majority of them of marriageable age, a circumstance that arose solely and simply from the carnage of the war years. To make matters worse, the economic position was bad. After two or three years of boom, slump succeeded slump. The number of unemployed rose to far above a million. Savage strikes, especially the strike of miners in 1926, to support which the largely unsuccessful general strike was called, undermined the country's economy, so that recovery was slow. The middle class was as hard hit as any. Increases in salaries scarcely kept pace with the increase in the cost of living, and for many men early marriage and the responsibility of a family were out of the question. In these circumstances many people were receptive to a new philosophy of life which might be seen to minimize some of their difficulties.

This was especially true of the middle class, which before the war had been the chief bastion of conventional living. Russell's ethical teaching in effect swept away the foundation of religion and with it the whole moral superstructure which had been erected on it. Agnosticism is always easy for the young. It was particularly so then, and made all the easier by the doubts about religion that had assailed many during the war.

Russell went further than this. Not content with undermining religious belief as such, he belittled the Christian ethic and described Jesus Christ as inferior to Socrates or Buddha in the wisdom of his teaching and the goodness of his life. He upheld the cause of sex freedom and the equality of women's rights in regard to sex and said on many occasions that he regarded pre-marital intercourse as an essential prerequisite for good living and happy marriage. He did not think that anyone should undertake the responsibilities of marriage without prior experience. Unmarried mothers should be treated in precisely the same way as married ones and regarded with equal respect. Trial marriages between undergraduates would lessen the tension of university life. In education he taught that an absolute minimum of discipline should be exerted on children and in no circumstances should corporal punishment be used. He believed that sex should be taught at the earliest possible age and made uninteresting to children—uninteresting, that is, in an obscene sense. He also believed that clever children should be segregated from others at the age of twelve and be trained for further education at a university without further examination.

The facts of his life show that Russell was always ready to practise his own precepts. He inherited the earldom in 1932 when his brother Frank died (apart from a conviction for bigamy on technical grounds, Frank had lived the conventional life of a businessman and company director), but still preferred to be known as Bertrand Russell (or Bertie to his more intimate friends). When he went to China to lecture at the University of Peking (by now his first wife had divorced him) he took with him as his travelling companion Dora Black, who later became his second wife. Although his lectures were outstandingly successful, he courted a good deal of criticism by his atheistic professions and by his association with Dora Black. The attitude of the numerous Chinese Missionaries, who at that time were responsible for a large measure of Chinese cultural life, was highly critical.

So, too, in education. He and Dora founded Beacon Hill School, the purpose of which was to fulfil the principles of education in which they both believed—the principles of complete freedom and the breaking down of inhibitions. This part of Russell's work received more Press publicity than any other and the publicity was by no means always favourable. The school set a fashion which is still not extinct and in this the Russells were certainly pioneers.

The outbreak of the Second World War found him and his third wife Patricia in the United States. There they stayed until 1944. In the stress of warfare little was heard of them during these years. Few except the intelligentsia and their personal friends thought of them. Bertrand's influence inevitably declined, though, as we shall see, later many of his social conclusions lived on in the atmosphere of strain and experiment that every war, and particularly a people's war, engenders.

His outlook on pacifism appeared to change completely between 1936 and 1940 but the change was not truly a change of mind but rather a change in the appraisal of the particular circumstances. He remained a pacifist at heart. On the other hand, he had always infuriated conventional pacifists—the bulk of conscientious objectors—by allowing that the use of force might sometimes be justifiable, especially if a world government were established and it became necessary to discipline some nation or group which showed signs of rebelling. That would be a case, in Russell's view, of helping the rebels to help themselves.

In 1936 one of Russell's most provocative books aimed at the popular market, *Which Way to Peace?*, was published. His message was amplified by a large number of Press articles. In this book Russell argued the case for pacifism in connexion with Nazi Germany. He regarded a future war as one in which a dominant part would be played by aeroplanes dropping bombs containing disease germs and poison gas. He believed that normal life would be impossible. In every way he exaggerated grossly the effects on civilization of a war in the air (one wonders whether perhaps he has similarly exaggerated in more recent years by equating the existence of the hydrogen bomb with the suicide of the human race). In practice none of the horrors which he expected came to pass. No one would be disposed to argue against the fact that war between nations brings death and destruction in its wake, but the number of casualties during the Second World War was little, if at all, greater than the number killed and injured throughout the world in a comparable time from road accidents in the 1960s.

Russell's other main contribution to the subject in 1936 was that a war must produce a military dictatorship, so that it would be a matter of exchanging a German Hitler for an English one. So he committed himself to the uncompromising statement that if Hitler were to attack Great Britain, German troops should be welcomed like tourists. He did not believe that Hitler would prove the monster that he had been depicted or that German troops would respond in anything but a friendly way to their welcome.

By the time of the Munich agreement he was already in the United States discharging engagements in the Universities of Chicago and California. From the other side of the Atlantic he proclaimed his agreement with the Munich compromise. Yet when war broke out he renounced his pacifism, maintaining that the defeat of Nazi Germany was an essential prerequisite for the establishment of peace and good life in the world at large.

His years in the United States were spent in lecturing and writing, although it was only at the academic level that he was notably well received. At one time few American journals would publish his articles. When he resigned from the University of California to become Professor of Philosophy in New York College, he was prevented from taking up his new appointment by a Court decision. A member of the public brought an action against the selection board in accordance with United States law and obtained a ruling that his appointment was invalid. The judge thought it was iniquitous that anyone who publicly advocated trial marriages for university students should be let loose to teach in an American university. Russell's stock remained low on the other side of the Atlantic for many years.

It was not perhaps as surprising as it seems at first glance that when he returned in 1944, having been reappointed in his absence a Fellow of Trinity College, Cambridge, he was received in Cambridge with enthusiasm. Within a few years he was regarded not only in academic circles but by many laymen as one of the country's most venerable and honoured philosophers. Honours were heaped on him in his seventies, academic and public. He was invited to give the first Reith Lectures by the B.B.C. in 1948. Two years later he was doubly honoured with the award of the Nobel Prize and of the Order of Merit. Earl Russell, O.M., was a very very different matter from Bertrand Russell, author of *Principia Mathematica*. He was no longer regarded as a rebel but as a forward-looking philosopher, convincing to all whose faith was undermined by one cause or another.

The explanation lies in the fact that a great change had taken place in the British way of life since Russell had begun to publish his ethical and political conclusions. The cause for which he had campaigned in his youth, that of women's rights, had been won. Divorce was now as easy for women to obtain as for men. Birth control was no longer a topic to be discussed behind closed doors, but was openly practised by millions of men and women. The often repeated statistic that every third first child is conceived out of wedlock shows at least that pre-marital intercourse is commonplace.

It is probable that during the Second World War and immediately afterwards far more young people would have commended themselves by their conduct to Russell than today. There has been a reaction against sexual licence, as there has been also against Russell's philosophy. Material conditions have changed and this change from a world of mass unemployment between the wars to the "opulent society" of the 1960s, holding out the possibility among other things of early marriages in all phases of society, has been one of the factors leading to reaction.

In the six years between his return to Cambridge and the award of the Order of Merit Russell made two further contributions: one to political thought, the other to ethical theory. In both cases the contribution was an amplification or qualification of conclusions he had reached long before. In politics he argued strongly for world government but held that the function of the world government should be merely to eliminate war. It should delegate its powers to national governments and these in return to regional governments, leaving the individual the greatest possible freedom of thought and action.

In ethical theory he added a new word to the English language—"compossible". The theories of compossibles did not appear in book form until 1954, when *Human Society in Ethics and Politics* was published, but the idea on which the book was based was much earlier. The right desires are those which are compossible with others, that is to say, it is right to satisfy a personal desire (resulting in pleasure) if the satisfaction of that desire does not interfere with other people satisfying their desires. The introduction of a new word does not necessarily constitute a new theory. Russell had always believed that creative impulses were good, possessive ones bad, and the theory of compossible desires has been compared with the hedonistic philosophy that the greatest good is the greatest happiness of the greatest number.

It has always been doubtful whether the spark that kindled the fire of Bertrand Russell's enthusiasm was a philosophical or a practical one. Admirers and detractors have for many years agreed, however, that his chief object in later life has been to secure the peace of the world. His admirers have maintained that his contribution has been an enormous one. His detractors have argued that his shock methods of drawing attention to his creed have sometimes defeated themselves. Some have questioned whether he has tackled the problem in the best

possible way, whether indeed one man, however great his influence, can without any authority except that of his own
personality, have any real influence on world opinion, or what
is perhaps more important, on the outlook of national governments.

No one has ever doubted his sincerity. When he was awarded
the Nobel Prize for Literature in 1950 few disputed his claims
as a writer. He had proved himself to be one of the most
eminent philosophers of his times. The award of the Nobel
Prize when he was in his seventy-eighth year might have been
expected to be the consummation of a long life but it was a
beginning rather than an end. The older he became the more
energetic he seemed to be in his passionate and practical
crusade to convert the world to his way of thinking, so far at
least as this was concerned with the peace of the world.

It is easy to see a similarity between his career and that of his
grandfather. Many believed that Lord John Russell's day of
glory was over when his first administration was dissolved. Yet
Lord John lived to be Prime Minister a second time against all
probability and retired ultimately with honour and distinction.
So Bertrand Russell, commonly regarded as an elder of
philosophy, a man whose days of influence were in the past,
asserted himself with renewed vigour to make a greater impact
on national thought and on international politics than he had
ever done before. As in the case of his grandfather, respect for
his courage and determination to serve others overcame all
other considerations.

After the Second World War he began to feel happier about
the future of the world than he had done at any time since 1914.
Russia did not make war on the Western World. The nuclear
powers of the West were in a position to threaten any aggressor
rather than to be threatened. In this Russell saw renewed hope;
he could not bring himself to believe that either side would in a
position of relative equilibrium unleash these destructive
forces, whatever provocation might be offered.

Then came news of the development of the hydrogen bomb. That acted as a trigger which brought all Russell's old fears to new life. The very existence of such devastating sources of destruction appalled him. He re-entered the world arena as a still vitally active contestant, though now well past his eightieth birthday.

His first and one of his most effective instruments for peace was forged in the summer of 1955. He was successful in obtaining the support of world-famous scientists, seven of whom had been awarded a Nobel Prize, who identified themselves with a declaration published by Russell, calling on all nations to renounce war as a means of settling their disputes. A measure of the scientific weight behind this declaration was that the signatories included Professor Einstein, who confirmed his adherence to the declaration only two days before he died. The international nature of the declaration was underlined by the fact that apart from Professor Einstein, two of the scientists were British, two American, one Polish, one French and one Japanese.

The declaration was sent to the head of all states possessing nuclear weapons and also to those states, including China, which might be expected to possess them in the future. It was a brilliant document which fulfilled at least a part of its purpose through the wide world publicity it received and the sympathy which was expressed by the Press of many countries. It brought home to people more clearly, perhaps, than ever before the horrors awaiting the civilized world in the event of an intensive war carried out with nuclear weapons. It pointed out that a war waged with hydrogen bombs might do more than bring civilization as we know it to an end. It might possibly be the end of the human race. If what the declaration called universal death were to come, this would be immediate only for a minority. For the majority it would involve the slow torture of disease and disintegration.

The signatories were emphatic in saying that they were not

speaking as members of a particular nation or creed but as members of the species Man, whose continued existence was in doubt. They were equally emphatic in their statement that not only the general public but many men in positions of political authority did not realize what was involved in such a war.

It was said by some critics that the declaration in itself said nothing that had not been said many times before: "We urge the governments of the world to acknowledge publicly that their purpose cannot be furthered by modern war", and again: "We urge them consequently to find peaceful means for the settlement of all matters of dispute." There is, of course, some truth in that criticism. It is equally true that the majority of people had not realized the full consequences of high-powered nuclear weapons and that the combined authority of these international scientists ensured awareness of the facts. This awareness revived the determination of the man in the street to resist the idea of war. Without the support of its people no nation dare contemplate war. In that sense Russell's campaign was a success and its influence was a lasting one.

His work for peace was far more immediately appreciated in other countries than in Great Britain and on the whole was taken more seriously. It was significant that in 1960 he was awarded the Sonning Prize, a Danish award for outstanding contributions to European culture. Russell was only the second recipient of this prize. The first was Dr. Albert Schweitzer. However dissimilar on the face of it the work of the two men may appear, there is an obvious ground for comparison between the superhuman efforts made by Dr. Schweitzer to relieve physical suffering in Africa and Earl Russell's efforts to save the world from unnecessary suffering, efforts which must rank as superhuman, if only on account of his advanced age.

His passionate determination to carry on what for him had become a guiding principle of his life was evidenced again by his part in the campaign for nuclear disarmament and by his unexpected and to many statesmen unwelcome intervention in the

Cuba crisis. Much of the preliminary work of launching the Campaign for Nuclear Disarmament (C.N.D.) was carried out by him with able assistance from the Rev. Michael Scott. A major development was the establishment in the latter months of 1960 of the Committee of 100. The purpose of the Committee was frankly non-violent civil disobedience, a policy to which, after all, Earl Russell was no stranger. The aim was to draw constant attention to the attitude of the people about nuclear weapons. The reason underlying the formation of so numerous a Committee was that if there were no specific office holders there would be less danger of the work of the campaign being brought to a halt through action directed against key personnel. Earl Russell signed a letter of invitation as President of the campaign and the Rev. Michael Scott signed a covering letter endorsing the invitation. Members were drawn from the ranks of people known to be sympathetic to the campaign's under-lying purpose. The Committee was responsible for ensuring that there would be at least two thousand present at any demonstration that was organized.

The Committee of 100 provoked major disagreement within the ranks of the organization responsible for the campaign for nuclear disarmament. Canon Collins, the national chairman, said that the civil disobedience campaign was contrary to the organization's policy. There was recrimination within the executive committee, followed by a temporary truce between the belligerents. Early in October 1960 Earl Russell and Canon Collins issued a statement to the effect that they would continue to work together. However, Canon Collins did not repudiate his disapproval of the Committee and before the end of October Earl Russell had resigned as President. "I find it impossible to work with the national chairman of the campaign," he said. After that, less and less was heard of the campaign for nuclear disarmament, more and more of the Committee of 100.

During 1961 a number of demonstrations were organized,

some of them involving a prolonged "sit-down" for the purpose of obstructing traffic. These demonstrations achieved one object, that of obtaining major publicity for the movement. On the principle attributed to Mr. Sam Goldwyn that any publicity is good publicity, the demonstrations were highly successful. The police on the whole were meticulous in their approach to the very real problem they presented, but on information that a demonstration at which ten thousand people were expected was to be held in Parliament Square, followed by a sit-down, the police took more drastic action than previously and arrested 32 members or adherents of the Committee of 100. They were accused of inciting members of the public to commit a breach of the peace.

Earl and Countess Russell were among the 32 accused, for neither Earl Russell nor his wife had ever spared themselves. They worked as hard as any and "sat down" with as much determination as any. All refused the magistrate's invitation to agree to be bound over. The magistrate thereupon imposed prison sentences. Five, including the Russells, were sentenced to two months' imprisonment, the remaining 27 to one month. There was an outcry in Court at the sentences, which in the case of Lord and Lady Russell were reduced to seven days after the submission of medical reports. The telegram sent by the Romford Labour Party to the Home Secretary was typical of the feeling of a large section of the population: "Shocked and shamed by treatment of octogenarian Russell. Urge immediate release." But no. The 89-year-old demonstrator began to serve his seven-day sentence in Wormwood Scrubbs, his wife in Holloway. They were far less disturbed than thousands of their sympathisers.

It was a brave gesture which made a great impression, as did the undoubted standing of some of the other members of the committee who were sentenced. These included the Rev. Michael Scott, Arnold Wesker, Dr. Fergus King, Mrs. Anne Kerr, a London County Councillor, and Miss Noel Buxton,

sister of Lord Noel Buxton, all people eminent in their various
spheres of activity. That was by no means the end of the Committee of 100 but it was its finest hour. In spite of the prison
sentences and in spite of a specific ban imposed by the police,
the demonstration in Trafalgar Square was held as planned on
17th September. But without the fire of the leaders the
demonstration was far less effective than expected. The police
kept the demonstrators on the move and arrested about a
thousand out of the twelve thousand who took part. There
were few incidents and most of the people arrested were fined
between £1 and £5 at Magistrates' Courts on the following
day.

The scene changes. A year has passed. And now in October
1962 the world is on the brink of war. Memories of the "Cuba
crisis" have faded a little but many still recall vividly the
atmosphere of confusion, of fear, which prevailed from the time
when President Kennedy in a nation-wide broadcast announced
a blockade of Cuba. The pretext for President Kennedy's action
was the discovery by aerial reconnaissance of rocket missile
installations being constructed on Cuba and of jet bombers
capable of carrying nuclear bombs being uncrated on Cuban
airfields. To the United States this appeared to be a direct
threat, for the weapons being installed, which were known to be
of Russian origin, could not be called defensive ones.

Opinion in Britain was divided. An official statement issued
by the Foreign Office blamed what it called the provocative
action of the Soviet Union. The Prime Minister supported
President Kennedy's action, but the leader of the Opposition
was uneasy at any nation taking unilateral action. Many
doubted the international legality of a blockade against a
sovereign state in times of peace. Mr. Kennedy repeated that no
diplomatic conversations could take place with Chairman
Khrushchev until the missile bases in Cuba were dismantled.
There was no doubt at all that the United States Government
had provided a *casus belli*, nor was there any doubt that if

Russia and the United States were at war the greater part of the civilized world would be involved.

This was the point at which Russell intervened. From his home in North Wales, he sent personal telegrams to President Kennedy, Mr. Khrushchev, Mr. Macmillan, then Prime Minister, and U Thant, Secretary-General of the United Nations. The appeal he made depended for its efficacy solely on Russell's reputation and on the respect with which he was regarded by the governments of the nations concerned. The text of the cable sent to Mr. Khrushchev made no secret of the fact that the philosopher blamed the United States for having precipitated the crisis. "I appeal to you not to be provoked by the unjustifiable action of the United States in Cuba. The world will support caution. Precipitous action could mean annihilation for mankind."

Mr. Khrushchev replied by return at considerable length. He expressed his gratitude for Lord Russell's concern at the aggressive action of the United States in pushing the world to the brink of war. "I should like to assure you," he said, "that the Soviet Government will not take any reckless decisions, will not permit itself to be provoked by the unwarranted action of the United States, and will do everything to eliminate a situation fraught with irreparable consequences." He ended, "I thank you once more for your appeal, prompted as it was by your concern for the destinies of the world."

It is remarkable, but not surprising, that the other recipients of Lord Russell's telegrams acknowledged them, though more briefly than Mr. Khrushchev, and showed beyond any possibility of doubt that his appeal was regarded seriously, in the belief that it represented the viewpoint of a vast number of people. The denouement was sudden. Unexpectedly the Russian Government agreed to withdraw the offending missiles from Cuba and to dismantle Cuban missile sites under the supervision of the United Nations. That was the end of the crisis. How far Lord Russell's appeal was responsible for the

Russian decision and for the far more conciliatory attitude of the United States Government in the following weeks can never be known.

The conclusion of the nuclear test-ban treaty, in Russell's opinion, lulled the civilized world into a false sense of security. It seemed to many that the work of the campaign for nuclear disarmament and of the Committee of 100 was now unnecessary. This he considered was a gross misconception. The United States and the Soviet Union had stock piles of thermonuclear weapons which could destroy organic life in every part of the world.

That was the background to the initiation in September of 1963 of the Bertrand Russell Peace Foundation and the Atlantic Peace Foundation. The purpose of the former was to envisage the causes of "cold war" and carry out research into ways of diminishing and ultimately eliminating the risk of hostilities. The aims of the Atlantic Peace Foundation were similar. It was created to carry out research in the areas most closely connected with the work of the Bertrand Russell Foundation.

Russell believed that anti-war movements had lived from hand to mouth not only in Great Britain but in every civilized country. Publicity had been frugal, the work of the peace organizations had been belittled. It was one of the purposes of these foundations to remedy that state of affairs by developing their own media of communication, not dependent upon the "governmental intimidated Press". There was, he said, substantial financial backing making possible plans for the publication of the foundation's own newspaper, which it was intended eventually to print in several languages, and possibly the establishment of a radio station.

This was a grandiose scheme which many commentators believed would never come to fruition. It did, however, emphasize once more Lord Russell's continuing struggle for the maintenance of peace in a nuclear age and underlined his practical attitude to the value of publicity. The Russell

19

philosophy might live on, the philosophy of peace might win the assent of scholars the world over, but the vital thing for Lord Russell was, as it had always been, the practical interpretation of this philosophy for the benefit of common man. His message now, just as it had been in the early years of the century, was a message of action for every human being.

Much of the social philosophy put forward in his early years had been regarded as contrary to the profound beliefs of the Church, but much of it had been accepted as the years passed. Bertrand Russell, the practical philosopher, had always been years ahead of his time, had by any reckoning made a substantial contribution to the changing pattern of conduct. It could well be that the practical approach to international affairs which was his preoccupation in the eighties and nineties might be accepted as commonplace by future generations.

In a broadcast interview in 1965 he said that the Russell Foundation had been started because demonstration marches had grown stale. It had, he thought, already achieved worthwhile results, especially in acting for the liberation of political prisoners. He said he was neither optimistic nor pessimistic about the future. He would not be content until there was an effective world government, but he realized that could not happen in his lifetime.

That was still his hope. No man could have worked harder to make his dreams come true.

CHAPTER TWELVE

Selling Woburn to the World

DUKE HERBRAND was the last of the farming Russells. He projected the traditions and image of the 19th-century Dukes far into the 20th century with an unflagging determination. An unyielding conservatism was characteristic of him as a man as well as in his position as head of the House of Russell—and that although he was liberal in politics, still following the Russell tradition. He succeeded to the dukedom in 1893 and died in 1940. Those forty-seven years span an era of change greater perhaps than any comparable period in English history. It was a period in which the way of living of the whole nation changed, when new traditions were born, and when the privilege of the aristocracy was undermined by many factors, economic as well as social.

Duke Herbrand never changed. Stubbornly he held to the canons of his ancestors. When he accepted change even in the minor things of life, such as lighting or heating, he accepted them with his mind but never with his heart, which was rooted for ever in the world of his youth, when to be Duke of Bedford was to be preordained to be great, when the word of a duke, however inept, was received with respect. That was the atmosphere in which he was brought up. It was the atmosphere that he strived to maintain, in semblance if not in fact, to the end of his life.

In order to do so he was compelled to live a lonelier and lonelier life, isolated from the changing pattern of thought and behaviour. He was secure only in his own castle, the traditional stronghold of Woburn; his word was still law with the people who worked for him as assistants and servants, an army of retainers never less than two hundred strong if one includes the outdoor workers as well as the indoor servants.

Such defiance of circumstances is regarded by some as a noble gesture, by others as evidence of supreme egotism. In the case of the 11th Duke it may well have owed something to both. In spirit Herbrand was certainly conservative to a degree that would be impossible in a man of less strength of character. He believed most sincerely in the way of life of his predecessors, in the dignity of the dukedom, and the necessity of maintaining proved institutions. He did not want change. There was no one and nothing to compel him to accept it in his private life. He had the money to run a 20th-century ducal household in 19th-century style and could always find people who would run it for him as he wished. The fact that inevitably he became out of touch with contemporary thought was not important to him.

That is only one side of his character. In his work as a master farmer and estate manager he was as progressive and receptive of new ideas as any Russell who had gone before him, still essentially a reforming Russell. Indeed, in every way he was a Russell cast in the traditional mould, forward-looking in a national sense, often generous to those who served him, but idiosyncratic in his own life, an indestructable permanent in a crumbling world. He stands out in the social history of the 20th century not so much because of what he achieved as because there were few, if any, who occupied a comparable position in a period that spans the business-as-usual years of the Edwardian era, the shock of the First World War, the years of depression between the two wars, and the outbreak of a people's war.

When he became Duke upper-class women were still ladies of the household and nothing more. He lived to see their emancipation and by a strange paradox his own wife contributed much to the vastly different ideal of feminine usefulness. He lived, too, through a period in which the philosophy of democracy often

degenerated to something akin to anarchy. While he was Duke
the horse gave way to the motor-car. The first aeroplane flew
long after he had succeeded. By the time he died air travel and
air warfare were commonplace.

In 1893 it was not regarded as either ostentatious or eccentric
to employ fifty footmen with powdered hair, red coats and
white breeches and to place one of these oddly attired gentlemen behind the chair of every guest at dinner. That was the
done thing. More than that, it was expected of a man in the
Duke's position. Nor was it considered extravagant to supply
each guest with an individual gold teapot for breakfast. The
routine of aristocratic life was determined down to the last
detail. It was not only customary; it was obligatory. Any change
suggested or necessitated was in the eyes of Herbrand and his
fellow peers a lowering of standards which must be resisted to
the uttermost. The outstanding achievement of Duke Herbrand
was that his resistance was more effective (however negatively)
than that of almost any of his fellow peers. There is something to
be said for his attitude of mind. Change is often associated with
decay and it is extraordinarily difficult at the time to distinguish
between the change that marks progress and the change that
marks with equal certainty regression.

In spite of this attitude the 11th Duke was a Whig. He chose
deliberately the occupation of farmer and rejected the opportunity to enter politics, though he was more than once offered
high office. He did not see how farming and public life could be
combined, and conceived his first duty to be to the Russell
estates and the Russell tenants. No one, however critical, could
describe him as other than devoted to his work, persevering, a
first-class manager and an excellent landlord. As mentioned in a
previous chapter, agriculture towards the end of the 19th century had not recovered from the acute depression that bedevilled it earlier in the century. It did not, in fact, recover until the
First World War, which brought it into the front line as the most
vital of all industries for survival. But it was a time of experiment

and innovation in farming methods, and the Duke gave every encouragement to new methods on his model farm and on the estates, encouraging tenant farmers to experiment themselves and often guaranteeing them against loss from doing so. His knowledge of farming was vast. It soon became his one and only interest, so that he struck acquaintances other than those engaged in agriculture as dull and unimaginative. In every community of farming people he was respected and often made challenging or provocative speeches.

He was for many years on the county council and served as chairman. He was indefatigable in promoting local charities and was created Knight of the Garter. He made only occasional appearances in the House of Lords, where he was regarded, oddly enough, as almost revolutionary in his views. The report of a speech of his in 1910 certainly suggests that in public, if not in private life, he was ahead of his times. He attacked heredity as the only qualification for membership of the House, foretelling the end of its usefulness unless the hereditary principle was abandoned. He also spoke in favour of land reform, though nationalization of the land was a bogey which he feared and detested. However, he certainly believed that the power of the hereditary landowners should be diminished and a leavening of more freeholders introduced to revivify agriculture.

Inevitably his views were unpopular in the highly traditional House of Lords. He made few, if any, more speeches after that year. However, he practised what he preached and provided the finance for a large number of his tenant farmers to buy their holdings on all the Russell estates. He also hived off many thousands of acres, selling the Thorney estate and parts of others.

He also sold the Covent Garden estate but his purpose in this case was principally to rid himself of what had been a thorn in the side of the Russells for several generations. The first decades of the century witnessed the growth of immoderate Radicalism, which reared its ugly head only to subside as many of the real grievances of the under-privileged were met. But during much of the time Herbrand was Duke the very fact of being a landlord was to be branded as an oppressor of the poor. And that is something which Herbrand certainly was not. Numerous attacks appeared in the Press, directed not so much at him personally as at previous Dukes for the allegedly extortionate rents which they obtained for the Covent Garden property. So he took the opportunity to sell it at a time when it seemed that investment in securities other than property was not only more profitable but less contentious. By the time of his death only the Woburn and Bloomsbury estates were intact, though substantial parts of the Tavistock estate also remained in Russell hands. The price he obtained for Covent Garden before the First World War is said to have been £2,000,000. It might be worth five to ten times that amount now.

Herbrand's early life was spent in the Army, in which he served with the same conscientiousness that he later showed in serving the estate. After a not undistinguished career in the Guards he was in 1886 aide-de-camp to the Marquess of Dufferin and Ava, then Viceroy of India. It was a job that suited him. He applied to the duties of organizing the viceregal establishment the same qualities as he brought to estate management. While in India he met Mary Tribe, daughter of the Archdeacon of Lahore, the girl whom he married and who proved to be the only woman in his life. The common interest in nature and the devotion to the countryside pursuits that brought them together were the only links forged between them for the rest of their long lives. Strong personal attachments were not possible with Herbrand's make-up; the emotional side of his character appears never to have had full expression.

They had an only son, christened Hastings, who became the 12th Duke, but there was never the exemplary family atmosphere at Woburn that had been associated with many of Herbrand's predecessors. The three protagonists of the drama, Herbrand, Mary and Hastings, went their own ways, drawing further and further apart as the years passed. Between the two wars it was apparent that this was the twilight of the Russell tradition, its hereditary leaders dogged by ill health and the ill wind of change.

Outside farming and the Woburn estate Herbrand's greatest contribution was made through the medium of the Royal Zoological Society. If he had a hobby it was zoology. He played a large part in the inception and development of Whipsnade Zoo and laid the foundations of the herds of exotic animals bred to a very different habitat from that of England which distinguish Woburn Park today. These included bison and Père David deer. The European Bison were a gift from the Czar, who was friendly disposed to the Russell family and made a friend of the Duke's cousin, Sir Odo Russell, when he was at the St. Petersburg Embassy. The Duke also introduced a herd of wild horses from the Gobi Desert. Woburn was, and still is, one of the most important private zoos in Britain and Duke Herbrand was encouraged perhaps by the enthusiasm of his wife, which equalled, if it did not surpass, his own.

Mary, for all her quietness, her acceptance of the Woburn regime, so different from that of the home of a clergyman in India, for all her apparent conservatism, was a portent of the times. She typified the emancipation of women quite as vividly as those who cast their first votes in parliamentary elections. Mary did not want to vote. She showed not the slightest interest in politics, but she did want to serve the community and demonstrate that a woman could be in the forefront of progress just as surely as a man. So although she is known best perhaps for the founding of the bird sanctuaries, she was also a genuine pioneer of the motoring and flying age. Herbrand did not take to the motor-car. It represented a form of progress with which he had no sympathy, in contrast with the application of the principle of the internal combustion engine to agriculture, which he favoured. But Mary was an enthusiastic motorist from the early 1900s, often insisting on driving alone along the roads of Bedfordshire, an almost unheard-of thing for a woman to do. She was, however, practical and quite prepared to do her own running repairs, indeed preferred to do so.

Like her husband, the Duchess had real ability of a practical kind and only needed the opportunity to develop it. Of this she gave absolute proof during the First War. She had always been interested in nursing and would probably have followed it as a profession if she had not married. But she never lost her interest and personally supervised the opening and administration of the Woburn Cottage Hospital, which was wholly financed by the Duke. She became a qualified radiographer and persuaded her husband to transform part of Woburn Abbey into a wartime hospital for wounded soldiers. The expense of the hospital was borne by the Duke. The Duchess gave her services as general administrator and organizer. It was a remarkable example of the efficiency of private enterprise in a national emergency. The Duchess is said not only to have overworked herself but inspired the nurses and medical staff to do the same, thinking nothing of being at the hospital for 14 hours a day.

The Duke worked almost equally as hard. With government approval he converted the Ampthill estate into a training depot for the Bedfordshire Territorial Regiment. Later Ampthill was taken over by the War Office as a Command Depot but the Duke continued to foot the bill for the troops' special amenities provided on the estate. In the early stages he met all the expenses except for pay and rations. Ampthill Park today is open to the public and thousands of visitors are drawn every year to the striking monument commemorating the Duke's work.

With the end of the war, life returned to normal at Woburn— or almost normal. The Duke continued to administer the estate efficiently, the Duchess continued to interest herself in the cottage hospital, in bird watching and motoring. But now the Duchess was almost stone-deaf, her only contact with people being through letters. The Duke took over entirely the running of the household as well as of the estate.

The Duchess's deafness was incidentally the cause of her

achieving quite unlooked-for fame as an airwoman. She found that flying alleviated the distressing noises in the head that were the worst part of her aural affliction. She took her first flight as a passenger in 1926 but two years later started to learn to fly herself and had an airstrip laid out in Woburn Park. Soon she was taking part with Captain Barnard, her flying instructor, in record-breaking flights across the world. One of their most memorable flights was to India and back, accomplished in eight days. In 1930 they completed the round trip to Cape Town in seventeen days. Both were record or near-record flights which achieved a great deal for aviation, if only because the interest focused on the "Flying Duchess" provoked a national enthusiasm for flying in itself.

Many of her later flights, like her expeditions in early motor-cars, were made alone. By 1937, when she was 71, she had completed 199 hours of solo flying. On 22nd March she set off on an hour's flight to complete her 200 hours. She was never seen again. Wreckage of her plane picked up off the coast of East Anglia showed that she must have flown out into the North Sea. The reason for her tragic death was never discovered.

With her death the Duke seems to have lost heart. Though he never admitted it, the estrangement between him and his son probably affected him almost as much as his wife's death. It must have irked him terribly—alone in the vast house though hemmed in and tended by scores of servants—to be so blind that he could not see his way from room to room without guidance. The threat of war depressed him. When it broke out in 1939 he could see clearly that the life of Woburn was approaching a crisis. Part of the stable wing was already occupied by units of a government department. Then he had a slight stroke and after a short period in which he made one final effort to adjust himself to impossible conditions, he died disappointed and quite helpless but wholly resigned. That was in August 1940, just when the prospects for victory in the war against Nazi Germany looked most gloomy.

His successor to the dukedom, his only son Hastings, found himself a Duke in little more than name. He knew practically nothing of the Russell estates or their management. The great house was in the hands of the War Office and more than £3,000,000 had to be found to satisfy the demands of death duties. That was an unpromising beginning. When to that is added the fact that Hastings had incurred the displeasure of many of his fellow peers and of the Press by his militant pacifism there was little chance of the orderly succession of events continuing with their base at Woburn Abbey.

In fact the 12th Duke never lived in Woburn Abbey. Although he took an interest in the estates—he was compelled by his position to do so—farming was not a subject on which he could conceivably be called an expert and most of the decisions relating to the estates were taken by others and rubber-stamped by him.

He was unfortunate in the background of his youth. Unlike most of the Russells, who were educated by tutors, he had been sent to Eton and from there had gone on to Balliol College, Oxford. He is on record as disliking both intensely, of being in fear of bullies more robust than himself, and of finding it impossible to make firm friends among youths of such very different tastes from his own. He seems to have been no more interested in women as women than Duke Herbrand. It was a surprise to his family and many of his acquaintances that he married. But married he was, to a charming lady, Louisa Whitwell, the daughter of an Oxford don whom he met while he was at Balliol. They had three children, the present Duke, a younger son, Lord Hugh Hastings, and a daughter, Lady Daphne. Though they continued to live as Marquess and Marchioness of Tavistock in the same house, first at Havant then at Peasmarsh, Sussex, for many years the gap between them grew ever wider, as it had between Duke Herbrand and his Duchess. At the same time the gulf between him and the Duke widened alarmingly. They had no single interest in common except perhaps in wild life, but that single mutual interest could never take the place of affection or respect.

The Duke wanted his son to embark on a military career with the same enthusiasm that he had when he was the same age. Hastings was indeed briefly in the Grenadier Guards but found the life utterly unsuited to his highly reflective nature and resigned his commission. Soon after the outbreak of war in 1914 he quarrelled finally with the family. By then he had become in conscience a pacifist though his ideas were as yet unformulated. He did, however, realise that he could help his country better than by, in his own words, "re-entering the slavery of army life". In the event he spent the greater part of the war running with his wife a Y.M.C.A. canteen attached to Portsmouth barracks, a canteen, incidentally, for which he paid out of his own income. Duke Herbrand had settled an income of £15,000 a year on him, the greater part of which he used right up to the time of his succession to the dukedom in furthering various charities and a great number of causes which he regarded as deserving. There was, however, perhaps inevitably in view of his pacifism, a complete break between him and his father, whom he did not see again for at least 20 years.

He heartily disapproved of his eldest son. Each regarded the other as quite mistakenly believing that they were always right. Certainly there was no sympathy of any kind between them. When Hastings succeeded he turned rather to his younger son, Hugh, to help him in the quite exceptional task of coping with the estates in wartime. There is no possible doubt that Hastings was utterly sincere. The trouble was that the causes which appealed to him were unpopular ones, several of them attracting a good deal of unwelcome publicity. His long-continued leadership of the Prisoners' Aid Society, however, was one of his activities between the wars that no one could criticize.

While at Oxford he had become interested in the Oxford Group Movement and continued a vigorous supporter of its philosophy. He was on less firm ground as a supporter of the

Social Credit Movement, which originated in Canada and which most people have now forgotten, though it loomed large in the pages of the popular Press for some years.

But it was as a pacifist that Hastings provoked most unfavourable comment. He was believed, rightly or wrongly, to be sympathetic to Germany and had aroused a good deal of criticism long before the Second World War by his public attempts to vindicate German conduct during the First World War. He has been described as an inveterate writer to newspapers. That is perhaps not an unfair description of a man who sought publicity for his views and found the correspondence columns of newspapers one of the most effective media for expressing them. It was probably unfair that the most publicized of his activities were ones capable of easy criticism. He prided himself, rightly, on doing a great deal of good work which received no publicity at all, work such as that for the Prisoners' Aid Society.

He inherited the Russell dogmatism, and unyielding determination. When in 1935 his wife brought an action for the restitution of conjugal rights, he successfully defended the action on the ground that he was justified in refusing to cohabit with her as she was unduly under the influence of another man, though there was no suggestion of unfaithfulness. Newspaper reports of the case were naturally full and detailed. The case provided ammunition for the many who in those years of grim depression inveighed against the decadence of the nobility and placed on their largely guiltless heads the responsibility for the woes and wrongs of the whole people. The inevitable result was that by the outbreak of the Second World War Hastings was as lonely a man as his father, convinced only of the inability of his fellow peers and social equals to understand the truth when it was put before them.

As the Marquess of Tavistock he was no mere cipher to be disregarded, as he might have been if he had been born with a lesser name. That explains why his fruitless labours for peace in the first year of the war were at least connived at by the government. He had a link with the head of the German Legation in Dublin through the German wife of an acquaintance of his. He was apparently sounded by the German Legation on the possibility of peace, assuming that Germany would join in international disarmament and revise its policy towards the Jews. The Marquess obtained the authority of the Foreign Secretary, then Lord Halifax, to visit Dublin and investigate the possibilities further. He travelled to Dublin early in 1940 but achieved nothing. The story was, however, published and convinced a great number of people that he was, if nothing worse, pro-Nazi.

Only a few months later the 11th Duke died. Duke Hastings was preoccupied for much of the next few years in negotiations with the trustees of the estate for paying the enormous sum of death duties. Disposal of further parts of the Russell estates was the only possible way out of the difficulty and part of Bloomsbury passed into other hands. But the full amount of the duties had not been paid by the time of his death.

Woburn Abbey continued to be used by a government department for the remainder of the war, while the Duke did what he could to manage the estate, although put at a disadvantage by the open conflict between himself and the War Agricultural Committee, which disapproved strongly both of the existence of a "park" and still more of the maintenance of non-meat-producing animals inside its fences. The zoo was one of the Duke's greatest interests and it is a tribute to the Russell doggedness that even when fodder was strictly rationed and the spotlight of publicity was on Woburn Park, sufficient of the herds were preserved to perpetuate the species. They might so easily have disappeared for ever.

The Duke was in conflict also at one time with the authorities in London because of his unwillingness for the iron railings round Russell Square to be removed and added to the nation's metal store. The "railings for war" movement may have been a slightly misplaced one but it had been hailed with enthusiasm and the Duke was one of the very few who attempted to stand his ground and preserve his railings. The reward for his persistence was that the statue of the 5th Duke in the square was defaced by irate citizens and rude messages scrawled over it.

After the war the Duke divided his time between a house in Woburn village and another in Scotland. He decided to make Woburn Abbey habitable again and intended to take up residence there. But even at the outbreak of war the house had been sadly in need of repair and redecoration. Years of government occupation did not improve matters. The discovery of dry rot in the fabric made things worse. Finally he decided on a virtual reconstruction. The east wing, which before then included the main entrance, was demolished, as were parts of the stable blocks, the riding school, the real tennis court and parts of the north and south wings. The work of restoration was still not complete when the Duke died, although it might well have been completed some time before had not yet another dispute arisen between the estate and the government over the use of rationed materials for rebuilding.

As in life, so in death, the 12th Duke achieved a blaze of publicity. He was on a visit to a house on the Tavistock estate, went out one morning to shoot, as was his custom, and failed to return. After a day-long search he was found shot by his own gun in undergrowth quite near the house. Why a sportsman of lifelong experience was scrambling through undergrowth with his gun unbroken, loaded and cocked was a mystery that has never been resolved. The coroner recorded a verdict of accidental death.

His eldest son John (generally known in the family as Ian), the 13th and present Duke of Bedford, who thus succeeded him in 1953, was even less equipped for the task ahead of him than his father had been on his succession. Moreover he faced an even larger bill for death duties, amounting to more than £4,000,000, with a great deal of the most easily expendable parts of the estates already sold. The complete break between his father and Duke Herbrand had precluded him from having even a remote knowledge of Woburn and the family estates until he grew to manhood.

Unlike his father, he had not even mixed with boys of his own age at public school. He had been brought up, if that is the word, by private tutors and, already showing age-old determination of the Russells to follow their own bent, refused to learn, did not even, in his own words, learn how to learn. Finally his father sent him to a London hostel to prepare for entrance to Cambridge University. But his new tutors were little more successful than his home tutors had been. He arrived in London with an insufficient income, and making the most of his first opportunity to mix with people was soon caught up in the whirl of London society and spent a great deal more of his time being entertained (and recovering from the entertainment) than in studying. Finally he sacked his crammers and abandoned the idea of going to the University.

At the age of 20 he had paid a few visits to Woburn but had found little more sympathy with his grandparents than from his parents. Naturally, perhaps inevitably, he fell in love. The lady of his choice was 13 years older than himself, a Mrs. Clare Hollway. Marriage was made possible by Mrs. Hollway's divorce but the suggestion was to all intents and purposes vetoed by both father and grandfather. However, the marriage took place and John, at the age of 21, found his allowance stopped by his father, with little to hope for from his grandfather. He was conscious of the indignity of living on his wife, who was still receiving alimony from her ex-husband. Though desperately ill-equipped for earning a living he found and kept a job in an estate agent's office.

Then the war broke out and, like his father, he joined the Guards—but only briefly. His physique was poor at the time and he was discharged as unfit and once more found himself looking for a job. Some help was now forthcoming from his grandfather, who undertook to pay the expenses attendant on the birth of his first child (a son christened Henry Robin Ian, the present Marquess of Tavistock) and to give him an allowance of £2,000 a year. Unfortunately his grandfather's death caused an interruption in the allowance while the details of his will were being sorted out and John took another job as a journalist on the *Sunday Express*. He had found his niche. He was good at the work because it suited him and he enjoyed it thoroughly. His married life was happy, too, up to a point. Clare bore him a second son, Rudolph Christian, in 1944, but her health was never good and tragedy once more engulfed the Russell life in September 1945. She had become increasingly dependant on sleeping pills. On 1st September 1945 she swallowed a massive overdose and never regained consciousness. What made the tragedy more poignant was that she and the Duke had had a silly and quite meaningless squabble just before she took the pills and had previously threatened half-jokingly to take her life. The coroner recorded an open verdict.

It was a grim prospect for John, bereft of the one woman whom he had loved in his life and with two small sons dependent on him, a catastrophe bad enough to distort the life of many men far tougher than the future Duke of Bedford. That he rose above the anguish of the moment and succeeded in making a new and full life for himself and his children is the greatest possible tribute to his character.

He was helped immeasurably by his second wife, Lydia, third daughter of Lord Churston and his wife Jessie Smithers, better known as Denise Orme, musical comedy star in the heyday of Daly's Theatre and later Duchess of Leinster. Lydia was the widow of a Captain Lyle, who had been a war casualty, and was the mother of three. There was a great mutual understanding between the two, both of them the victims of tragic bereavement. They were married early in 1947, had a son Francis in 1950 and lived together with their six children happily and successfully for many years. The marriage won the approval also of

20

the Duke of Bedford and until the latter's death relations between him and his son were more cordial than they had ever been.

John and his wife shared a feeling for making a new start in a new world. England did not hold very much except sad memories for either of them. So with the characteristic Russell (and incidentally Yarde-Buller) contempt for a humdrum way of life they did just that. They pooled their resources and emigrated to South Africa to become successful fruit farmers in Cape Province.

And there they might well have stayed indefinitely. The Duke recalls this period of self-inflicted exile as one of the happiest in his life. They made many friends, liked the climate and had no financial worries. It was a rewarding and useful interlude in the lives of both of them and served to give John a maturity of outlook and a practical approach to everyday affairs that stood him in good stead when he had to undertake the responsibilities of the dukedom.

The news of Duke Hastings' entirely unexpected death was a great shock. It was also, inevitably, a call to arms, as it were— the signal for a complete and at first most unwelcome change in the whole way of living of the new Duke of Bedford—the 13th Duke and 17th Earl.

The problems that awaited him on his return to England were uncommonly daunting. The dukedom is hereditary, the Russell estates are not. That is an over-simplified way of expressing the legal position but it is near enough to the truth. The estates were placed in the guardianship of Trustees by the 6th Duke and these Trustees have absolute discretion in their administration. In practice the Duke is normally tenant for life but provisions made by the 11th and 12th Dukes placed the present Duke in the position of being compelled to seek the approval of the Trustees for the slightest capital expenditure. The position was aggravated by the incidence of death duties for the second time in less than fifteen years. Upwards of £4,000,000 had to be found by the Trustees. This meant, of course, the dismemberment of the surviving part of the original Russell estates. Thorney and Covent Garden had been sold in the time of Duke Herbrand. Now Chenies was sold, together with the fertile agricultural land surrounding the house. Only Woburn and parts of the Tavistock and Bloomsbury estates remained.

That was the measure of the difficulties facing the new Duke and the Trustees. The latter favoured dispersing of Woburn, if possible making over the Abbey and its historic contents to the National Trust. The Duke opposed this suggestion with every means of persuasion and argument. "Over my dead body" might have summed up his personal attitude compounded equally of reason and emotion. He believed that to survive as a great family the Russells must retain Woburn as an heirloom and home. He had an intense love for the house and its treasures. Partly as a result of his determined attitude and his unwillingness to be a tenant of the National Trust, negotiations fell into abeyance. His solution of the financial problem was twofold, first to dispense of as much of Bloomsbury (or other remaining estates) as absolutely necessary to meet current liabilities, second to make Woburn pay for itself—more to make it contribute substantially to the Trustees' funds.

So the 13th Duke of Bedford made selling Woburn to the world his life's work—the only means by which it could be retained in the family. And he brought immense energy and determination to the Stately Homes business with outstanding success, using modern sales and advertising methods to attract his customers and, incidentally, revolutionizing the previously accepted methods of "entertaining" visitors to England's historic houses. His approach has always been personal; he has treated his paying customers as guests. That explains a large measure of his success. The quality of the "goods" he is offering completes the explanation.

But that takes no account of the hard work and anxiety which preceded the opening of Woburn Abbey to the public. When he had received the lukewarm approval of the Trustees for the capital expenditure necessary to make Woburn suitable as a public show-place he and his wife set to work day and night to prepare the "exhibits" with help from friends and members of the estate staff.

It was a gigantic task, for Woburn had not been a home since Duke Herbrand died and the work of demolition and reconstruction initiated by Duke Hastings had not, as already mentioned, been completed by the time John succeeded. Nothing, positively nothing, was in place; the family heirlooms were either in store or disposed in no sort of order about Woburn. What the Duke and Duchess set out to do was to arrange the family portraits and family possessions in such a way that a visitor passing through the house on a predetermined route might form a mental picture of life at Woburn in its heyday and at the same time grasp the essential facets of the family's history from Tudor times to the present day and some of the events that shaped its history or affected the lives of its individual members. The itinerary was designed to be at once a tribute to a noble family and its achievements and an illustration of life in a great house. Simultaneously, new roads were built across the park, so that visitors could share in its beauty as in the beauty of the house and catch a glimpse of the rare animals which still make Woburn Park one of the finest private zoos in the country.

Woburn was opened to the public in the spring of 1955. In the first year it welcomed almost 200,000 visitors. In the following ten years it went from strength to strength, becoming probably the most successful and remunerative of all the historic homes open to the public. Its success was as gratifying to the Trustees as it was to the Duke. That it has remained the ducal residence as well as a famous show-place is the real justification of the Duke's faith and the root cause of his dedication to work which is exacting and often arduous.

Woburn has been truly a family home since the present Duke took up residence there, though Robin, the Marquess of Tavistock, has been educated chiefly abroad. He was at boarding-school in Switzerland, where he made many friends from the States, and persuaded his father to let him go to High School in America and later to Harvard University.

The 13th Duke clearly believes that publicity pays. He has made innumerable broadcasts and television appearances; he has undertaken exhausting lecture tours in the United States and elsewhere, "selling Woburn to the world"; he can often be found in the Abbey "shop", which sells souvenirs or autograph-ing books for visitors; he frequently "makes the rounds" of the house with a word and a smile for every visitor he meets. And he is wonderfully supported by the Duchess, his third wife Nicole, just as he was in the early stages by his second wife. With practical French common sense she helps to organize the never-ending round of chores which are an inevitable part of receiving many hundreds of thousands of people every year. Whether presiding at a fashion show (for Woburn has become the venue of many special events) or entertaining guests, she has impressed her personality on thousands of visitors. Snobbery in any form is anathema to her as to her husband.

What is there about Woburn that makes it such a very special place? Certainly publicity has helped to bring the customers; it still does. But many return again and again by coach or car to spend a day or an afternoon in the park or house. It is, I think, apart from its air of welcome, that it has something to offer everyone of all tastes and ages from whatever walk of life. And, of course, Woburn is *always* open, yes, even on Christmas Day. That is important. In the Duke's words, "We welcome you to our home *any* day of the year"—a perfect slogan for its purpose.

The Duke's first concept of a popular country venue for jaded townspeople and their children from London and the Midlands has been maintained. There were more than three million visitors in the first eleven years that the house was open. He has often been criticized for "commercializing" Woburn. Of course Woburn is a commercial venture, and a very successful one. It has to be. And a commercial undertaking simply must be run on commercial lines in this day and age of intense competition. The Duke is on record as saying, "What I have dedicated my life to has but nothing to do with art", and again, "I believe in giving the people what they want. Is that so bad?" In fact, one supposes he would instal "a juke-box in the ballroom for the Elvis Presley fans" if there were a ballroom in which to instal it and if it were good business to do so. There is at least (and always has been) a children's playground and pets' corner and boating on the lake. And there have been many novelties such as rides by stagecoach round the park and safaris by jeep! And, of course, picnic places at strategic points in the park.

But that is only one side of Woburn. The other is represented by about £2,000,000 worth of art treasures and objects of historic interest which can be seen at leisure for a few shillings. There is a unique dinner service of Sèvres china, magnificent plate, an 18th-century Chinese room with Chinese wallpaper (made about 1750) of exceptional beauty and an outstanding collection of 21 Venetian scenes painted in 1746–50 by Canaletto for the 4th Duke and originally hung in Bedford House, Bloomsbury. There are literally thousands of other treasures. Above all, there is the collection of family portraits which bring to vivid life the men and women whose achievements (and follies) are recorded in the pages of this book, all painted by the foremost portrait artists of their generation.

The future of Woburn Abbey, its continuance as the home of the Russell family as it has been for nearly three centuries, can never be assured, though it is much brighter than it was a decade ago. John the 13th Duke has at least underlined the fact which many generations of the family have proved, that when a Russell puts his hand to the plough, whether agricultural, political or commercial, he does so with determination and infinite stubbornness and with implicit faith in the rightness of his cause. The end product has always been memorable, often brilliantly, sometimes unexpectedly successful.

BIBLIOGRAPHY

The following are some of the books which I have found most helpful in compiling this story of the Russell Family.

Historical Memoirs of the House of Russell, by J. H. Wiffen; Longmans Green, 1833.

Two Centuries of Family History, by Gladys Scott Thomson, M.A.; Longmans Green, 1930.

Life in a Noble Household, by Gladys Scott Thomson, M.A.; Jonathan Cape.

The Russells in Bloomsbury, by Gladys Scott Thomson, M.A.; Jonathan Cape.

Family Background, by Gladys Scott Thomson, M.A.; Jonathan Cape.

Woburn and the Russells (for young people), by Gladys Scott Thomson, M.A.; The Pilgrim Press, 1956.

Lord John Russell, 1792–1878, by Stuart J. Reid; Sampson Low, 1895.

The Life of Lord John Russell, by Spencer Walpole; Longmans Green, 1889.

Bertrand Russell, by Alan Wood; A. & D. Whitfield, 1957.

Bertrand Russell, A Life, by Herbert Gottschalk; John Baker, 1965.

A Silver Plated Spoon, by the Duke of Bedford; 1959.

William, Lord Russell, by Lord John Russell; 1820.

Amberley Papers.

The Draining of the Fens, by H. C. Darby; Cambridge University Press, 2nd edition, 1956.

The Story of a Great Agricultural Estate, by the Duke of Bedford (11th); John Murray, 1897.

Britannia, by W. Camden; 1610.

History of the Drainage of the Fens, by S. Wells; (2 vols.) 1830.

Letters of Junius.

An Historical Geography of England before 1800, by H. C. Darby; Cambridge University Press, 1951.

English Social History, by G. M. Trevelyan; Longmans Green, 2nd edition 1946.

The Expansion of Elizabethan England, by A. L. Rowse; Macmillan, 1955.

The England of Elizabeth, by A. L. Rowse; Macmillan, 1951.

Tour through Great Britain, by Daniel Defoe; 1724.

The Diary of Samuel Pepys, 2 *vols*; Everyman's Library, J. M. Dent & Sons.

The Diary of John Evelyn; Oxford University Press, 1959.

Georgian London, by John Summerson; Pleiades Books, 1945.

Life in Georgian England, by E. N. Williams; Batsford, 1962.

London Houses from 1660 to 1820; Richardson.

INDEX

Aberdeen, Lord, 253*f.*

Agricultural Holdings Act, 224

Agriculture, 208*f.*, 292*f.*

Alabama Affair, the, 255

Amberley, Viscount, 259

American Civil War, 255

Amersham, 58

Ampthill, 297

Androse, Richard, 87

Anjou, Duke of, 86

Anne, Queen, 155

Anti-Corn Law League, 244*f.*

Aragon, Queen Katherine of, 41, 63, 78

Arc, Joan of, 28

Argyll, Duke of, 84, 142

Arlington, Lord, 135, 136

Armagh, Archbishop of, 197, 199

Armagh, Siege of, 95

Ashley, Antony (Lord Shaftesbury), 134, 140*f.*

Atlantic Peace foundation, 289

Barnard, Capt., 298

Beacon Hill School, 277*f.*

Beaufort, Henry, Bp. of Winchester, 27

Bedford, the, ship, 182*f.*

Bedford, Dukes and Earls of, *see* Russell

Bedford House, 87, 161*f.*, 172, 173*f.*, 175, 179, 181, 183, 185*f.*, 209

Bedford Level, 104*f.*

Bedford Old and New Rivers, 13, 100, 108, 109*f.*

Bedford Square, 185*f.*

Bedfordshire Territorial Regt., 297

Bermondsey, 181*f.*

Berwick, near Swyre, 17, 20, 36, 37, 39, 40

Besançon, 50, 51

Bessborough, Lord, 248*f.*

Bison at Woburn, 296

Black, Dora, *see* Russell, Dora

Blenheim Palace, 174*f.*

Bloomsbury, 14, 166*f.*, 169, 171*f.*, 183*f.*, 187, 209, 295, 302, 307

Boleyn, Anne, 63, 78

Bordeaux, wine from, 22, 34

Bosworth, battle of, 35

Bothwell, Earl of, 83

Bourbon, Charles, duke of, 49*f.*

Bridgewater, Duke of, 174

Briquebec, William Bertrand, 25

British Museum, 185

Bromley Common, 219

Brooke, Lord, 122*f.*

Buckingham, Duke of, 30

Burgundy, Duke of, 30

Burke, Edmund, 62*f.*, 202

Burnet, Bishop, 149, 156, 159

Burton, James, 186*f.*

Bute, Lord, 200*f.*

Cabal, the, 13, 134

Calais, 34, 45*f.*, 77

Campaign for Nuclear Disarmament (CND), 285*f.*, 289

Campeggio, Cardinal, 61

Canaletto, 179, 310

Canning, George, 206, 238

Carew, Sir John, 41

Caroline, Queen, 237

Carter, Admiral, 153

Castlereagh, Lord, 236

Catholic emancipation, 205, 207, 229, 239

Cato Street Conspiracy, 236

Cattle on Russell estates, 218*f.*

Chamberlain, Joseph, 267

Chandos, Lord, 117

Charles I, 103, 105*f.*, 118*f.*, 163*f.*

Charles II, 132*f.*

Charles V, Emperor, 48*f.*, 76

Charles IX of France, 79

Charles of Austria, Prince, 72

Chartists, 249*f.*,

313

Chatham, Earl of, *see* Pitt, W.
Chatillon, battle of, 34
Chenies, 57*f*., 87, 88, 89, 160, 307
Cheverell family, 35
Churches, 177*f*., 188, 222*f*.
Churchill, John, *see* Marlborough
Churston, Lord and Lady, 305
Civil War, the, 13, 127*f*.
Clarendon, Earl of, 125, 134
Clarendon, Lord, 249
Clement, Pope, 59*f*.
Cleeves, Anne of, 66
Clifford, Lord, 135
Coke, Thomas, Earl of Leicester, 15, 215
Collins, Canon, 295*f*.
Common lands, 219
Communism, 266
Corn Laws, 220, 235, 244*f*.
Country Party, 13, 135, 138*f*.
Court Party, 135
Covenanters, 122*f*.
Covent Garden (Convent Garden), 14, 68, 158, 160*f*., 169, 176*f*., 181, 183, 188, 294
Coverdale, Miles, 73
Cox, Sir Richard, 198
Cranmer, Thomas, 65*f*.
Crimean War, 253*f*.
Cromwell, Oliver, 107, 108
Cromwell, Thomas, 55, 56*f*., 62*f*., 66
Crowland, 100*f*., 112*f*.
Cuban crisis, 287*f*.
Cubitt, Thomas, 187
Cumberland, Duke of, 194, 195, 201
Cumberland, Earl of, 90

Danby, Earl of, 149, 151
Dancy, Lord, 136
Darnley, Lord, 78, 81, 84
Dartmoor, Close of, 65
Dartmouth, 32
Declaration of Indulgence, 135
Declaration of Right, 150
de la Pole, Richard ('The White Rose'), 46*f*.
de la Tour family, 20*f*.
Denver, 100, 104, 108, 113
de Rosel family, 24, 25
Derby, Lord, 253, 256

Deverell family, 21
Devonshire, Earl of, 149, 150
Digby, Lord George, 127
Disraeli, Benjamin, 253, 254
Dorchester, Dorset, 17
Drainage, experiments in land, 220
Drury, Sir William, 97
Dublin, 92
Dudley, John, Earl of Warwick, later Duke of Northumberland, 66*f*., 68
Dudley, Lord Guildford, 69
Dudley, Lord Robert, Earl of Leicester, 81*f*., 90, 96
Dufferin and Ava, Marquess of, 295
Duke of Bedford, the, whaler, 182
Durham Letter, the, 252*f*.

Earith, 104, 108, 115
Edgehill, battle of, 127
Edinburgh Castle, siege of, 97
Education, 215, 222*f*., 245, 247, 257, 263, 264, 277*f*.
Education Act, 1870, 222*f*.
Edward VI, 12, 27, 31*f*., 43, 66*f*., 72, 73
Einstein, Albert, 283
Elementary Education Act, 257
Eliot, T. S., 259, 268
Elizabeth I, 12, 71*f*., 77*f*., 102, 161
Eldon, Lord, 236*f*.
Ely, Isle of, 101, 107, 112
Enclosures, 219
Enniskillen, surrender of, 92
Essex, Earl of, 88, 94, 95, 122, 127*f*., 141
Estate management, 208*f*., 292
Evelyn, Sir John, 169, 214
Exclusion Acts, 13, 130, 140, 141
Exeter, 32*f*., 65, 67, 87

Fabian Society, 265, 267
Factory Acts, 247
Farmers, Russells as, 208*f*., 292*f*.
Fenians, 257
Fens, the, 13, 99*f*., 117, 160, 210*f*.
Fenwick, Sir John, 154
Field of the Cloth of Gold, 11, 47
'Finality Jack', *see* Russell, Lord John
Finances of the Russell family, 224, 295, 297, 303, 305, 306*f*.
Flitcroft, Henry, 177*f*., 216
Forestry, 213*f*.

Forster, Julia, m. Sir Francis Russell, q.v.
Fox, Charles James, 202, 203f.
Fox, Henry, 195f.
Francis I, of France, 46f.
Francis II, of France, 79
Free Trade, 246, 267
Froxmere, John, 37
Fruit farming, at Woburn, 225; in South Africa, 306

Galway, Earl of, 191
Gascoyn, Stephen, see Russell, Stephen
George, David Lloyd, 272
George, of Hanover, later George I, 158, 178
George II, 192, 199
George III, 15, 200, 227, 236
George IV, 227
German Social Democracy, 265
Gibbs, James, architect, 177, 178
Gladstone, W. E., 255f.
Glendalough, battle of, 92
Gloucester, Humphrey, Duke of, 27
Gordon Square, 187
Gostwick, Sir John, 75
Grafton, Duke of, 185, 201
Grampound, disenfranchisement of, 236f.
Grass, experiments with, 217
Great Level, the, see Fens
Great Russell Street, 171, 175f., 180, 184
Grenville, George, 200, 203f., 229
Grey, Lady Jane, 69, 73, 75, 76
Grey, Lord, 228, 232, 239f.
Guild of St George, 33, 63

Habeas Corpus Act, 136, 234
Hampden, John, 122
Hampden, Lord, 143
Harrington, Sir John, 88
Hawksmoor, Nicholas, architect, 178
Haxey, Sir Thomas, 19
Henry VII, 11, 41f.
Henry VIII, 11, 41, 43, 44f., 74
Herring, Elizabeth and John, 35
Hertford, Earl of, 127
Hobby, Elizabeth, m. Sir William Russell, q.v.

Holbein, portrait by, 71
Holland, Earl of, 128
Holland, Henry, architect, 218
Holland House, 230f.
Holland, Lord and Lady, 230f.
Hollway, Mrs Clare, m. 13th Duke of Bedford, q.v.
Honiton, battle at, 67
Horticulture, 211f.
Howland, Elizabeth, m. 2nd Duke of Bedford, q.v.
Human Society in Ethics and Politics, 281
Hume, Lord, 84
Hussey, Lord, 63
Hydrogen bomb, the, 283f.

Irish Church, Disestablishment of, 257
Irish Question, 229, 239, 242f., 248f., 256f., 260

James II, 142f., 151f.
James VI of Scotland, later James I, 78, 89f., 103, 118f., 161f.
Jennings, Sarah, Duchess of Marlborough, 157, 174f., 181
Jerningham, Anne, see Russell, Anne
Jerningham, Sir Richard, 47f., 57
Jones, Inigo, 14, 162f., 169, 173

Kennedy, President, 287f.
Kildare, Earl of, 93
Kildare, Lord, 197
King's Lynn, 104, 113, 115
Kingston, Russell, Dorset, 23, 87, 105
Khrushchev, Nikita, 287f.

La Hogue, battle of, 153
Land drainage companies, 221
Landlords, Bedfords as, 190f.
Laud, Archbishop William, 122, 125
Lauderdale, Duke of, 134
Lautrec, General, 61
Leinster, Duchess of, see Churston
Leicester, Earl of, see Coke, Thomas
Leicester, Earl of, see Dudley, Robert
Leith, Treaty of, 79, 84
Limitations, Bill of, 140
Little Russell Street, 171
Liverpool, Lord, 206, 237f.
London, Great Fire of, 170

Long, Elizabeth, m. Sir William Russell, q.v.
Long, Sir Henry, 90
Long Parliament, the, 124f., 126, 131
Louis XIV, 134, 136f.
Louis Napoleon, 250
Louisburg, Capture of, 193
Luddites, 235
Lumley, Lord, 149
Lynn Law, the, 104f.

Macmillan, Harold, 288
Madrid, Treaty of, 59, 194
Malmesbury, William of, 112f.
Manchester, Earl of, 130
Marlborough, Duchess of, see Jennings
Marlborough, Duke of, 151, 157
Marlborough, George, Duke of, 181
Marlborough House, 174
Marxism, 265, 274
Mary, Queen of Scots, 78f.
Mary Tudor, Queen Mary, 12, 48, 69f., 72, 75f.
Mary, Queen of William III, 137, 142f., 148, 152, 154
Maynard, Lord and Lady, 218
Melbourne, Lord, 242f.
Mildmay, Sir Walter, 82
Mill, John Stuart, 262
Miller, Philip, 214
'Ministry of All the Talents', the, 213f.
Modena, Mary of, 147f.
Monk, General, 131
Monmouth, Duke of, 130, 141f., 147
Moor Park, 210
Morrison, Jane, m. Edward, Lord Russell, q.v.
Morton, Bishop, 102
Morton's Leam, 102, 104, 113
Mountjoy, Lord, 46, 96
Municipal Reform Act, 243
Murray, Earl of, 81f., 84
Mutiny Act, 205
Myddelton, Sir Hugh, 180

Napoleon Bonaparte, 204, 231, 233, 234
Naseby, Battle of, 132
National Trust, the, 307
New River Company, 180
Newbury, battle of, 128

Newcastle, Duke of, 193, 194, 195f.
Nicholas, Csar of Russia, 253
No Conscription Fellowship, the, 270f.
Norfolk, Duke of, 85f.
Norris, Sir John, 93f.
Northumberland, Duke of, see Dudley, John

Oates, Titus, 139
O'Brien, Smith, 249
O'Connell, Daniel, 243, 248f.
Olaf the Sharp-eyed, 25
Old Pretender, the, 147
Old Sarum, 228
Orange, William of, later William III, 13, 137, 142, 143f., 147, 152, 154
Orford, Earl of, 211
Orme, Denise, see Churston
Ouse, Drainage Board, 110
Oxford Group Movement, 300
Oxford Movement, 251f.

Pacifism, 268f., 278f., 300f.
Palmer, Robert, 186
Palmerston, Lord, 250f, 252, 253, 254, 255, 256
Passfield, see Webb, S.
Pavia, battle of, 52f.
Peace of Paris, 1814: 183, 200, 201, 233; 1815: 234; 1856: 254
Peel, Sir Robert, 238f., 242f., 253
Pelham, Henry, 193f.
Pembroke, Earl of, 150, 158
Pembroke Lodge, 257, 260f.
Peninsular War, 231f.
Penrhyn, Disenfranchisement of, 238
Pepys, Samuel, 169
Père David deer, 296
Peterloo Massacre, 235
Petition of Right, 13, 120
Philip, Archduke of Austria, 11, 41f.
Philip of Spain, 69f., 76f., 94f.
Pilgrimage of Grace, 11, 63f.
Pitt, William, Earl of Chatham, 194, 195f., 203f.
Pitt, William, the Younger, 228
Pius V, Pope, 86
Pius IX, Pope, 251f.
Poole, 35

Popish Plot, the, 139
Portland, Duke of, 205
Portsmouth, Duchess of, 143
Potato famine, 1846, 248
Poynings, Sir Edward, 46
Prayer Book, the, 72*f.*
Principia Mathematica, 262, 266, 280
Principles of Social Reconstruction, 271*f.*, 273
Prisoners' Aid Society, 300*f.*
Problems of Philosophy, 266
Puritans, 122*f.*, 134
Pusey, Dr. Edward, 251*f.*
Pym, John, 122, 125, 126

Queen's Party, the, 237

Raphael, 179
Reform Bills, 236*f.*, 240*f.*, 255
Reform Act, 1832, 241
Regency Bill, 201
Restoration, the, 132*f.*
Restoration Parliament, 13
Rich, Lord, 75
Richard II, 19
Rizzio, murder of, 82
Rockingham, Lord, 201
Roman Catholic Church in England, 251*f.*
Rotherhithe docks, 182
Rotten boroughs, 227
Rouvigny, Marquis de, 138*f.*
Royal Agricultural Society, 217, 219, 221, 224
Royal Horticultural Society, 225
Royal Zoological Society, 296
Russell, the, ship, 182
RUSSELL, Alice, wife of Stephen Russell, 20
RUSSELL, Alys (or Alice), wife of James Russell of Berwick, 38*f.*
RUSSELL, Anne, daughter of Francis, 2nd Earl of Bedford, 75, 82
RUSSELL, Anne, Lady George Digby, 127
RUSSELL, Anne, d. of Duke of Bridgewater, wife of Wriothesley, 3rd Duke, 174
RUSSELL, Bertrand, 3rd Earl R., 230, 258*f.*

RUSSELL, Bridget, wife of Francis, 2nd Earl of Bedford, 87
RUSSELL, Caroline, d. of John, 4th Duke of Bedford, 181, 201
RUSSELL, Cristina, d. of Henry R., 35
RUSSELL, Clare (*née* Hollway), 1st wife of John, 13th Duke of Bedford, 304
RUSSELL, Daphne, d. of 12th Duke of Bedford, 299
RUSSELL, Dora, 2nd wife of Bertrand, Earl Russell, 277*f.*
RUSSELL, Edward, 1st Lord Orford, 142, 143*f.*, 166
RUSSELL, Edward, Lord Russell, 75, 90
RUSSELL, Edward, 3rd Earl of Bedford, 1574–1627, 23, 88*f.*, 167*f.*, 210
RUSSELL, Elizabeth (or Alice), wife of John R. of Berwick, 37
RUSSELL, Elizabeth, Baroness Russell (*née* Hobby), 96*f.*
RUSSELL, Elizabeth, d. of above, 96*f.*
RUSSELL, Elizabeth, d. of Francis, 2nd Earl of Bedford, 75
RUSSELL, Elizabeth (*née* Long), wife of Sir William R., 90
RUSSELL, Elizabeth (*née* Howland), wife of 3rd Duke of Bedford, 172, 181
RUSSELL, Sir Francis, 75, 87, 97*f.*
RUSSELL, Francis, 2nd Earl of Bedford, 1527–85, 12, 66, 70*f.*, 215
RUSSELL, Francis, 4th Earl of Bedford (d. 1641), 13, 14, 99*f.*, 117*f.*, 163*f.*, 210
RUSSELL, Francis, son of above, 125
RUSSELL, Francis, son of 4th Duke of Bedford, 201
RUSSELL, Francis, 5th Duke of Bedford, 1765–1802, 14, 185, 187*f.*, 190, 201*f.*, 216*f.*
RUSSELL, Francis, 7th Duke of Bedford, 1788–1861, 202, 220*f.*, 226
RUSSELL, Francis, s. of 13th Duke of Bedford, 305
RUSSELL, Frank, 259, 261, 277
RUSSELL, Gertrude, wife of 4th Duke of Bedford, 185*f.*
RUSSELL, Hastings, cousin of 8th Duke of Bedford, 221

RUSSELL, Hastings, 9th Duke of Bedford, d. 1891, 221*f.*

RUSSELL, Hastings, 12th Duke of Bedford, d. 1953, 295, 299*f.*, 306

RUSSELL, Henry, d. 1463, 17, 26*f.*

RUSSELL, Henry, s. of John R. of Berwick, 38

RUSSELL, Henry Robin, s. of 13th Duke of Bedford, 305, 308*f.*

RUSSELL, Herbrand, 11th Duke of Bedford, d. 1940, 116, 214, 221, 291*f.*

RUSSELL, Hugh Hastings, s. of 12th Duke of Bedford, 297*f.*

RUSSELL, Isabella, 23

RUSSELL, James, 17, 36

RUSSELL, James, s. of John of Berwick, 38*f.*

RUSSELL, Jane, Lady R. (*née* Morrison), 90

RUSSELL, Joan, d. of Henry R., 35

RUSSELL, John, of Berwick, c. 1430–1505, 17, 35, 36*f.*

RUSSELL, John, of Kingston Russell, 23

RUSSELL, John (Gyle), of Dorchester, 24

RUSSELL, Lord John, 1st Earl R. ('Finality Jack'), 15, 190, 202*f.*, 206*f.*, 226*f.*, 259

RUSSELL, John, 1st Earl of Bedford, 1486–1555, 11, 17, 39, 40*f.*

RUSSELL, John, Baron R., 75, 96*f.*

RUSSELL, John, s. of 3rd Duke of Bedford, 174

RUSSELL, John, 4th Duke of Bedford, 1710–71, 15, 175*f.*, 179*f.*, 182*f.*, 191*f.*, 209, 212*f.*

RUSSELL, John, 6th Duke of Bedford, d. 1839, 25, 202*f.*, 218*f.*, 226

RUSSELL, John (Ian), 13th Duke of Bedford, 28, 189, 299*f.*, 303*f.*

RUSSELL, Katharine, d. of Lord Chandos, wife of 4th Earl of Bedford, 117

RUSSELL, Louisa (*née* Whitwell), wife of 12th Duke ('The Flying Duchess'), 297*f.*

RUSSELL, Lucy (*née* Harrington), wife of 3rd Earl of Bedford, 88, 89*f.*

RUSSELL, Lydia (*née* Churston), wife of 13th Duke of Bedford, 305*f.*

RUSSELL, Margaret, 23

RUSSELL, Margaret (*née* Gostwick), wife of 2nd Earl of Bedford, 75

RUSSELL, Mary (*née* Tribe), wife of 11th Duke of Bedford, 295*f.*

RUSSELL, Sir Maurice, 23

RUSSELL, Nicole, wife of 13th Duke of Bedford, 309

RUSSELL, Sir Odo, 296

RUSSELL, Patricia, wife of Bertrand R., 278

RUSSELL, Rachel, Lady Vaughan, 171

RUSSELL, Robert, or Kingston Russell, 24

RUSSELL, Rudolph Christian, 305

RUSSELL, Sackville, 10th Duke of Bedford, d. 1893, 221

RUSSELL, Stephen, of Dorchester and Weymouth (Stephen Gascoyn), 17*f.*, 183

RUSSELL, Sir Theobald, 23

RUSSELL, Thomas, 38, 39

RUSSELL, Thomasine, 39

RUSSELL, William, s. of Henry R., 17, 35

RUSSELL, Lord William, 117, 132*f.*, 143*f.*, 146, 148, 171, 226, 236

RUSSELL, William, Baron Thornhaugh, 117

RUSSELL, William (d. 1683), 13, 14

RUSSELL, Sir William, 75, 90*f.*

RUSSELL, William (d. 1700), 5th Earl and 1st Duke of Bedford, 13, 99, 107*f.*, 125*f.*, 143*f.*, 172, 182, 209*f.*

RUSSELL, William, s. of 1st Duke of Bedford, 171

RUSSELL, William, s. of 2nd Duke of Bedford, 174

RUSSELL, William, s. of 3rd Duke of Bedford, 174

RUSSELL, William, Lord Tavistock, s. of 6th Duke of Bedford, 202, 207

RUSSELL, William, 8th Duke of Bedford (d.1872), 221

RUSSELL, Wriothesley, 2nd Duke of Bedford (1680–1711), 172*f.*, 190*f.*, 211*f.*

RUSSELL, Wriothesley, 3rd Duke of Bedford (1708–1732), 174*f.*, 191

Russell nose, the, 71

Russell Peace Foundation, Bertrand, 289

Russell Square, 14, 187, 302
Russels of Mappowder and Bridport, 24
Rye House Plot, the, 13, 142, 146
Ryswick, Treaty of, 155

Sacheverell, Dr, 191
St George's Church, Bloomsbury, 178
St Giles Church, Bloomsbury, 177*f.*
St Ives, Hunts., 105
St John, Sir John, 75
St Paul's Church, Covent Garden, 188
Salmon, Robert, 217
Sandwich, Earl of, 193, 195, 201
Sanger, Charles, 262
Sapcote, Sir Guy, 157
Saville, Lord, 123*f.*
Say, Lord, 122*f.*
Sceptical Essays, 273*f.*
Schools, 215, 222*f.*, 247, 257, 277*f.*
Scott, Rev. Michael, 285, 286
Scott, Sir Walter, 203
Security, Act of, 157
Sedgemoor, battle of, 147
Sewers, Commissioners of, 102, 105, 106, 110
Shaftesbury, Earl of, *see* Ashley
Shaftesbury, Russell land at, 20
Sheep-shearings at Queensferry, 218; at Woburn, 216*f.*
Ships named after Russells, 182
Short Parliament, the, 123
Shrewsbury, Earl of, 81, 84, 147*f.*, 151
Sidney, Algernon, 142
Sidney, Henry, 149
Sidney, Sir Philip, 90
Sigurd, Hring, King of Sweden, 25
Sinclair, Sir John, 218
Slave Trade, the, 204
Sloane, Sir Hans, 212
Smith, Alys, *see* Russell, Alys
Smith, Rev. Sydney, 230
Smithers, Jessie, *see* Churston
Smithfield, Club, 218
Smugglers, 32*f.*
Social Credit Movement, 301
Somerset, Duke of, Lord Protector, 66*f.*, 68, 73, 74
Southampton, Earl of, *see* Wriothesley
Southampton House, 167*f.*, 173*f.*
Southampton Row, 176, 185

Spa Fields, riot, 235
Speculative Society, the, 232
Spencer, Lady Diana, m. John Russell, *q.v.*
Spurs, Battle of the, 45*f.*
Stannaries, Court of, 65
Stamp Act, 200
Star Chamber, 13, 120*f.*
Stately Homes business, 307*f.*
Stour Provost, Court of, 36, 37
Strafford, Earl of, 123*f.*, 126
Streatham, 173*f.*
Stubbs, John, artist, 215
Suffolk, Duke of, 50
Suffragette movement, 276*f.*
Sunday Express, 305
Sunderland, Earl of, 174
Surrey, Earl of, 48*f.*
Swyre, 17, 20, 36

Talbot, Lord, 30
Tavistock, 65, 87, 126, 132, 160, 183, 187, 202, 233, 236, 295, 303, 307
Tavistock, the, ship, 182
Tavistock, Lord, 236
Tavistock Square, 14
Tavistock Street, 187
Temple, Sir William, 89
Test Acts, 130, 135, 239
Thorney (Abbey), 68, 101, 108*f.*, 110, 117, 160, 172, 208*f.*, 294
Thornhill, Sir John, 179
Thrond, Lord of Trondheim, 25
Torrington, Herbert, Earl of, 150
Townshend, 'Turnip', 15, 213
Tournai, 46*f.*
Tourville, Admiral, 153
Treason Felony Act, 249
Trenchard, Sir Thomas, 41*f.*
Trevelyan, Charles, 262, 273
Trevelyan, George, 262
Tribunal, the, 272
Triple Alliance, 134
Tyler, Sir William, 55
Tyler's Rebellion, Wat, 19
Tyrone, Earl of, 93*f.*

Unemployment, 235, 276
Union, Act of, 157*f.*, 229
U Thant, 288

Utilitarianism, 262

Vaughan, Francis, Lord, 171
Vaughan, Rachel, Lady, 133, 171*f*., 174, 178
Vermuyden, Cornelius, 13, 103*f*.
Vetri, Castel, horticulturist, 210
Victoria, Queen, 227, 246, 251
Vinegar Hill, 229
Voelcker, Dr, 221

Walpole, Sir Robert, 192
Ward, James, 215
Ward, William, 87
Warwick, Countess of, 88
Warwick, Earl, *see* Dudley, John
Water supply, 180
Webb, Sidney and Beatrice (later Lord and Lady Passfield), 266
Wellington, Duke of, 206, 229, 231, 233, 239*f*.
Wells brothers, 181*f*.
West, rebellion in the, 67
Weymouth, 17, 19, 22, 26, 27, 30, 32, 33*f*., 181, 183
Whaling, 182
Which Way to Peace?, 278
Whipsnade Zoo, 296

Whitehead, A. N., 262, 266
Whood, painter, 190
William III, *see* Orange, William of
William IV, 241*f*.
Winchester, 62
Wise, Alys, *see* Russell, Alys
Woburn Abbey, 14, 67, 71, 85, 87*f*., 129, 143, 160, 163, 172, 173, 175, 180, 183, 185, 191, 195, 203, 205, 208*f*., 292*f*.
Woburn Agricultural Society, 217
Woburn Square, 14, 187
Woburn Walk, 187*f*.
Wolsey, Cardinal, 11, 46*f*.
Wriothesley, Thomas, 1st Earl of Southampton, 167*f*., 175
Wyatt, Sir Thomas, 69, 76
Wyke Regis, 34

York, James, Duke of, 13, 133, 135, 139*f*., 146*f*., 172
Young, Arthur, 114, 217*f*.
Young Ireland Party, the, 243, 249
Young Pretender, the, 192*f*.

Zucchero, portrait by, 71
Zutphen, battle of, 90